THE LEADER'S IMPERATIVE

The Leader's Imperative

Ethics, Integrity, and Responsibility

◆

EDITED BY J. CARL FICARROTTA

PURDUE UNIVERSITY PRESS
West Lafayette, Indiana

05 04 03 02 01   5 4 3 2 1

⊖ The paper used in this book meets the minimum requirements of American National Standard for Information Sciences—Permanence of Paper for Printed Library Materials, ANSI Z39.48-1992.

Printed in the United States of America

Library of Congress Cataloging-in-Publication Data

The leader's imperative : ethics, integrity, and responsibility / edited by J. Carl Ficarrotta.
    p. cm.
Includes bibliographical references and index.
    ISBN 1-55753-184-6 (alk. paper)
   1. Military ethics. 2. Leadership. 3. Integrity. 4. Responsibility. 5. Command of troops. 6. United States—Armed Forces—Officers—Conduct of life. I. Ficarrotta, J. Carl, 1957–
    U22 .L36 2000
    355.3'3041—DC21
                                                    00-008224

Contents

The Just War Tradition and
Moral Problems Outside Warfare

Thinking about Hard Cases

Traditions in Moral Education

Preface

Military academies aim to educate for leadership. As a nation, we hope that even those graduates who do not serve full careers in the military will eventually assume positions of leadership in other institutions. The essays in this volume are a complete collection of the distinguished lectures in ethics given at the US. Air Force Academy from the fall of 1988 to the spring of 1999. While there is no single theme that runs through the entire collection, each essay has a common purpose: each lecturer was, in his or her own way, attempting to contribute to the ethical education of our nation's future leaders. The contributors come from a variety of backgrounds (the series has enjoyed the participation of distinguished academics, high-ranking military officers, judges, university administrators, and political office holders) and in this volume we can read what some leading thinkers from these various backgrounds have to offer on the subject of ethics and leadership.

The two lectures are managed by the Academy's Department of Philosophy. The Joseph A. Reich, Sr., Distinguished Lecture on War, Morality and the Military Profession began in 1988 and is delivered each fall. The late Joseph A. Reich, Sr. was a distinguished and long-time resident of Colorado Springs, Colorado, and was instrumental in bringing the Air Force Academy to that city. The Reich lecture series is supported though an endowment fund from Mr. Reich and his family, which is administered by the Air Force Academy Association of Graduates. It honors "Papa Joe," as he was affectionately known, for his many years of dedicated service to the Academy, the Colorado Springs community, and the United States. The Alice McDermott Memorial Lecture in Applied Ethics has been given each spring, beginning in 1991. The McDermott lectures are in memory of Alice Patricia McDermott, deceased wife of the Academy's first Dean of the Faculty, retired Brigadier General Robert F. McDermott. Mrs. McDermott was intensely involved in the lives of cadets and was a strong, positive role model for all the young people that knew her. When General McDermott assumed the presidency of USAA, the McDermotts moved to San Antonio, where she continued her tireless volunteer efforts with St. Luke's Hospital, the Cancer Center Council, The Southwest Foundation Forum, Ronald McDonald House, the San Antonio Symphony League, and Project ABC. The McDermott series is funded by the Major General William Lyon Chair in Professional Ethics.

THE LEADER'S IMPERATIVE

First Things

1

Three Moral Certainties

John T. Noonan, Jr.

What do I mean by "moral certainties"? I mean things that we are sure of by means other than mathematical calculation or logical deduction, where following the rules of the system assures certainty, and other than physical sensation, where we trust our senses to know that we have two hands and walk on earth. We are morally certain that there is a Julius Caesar and morally certain that there is an Uzbekistan. On a personal level most of us are morally certain that our parents love us. Moral certainty depends on experience, but the certainty exceeds the experience. To be morally certain of something is not to be infallibly right but to be sure enough of it to act confidently in the belief that it exists. We have, obviously, a multitude of moral certainties. I should like to elaborate on three moral certainties that we have in our moral life. These certainties are in a double sense moral. They affect our moral life, and they have a certainty of the kind I call moral.

I will begin with a story. In 1942 the German army was occupying Poland. Far behind the lines was the small Polish city of Józefów. In June, Police Battalion 101, a unit of five hundred men of the occupying force, received orders to round up and kill every Jew in Józefów.[1] Every Jew meant every Jew, regardless of gender, health, or age. The order was carried out. The Jews were taken from their homes to the town square and methodically shot. Babies were bayoneted. In all over twelve thousand persons were put to death.[2] These killings are described with documentary detail by Daniel Joseph Goldhagen in his book *Hitler's Willing Executioners*.

Focusing on particular events Goldhagen highlights the personal decisions of those who took human lives in the course of the Holocaust, a mass event whose enormity, the destruction of over five million Jews, is such that it may blunt our sensibilities or cause us to blank out. Just as it may be far easier to understand the expenditure of $1,000 than the expenditure of $1,000,000,000, so the smaller killings can be better grasped. So Goldhagen takes pains to describe the action of Police Battalion 101's commander, Major Wilhelm Trapp, who told his men that anyone who did not think himself able to engage in the killing would be excused without reprimand.[3] Several men took advantage of this order. The rest were willing executioners.

What is one's first reaction on reading or hearing of this event? I am not sure, but I think it is to ask, "Had the Germans discovered some sabotage going on in Józefów or had there been some guerilla action against the German invaders for which this response was deemed appropriate reprisal?" Inexcusable as such massive retaliation would have been, whatever the stimulus, we still do not want to believe that it did not have the slightest military justification. Nothing of a military nature had, in fact, occurred. The Jews of Józefów were not different from other civilians in the occupied area. They were killed because of deliberate Nazi policy.[4]

When we find on such investigation that the victims were totally blameless and that the order to kill was deliberate policy, we think—nearly all people will think—that the killings were murder, the intentional taking of human lives without justification. The killings were acts of evil. We do not need to know the international law of war or the law of the Third Reich to reach this conclusion. We are morally certain. That certainty is part of a larger moral certainty: evil acts are done in the world.

Let me drive home this large and simple truth with other examples of mass murder from this century. In the period from 1916 to 1918 the government of Turkey turned against the Armenians, a minority of 2,000,000 persons distinguished by religion, ethnicity, and culture from the Moslem majority. The Armenians had lived for centuries within the Ottoman Empire. Still, 320,000 were killed intentionally; another 680,000 or more died as a result of starvation.[5] Over half of the Armenians in the empire did not escape death, a fact that the Turkish government still does not admit.

In the period 1926 to 1953 of Josef Stalin's rule of the Soviet Union the Communist regime killed purposefully at least 1,000,000 persons; another 19,000,000 died of starvation.[6] The victims of the killings were enemies identified by social class or status or political opinion and, in the case of Polish and Ukrainian victims, by ethnic difference.

In 1994 in Rwanda the Hutu government organized a three-month massacre of the Tutsi population. The Tutsis looked different from the Hutus, were alleged to be racially different, and had been the Hutus' social superiors. Of a Tutsi population of 930,000, this brief campaign of killing put to death 850,000.[7] According to Gérard Prunier, this was "one of the highest casualty rates of population in history from non-natural causes."[8]

I do not need to be exhaustive—to detail the Japanese rape of Nanking and killing of more than 260,000 Chinese,[9] the Cultural Revolution in China and the killing of 7.7 million Chinese,[10] the regime of the Khmer Rouge and the deaths of 1.5 million Cambodians.[11]

Morbid fascination may be the result of this catalogue of horrors that has marked the twentieth century, most of them in my lifetime; but they are horrible to dwell upon, and memory of them—the atrocities against the Armenians, for example—fades. I recall these events now to ask, "Is not each of these events evil? Does not any human being hearing of them judge them to be aberrations from humanity, fanatic explosions, massacre on a massive scale? If the killing of the Jews of Józefów demonstrated deeds of evil, are not all of these unjustified killings the amplest possible confirmation that evil exists and can be recognized as existing?"

Mass murder, it is now evident, knows no boundaries, is not the province of any particular ethnic, religious, national, or ideological group. Turkey, the Soviet Union, Germany, and Rwanda nurtured and harbored the murderers. Nazis and Communists, entrenched imperialists and tribal juntas, have alike been guilty. Some of these slaughters took place against the background of a war (the killing of the Armenians and of the Jews), but none of them was necessary to fighting the war, none was occasioned by military necessity. The motives for the murders were varied—religious and ethnic in Turkey, ideological and class in the Soviet Union, ethnic and ideological in Germany, ethnic and class in Rwanda. Characteristic of each case is the marking of the victims as different from their murderers. A sign was put upon them—literally in Germany, figuratively in the other cases—declaring the difference: "They are not us." It has been essential to mark the victims in this way so that the murderers will not see them as human beings like themselves. Not see them as themselves—that is the trick, if "trick" is not too trivial a description of the act by which a species of subhumanity is created. The "not seeing" is easier if the victims are physically out of sight, but essentially the "not seeing" is a mental act by which those to be killed are no longer regarded as human beings like the killers. Creation of a species of subhumans has been the way the killers have salved or stifled their consciences.

For I have no doubt that the killers, like their victims, had consciences. I am sure that the killers had consciences because they were human beings. If you and I recognize that their acts were evil, it is because our human consciences convey this judgment to us. Because they were human beings, the killers must have had the same basic human equipment for detecting evil.[12] If they failed to do so as they entered on mass slaughter, it must have been that in delusion or self-deceit they took their victims to be subhumans they could kill at will.

Have I gone too far and too fast in assuming that you will agree that these deeds were deeds of monstrous evil and that it is your conscience that tells you so? Let me go back to the story I started with and Goldhagen's book, *Hitler's Willing Executioners*, from which the story comes, because the book gives me pause. The book first appeared in the United States and, when reviewed in Germany, caused a furor. Who was this American to pass moral judgment on German soldiers? For the German translation Goldhagen wrote a special foreword, disclaiming moral judgment. He wrote, "It is because the task of this investigation is historical explanation, not moral evaluation, that issues of moral guilt and responsibility are never directly addressed."[13] As if he were making no moral judgments all the time he described the killings! He went on to note that after the war a court of the Federal Republic of Germany had tried the killers of Józefów and had found them guilty under German criminal law.[14] The judgment, then, was the law's, not his. In the same spirit he wrote of other Germans—those who were not at Józefów but who may have in their hearts approved the deeds—that the moral judgment "is to be left to each individual who wants to render moral judgments, just as each individual today is left to evaluate his or her contemporaries who harbor reprehensible views and tendencies."[15] There you see what is at work: he makes the moral judgment that the views are reprehensible, but he does not make a moral judgment for anyone else, it is up to each individual. In that hesitancy I see the modern problem.

Goldhagen does not say what a believing Jew or Christian would say: The deeds of the men of Police Battalion 101 were sins. They were offenses against God and against neighbor. They violated God's commandment, "You shall not murder."[16] Similarly, a believer would say that those who harbored in their hearts the desire to destroy the Jews were sinners, their thoughts were known to God and hateful to God.[17]

So at the end of the twentieth century, in the face of moral evils of unspeakable horror, of which the killing of the Jews of Józefów is a specimen, an author who has the courage to describe the evil deeds and chart the evil thoughts does not condemn the deeds and the thoughts in unconditional terms. He leaves the evaluation of the thoughts to each individual.

Who can fault Goldhagen? In our secular society, what else has authority except the law and one's own sense of rightness? Goldhagen seems to speak for his generation. In 1997, Richard Posner, a representative spokesman of an earlier generation, a distinguished graduate of Yale, gave the Holmes Lectures at Harvard Law School, attacking "academic moralists" and deriding their pretensions.[18] All morals, Posner maintains, are local; none are so universal as to be applied across the board.[19] Posner disavows being an amoralist or nihilist; he admits to having his own local morals,[20] those appropriate to a graduate of Yale College and Harvard Law School and the chief judge of a federal appeals court in Chicago. But he will not claim that his morals are better than another's. As to whose morals are better, he is neutral. As a corollary of this neutrality, he argues that law must be kept clear of the contamination that comes from taking morals "too seriously."[21] The purity of law, unaffected by moral content, appears as a desideratum. Posner's fine lectures are a splendid presentation of a position in which God is unmentioned and relativism reigns. His approach to moral judgments coincides with Goldhagen's. Moral certainties disappear.

Yet Goldhagen and Posner *are* possessed of moral certainties. Posner, as much as Goldhagen, wants to condemn the conduct of the Nazis. At one point he describes our "revulsion" against the Nazis, which he attempts to relativize as "understandable without reference to morality, being based on altruism for the victims and fear of the perpetrators."[22] (I do not understand why he excludes altruism from morality.) At another point he maintains that Hitler can be condemned because his regime failed; Posner takes the failure to be proof of the lack of functionality in his system and sees this lack as a moral failure.[23] Posner relies on the retrospective judgment that the Nazi regime was immoral because it did not survive. He uses the same kind of argument to show that Communism in Russia was wrong: it finally collapsed.

The difficulty with this sort of argument is that no regime, no society, no way of life survives forever. Hitler's regime had a dozen years of life, Soviet Communism seventy, the slaveholding South two and a half centuries. Was each regime immune from criticism while the society lasted and then shown to be immoral by its failure to be immortal? There is little demonstrable connection between social morality and social mortality.

Goldhagen's use of the law of Germany suffers from the same weakness as

Posner's criterion of survival. If Hitler had won the war, German law would not have condemned the men of Police Battalion 101. It was only Hitler's failure that brought a different reading of the law into play. The condemnation of their conduct is made, in Goldhagen's presentation, to rest on a result as arbitrary as the survival of the regime, for the result he relies on came about only by the destruction of the regime.

Inadequate as their criteria are, Goldhagen and Posner are clear in their judgment of the Nazis and expect their readers to share their judgment. Does not each silently appeal to a standard of judgment that is not local and relative, that is more stable than shifts in a regime? I infer that they must, or they could not speak with the moral certainty they do in condemning Nazi barbarism and wickedness. Indeed, would they speak at all if their moral judgments were merely private preferences?[24] They speak—they voice positions—because they share these positions with what they hope is humanity.

Let me support that inference further in Goldhagen's case by his conviction that the thoughts of those Germans who wanted the Jews dead were reprehensible. On what criterion does his own clear judgment rest? One reason for morally condemning thoughts that have resulted in actions is that they predispose to action. Wish a particular group or class dead, and if the opportunity occurs, one may help effect the wish by killing or by not impeding killing. If the killing is bad, then the predisposing thoughts that facilitate it must be bad. Although law condemns only the act, not the predisposition, a good moralist will condemn both.[25]

Predisposition, however, does not always lead to action or culpable inaction. The thought held as wish, as morbid fantasy, may never have the chance to affect conduct. Neither Goldhagen nor we can say with confidence how many Germans held these thoughts that never ripened in any way. Yet Goldhagen says with moral certainty—and invites his readers to join him in saying—that the thoughts were "reprehensible." Why? Why should those harboring the bad thoughts be morally condemned for thinking?

Before offering an answer to that question, let me offer three propositions that are relevant to an answer:

There is no judgment without a judge.
There is no judge without a law.
There is no law without a lawgiver.

Albert Camus's *La Chute*[26] may be taken as an elaborate demonstration of the truth of these propositions. Its protagonist is a lawyer, Jean-Baptiste Clamence, who describes himself as a judge-penitent. He is conscious of guilt for something he has done or not done, either killing his mistress or not preventing her suicide. But his judgment on himself is vacuous and his penitence is unavailing. His judgment on himself is empty because judgment requires impartiality; no one can be a judge in his own case. His penitence is unavailing, for there is no one to whom he can say he is sorry. His regret hangs meaninglessly in the air. There is only his fall. There is no judge to judge him, there is no law to empower a judge to judge him, there is no lawgiver to give such a law. Camus's judge-penitent is in the position of those who would condemn the Nazis and have only local, retrospective, state-made criminal law on which to rely. They have in effect neither judge nor law nor lawgiver.

The ultimate thrust of my argument, as by now may be obvious, is that the foundation of our moral certainty about moral evil comes from the existence of a law written in our hearts and known by our consciences; and if there is a law, there is a lawgiver. The extensive existence of evil is taken by some to be evidence that the world is a chaos formed by chance, without rhyme or reason; that it is, as an irreverent German movie title puts it, a case of "every man for himself and god against all."[27] I argue to the contrary. The extensive existence of evil proves the existence of a God who has given human beings a law. Without that law we would not recognize at once and without difficulty the evil of mass murder whoever its perpetrators are, whoever its victims are. No local transient custom, no special bias, accounts for the universal condemnation. Our moral certainty of the evil points to the second moral certainty I hold we have in the realm of morals: that our acts and thoughts are subject to a law established by a lawgiver who is not human.

In the context of our civilization, for Jews and for Christians, the name of that lawgiver is God. Our morals begin with the commandments attributed to God. In that context, the most relevant is the commandment sometimes translated, "You shall not kill," but better translated, "You shall not murder."[28] The people to whom the commandment was originally addressed, and to whose care its preservation is owed, engaged in various kinds of killing without compunction. They ate animals, they practiced capital punishment, they conducted wars.[29] "You shall not murder" was how the commandment was understood.

The commandment was reinforced by the story that opens the Hebrew Bible: The Creator creates human beings in the image of the Creator.[30] In a metaphor that is obscure but illuminating, human beings are presented as reflections of a divinity. For that reason their dignity, including the life of each, is special.

What constitutes murder, on what occasions the taking of human life is morally justified, underwent development in the biblical context[31] and has undergone development in the course of civilization. American law, for example, carefully distinguishes degrees of malice in killing and treats criminal negligence in bringing about a death as less than reckless indifference resulting in death, and each less than intentional killing, although all are species of homicide.[32] The necessity of capital punishment has been sharply criticized.[33] All morals have a dynamic capacity to develop and to interact with human law. The moral certainty that the unjustified taking of human life is evil, the moral certainty that a law inscribed in our being condemns it—these two moral certainties remain.

Admitting the fact of moral development that judges what kind of killing constitutes murder appears to reveal a weak point in my argument. I have assumed that each of the mass killings I condemn was not justified. But were the killings not justified in the eyes of the killers? Innocent as the victims appear to us, would their killers not have justified dispatching the victims in terms of national security or the class struggle? In every age and in all parts of the world there have been killings organized and carried out by governments—killings not regarded as murder because they were regarded by the state as justified. In this way in medieval Europe incorrigible heretics were thought to be rightly punished by death; even in seventeenth-century Boston Quakers were hanged on Boston Common because they were heretics who, contrary to law, had returned to Massachusetts.[34] In this way in the nineteenth century American Indians were dispossessed and killed if they resisted too much. In this way today in California and thirty-six other states criminals are executed for their bloody deeds.[35] No one who kills on behalf of the state is regarded as a murderer; the state has decided that the killing is justified. Justification for the killing—not the killing itself—appears to be at the nub of the moral judgment of whether or not a killing is murder.

I agree that as to justification there has been development and as to some justifications no universal human agreement exists. Nonetheless I argue that common human characteristics—age, gender, physical condition, mental capacity—can never be justification for killing. These characteristics never sufficiently distinguish one group of human beings from another. It would be irrational anywhere to kill those under five feet or all the redheads. By a parity of reasoning it is irrational to kill those identified by other characteristics they cannot change, such as ethnicity. If ethnicity is an excuse for killing, then every section of the human race is eligible for extermination. Finally I argue that experience has taught us that to enforce religious faith by death is to contradict the foundation of faith and that to achieve justice in the social structure by death is to be unjust. In sum, the justifications advanced for the massacres of our century do not bear rational examination. To accept these justifications in the light of the law inscribed and developed within us is to violate that law.

I speak of a law inscribed in our being, and I come to the third moral certainty I want to set before you today: that our moral life is conducted in our minds. I spoke earlier of a law written in our hearts, as I just now spoke of a law inscribed in our being. Clearly, these references are metaphorical. You can take the heart out of a human body and hold it in your hand, as a cardiac surgeon does during surgery, and you will find no text on its surface. You can examine the anatomy of our being without finding a single inscription. You can look at every movement in our brain without being able to detect a moral thought.

In the last twenty years the neurosciences have made extraordinary progress in the mapping of the brain, locating, for example, the amygdala as the place where emotions of anger and anxiety are processed, and charting the effect of dopamine on certain synapses. Analogies with the workings of computers have aided these scientific endeavors in understanding the neural connections and processes. These successes, and the greater successes they promise, have encouraged some to conclude that eventually the mind will be explained as a complex of interacting neurons—or rather, the mind will be dropped from the explanation as unnecessary. With the disappearance of mind will go such notions as the will, intention, and thought, already concepts linguistically relegated by aggressive materialists to the category of "folk psychology."[36]

As this intellectual battle over the implications of the neurosciences takes shape, it is obvious that our morals, like our law, are vitally dependent on intangible dynamisms, including will, intention, thought, and conscience. None of the processes by which law measures our acts, by which moral judgments are made, are identical with the physical processes of the brain. To look for them in the brain is like Khrushchev asking if the cosmonauts found God beyond the atmosphere. Neither God nor a human intention is a measurable physical substance. That we so easily use metaphors to describe the mind—that we *must* use metaphors to describe the mind—is some evidence that neither our law nor our morals depend on the conviction that the mind and the brain are identical. Why do we speak of the law in our hearts unless we are using metaphor to capture invisible realities not capturable by quantitative measurements?

The criminal law is insistent that it judges acts, not thoughts; but there is no human act unless a thought determines it.[37] Purpose is joined by thought to physical movement to form a human act that the criminal law can judge. The same is true of morals. A physical movement—a letting go of one's hands, for example—is not a moral act. It is only when thought provides purpose that moral judgment is possible. Then, for example, pulling the trigger on a gun can constitute murder or lawful self-defense; it depends in great part on the purpose of the action.

Going even further, I maintain that in morals, thoughts by themselves can be judged. They can be judged because they predispose one to later actions. They can be judged because they themselves violate the law inscribed in our being. To think that all the Jews or Armenians or capitalists or Tutsi should be killed is already to dehumanize them; to hate to the point of desiring extermination of the hated humans is to commit murder in the heart. The offense, invisible to others, is seen by the invisible giver of the law, who is also its judge. That is the third moral certainty I offer to you.

In capsule, I have shown four large instances of killing where the creation of a subhuman class for living human beings no longer seen as human constitutes irrational justification, and that every human being can recognize the killing of them as evil; that unlike the unnecessarily reticent Goldhagen, the relativizing Posner, and the frustrated judge-penitent of Camus, I believe the evil is recognized because it violates an interior, invisible law of our being; and that that law has been provided by a lawgiver, who will judge the violations of the law, be they purposeful murder or the thought of purposeful murder. We are morally certain of the evil, of the law, of the lawgiver-judge of our hearts.

Notes

1. David Jonah Goldhagen, *Hitler's Willing Executioners: Ordinary Germans and the Holocaust* (New York: Knopf, 1996; reprint, New York: Vintage Books, 1997), 211.

2. Ibid., 219.

3. Ibid., 214.

4. Ibid., 212.

5. Robert F. Melson, *Revolution and Genocide: On the Origins of the Armenian Genocide and the Holocaust* (Chicago: University of Chicago Press, 1992), 147.

6. Steven Wheatcroft, "The Scale and Nature of German and Soviet Repressions and Mass Killings, 1930–45," *Europe-Asia Studies* 48 (1996): 1319.

7. Gérard Prunier, *The Rwanda Crisis: History of a Genocide* (New York: Columbia University Press, 1995), 264–65.

8. Ibid., 265.

9. Iris Chang, *The Rape of Nanking: The Forgotten Holocaust of World War II* (New York: BasicBooks, 1997), 4.

10. Rudolf J. Rummel, *Death by Government* (New Brunswick, N.J.: Transaction Publishers, 1994), 100.

11. Ben Kiernan, *The Pol Pot Regime: Race, Power, and Genocide in Cambodia under the Khmer Rouge, 1975–79* (New Haven, Conn.: Yale University Press, 1996), 460.

12. See Goldhagen's discussion of the moral objections that the men of Police Battalion 101 had to the mass slaughter of Poles and to the presence of an officer's pregnant wife at a mass killing of Jews in Miedzyrzec (239–43).

13. Goldhagen, 481 (included as appendix 3 in the Vintage Paperback edition).

14. Ibid., 546–47.

15. Ibid., 482.

16. "You shall not murder" (Deuteronomy 5:17, Revised Standard Version).

17. "You have heard that it was said to those of ancient times, 'You shall not murder'; and 'whoever murders shall be liable to judgment.' But I say to you that if you are angry with a brother or sister, you will be liable to judgment; and if you insult a brother or sister, you will be liable to the council; and if you say, 'You fool,' you will be liable to the hell of fire" (Matthew 5: 21–22, RSV). "Indeed, the word of God is living and active, sharper than any two-edged sword, piercing until it divides soul from spirit, joints from marrow; it is able to judge the thoughts and intentions of the heart" (Hebrews 4:12, RSV).

18. Richard A. Posner, "The Problematics of Moral and Legal Theory," *Harvard Law Review* 111 (1998): 1637, 1639–40. See also Richard A. Posner, *The Problematics of Moral and Legal Theory* (Cambridge, Mass.: The Belknap Press of Harvard University Press, 1999).

19. Posner, "The Problematics of Moral and Legal Theory," 1640.

20. Ibid., 1644.

21. Ibid., 1695.

22. Ibid., 1692.

23. Ibid., 1653–54.

24. See ibid., 1655 (Posner's response to this objection).

25. See, for example, Stanley Hauerwas's work, relying on Aristotle and Aquinas to emphasize the importance of the development of character, or right dispositions, to the moral life. Stanley Hauerwas, *Character and the Christian Life: A Study in Theological Ethics* (Notre Dame, Ind.: Univ. of Notre Dame Press, 1994), 70: "Aristotle and Aquinas were using the word 'habit' in quite a different way than current usage dictates. For Aristotle a habit is a characteristic (*hexis*) possessed inwardly by man, defined as 'the condition either good or bad in which we are, in relation to our emotions.' These characteristics which form the virtues are dispositions to act in particular ways."

26. Albert Camus, *The Fall*, trans. Justin O'Brien (1956; New York: Vintage International, 1991).

27. *Every Man for Himself and God against All* (1975) (director Werner Herzog).

28. Deuteronomy 5:17, RSV.

29. "From among all the land animals, these are the creatures that you may eat . . ." (Leviticus 11:2, RSV). "Whoever strikes a person mortally shall be put to death" (Exodus 21:12, RSV). "Then they devoted to destruction by the edge of the sword all in the city, both men and women, young and old, oxen, sheep, and donkeys" (Joshua 6:21, RSV).

30. "This is the list of the descendants of Adam. When God created humankind, he made them in the likeness of God" (Genesis 5:1, RSV).

31. Brevard S. Childs, *The Book of Exodus: A Critical, Theological Commentary* (Philadelphia, Pa.: Westminster Press, 1974), 419–21.

32. See, e.g., McKinney's *Consolidated Laws of New York*, Penal Code §125.10 (St. Paul: West, 1999): "A person is guilty of criminally negligent homicide when, with criminal negligence, he causes the death of another person."; Penal Code §15.05: "4. 'Criminal negligence.' A person acts with criminal negligence with respect to a result or to a circumstance described by a statute defining an offense when he fails to perceive a substantial and unjustifiable risk that such result will occur or that such circumstance exists. The risk must be of such nature and degree that the failure to perceive it constitutes a gross deviation from the standard of care that a reasonable person would observe in the situation."

33. See, e.g., John Megivern, *The Death Penalty: An Historical and Theological Survey* (New York: Paulist Press, 1997), 5.

34. John T. Noonan, *The Lustre of Our Country: The American Experience of Religious Freedom* (Berkeley and Los Angeles: University of California Press, 1998), 51–54.

35. Center for Capital Punishment Studies, London, *The International Sourcebook on Capital Punishment, 1997 Edition* (Boston, Mass.: Northeastern University Press, 1997), 247.

36. See John Searle, "What's Wrong with the Philosophy of Mind," in *The Mind-Body Problem: A Guide to the Current Debate*, edited by Richard Warner and Tadeusz Szubka (Oxford: Blackwell, 1994), 281.

37. See, e.g., Ludwig Wittgenstein, *Philosophical Investigations*, trans. G. E. M. Anscombe, 3d ed. (New York: Prentice-Hall, 1958), 217: "The intention *with which* one acts does not 'accompany' the action any more than the thought 'accompanies' speech. Thought and intention are neither 'articulated' nor 'non-articulated'; to be compared neither with a single note which sounds during the acting or speaking, nor with a tune."; Hauerwas, 67: "The intention becomes morally significant only because by it we are formed as agents of the act. . . . For Aristotle and Aquinas the ethics of character is bound up with the ability of men to give reasons for their actions. For them the reasons given for an action cannot be incidental to the action."

2

"Turning" Backward

The Erosion of Moral Sensibility

JOHN J. MCDERMOTT

I have to say that I am aware that my presentation of a stand-up, belt-it-out in public lecture at this time has the odor of a troglodyte. We seem to be caught between two depressing "stools" (the pun is intended); the first features the glitz of pop-culture, showboat sports and preening politicians. The second features the dreary data-bases of academic analyses and in-house jargonic puff. In the first, eros has degenerated into ahistorical sleaze and in the second, eros has disappeared. For those among us who believe in intellectual passion rather than settling for intellectual inquiry, I say that we are a remnant and as such, so be it, for we believe that the integrity of the journey is all that we share so as to live, move and have our being.

The remarks which follow have as their ambience my having to re-think and thereby re-live my tried and assumedly true assumptions as a result of being savagely derailed from the neat clicking wheels of a life onward and up-ward. Some ten years ago having, as they say, bottomed out, one is then faced with the other side of the Janus directly, asking not just second questions but even third questions. Life, as philosophy, echoing William James, is the habit of always seeing an alternative. A life and person threatening experience (they are not identical—each of us needs both at some time) effects a profound transformation of what one already "knew" to be so but did not "know" to be so. The American poet, Wallace Stevens has it best:

You have a blue guitar
You do not play things as they are
. . . Things as they are
Are changed upon the blue guitar

And so, I offer here, some comments on the obvious, the quotidian, put sufficiently different, I trust, so as to prompt you to ask at least a second question.

Preamble

Remember that in life you ought to behave as at a Banquet.
—Epictetus, *The Enchiridion* - XV

In a relievedly brief vein, I offer here my personal stance as a context for the diagnosis to follow. I am not a Cassandra, who in the *Agamemnon* of Aeschylus, stands in the chariot facing the great doors of the palace which homes the House of Atreus, and issues her prophecy of doom. Although I can be Cassandra-like, especially on the vexing problem of world population, I keep going in the hope of better times. Conversely, I am not the eighth dwarf who awakes every morning singing, "Hi-Ho, Hi-Ho, it's off to work we go" and then proceeding to tell us that if you sing all day long, your troubles will go! Work may save, but it can also punish. Consequently, please hear my remarks tonight as neither pessimistic nor optimistic. Rather, take them as melioristic, a sort of moral dew-line, an early (late?) warning system for me and for thee!

In the parlance of medical practice, it is now virtually a truism that compassionate care in the face of serious medical illness requires the presence of a wounded healer. The analogy to the moral question has not been forthcoming but it is pertinent and overdue. I put it this way. Moral pedagogy requires the presence of a judge-penitent, in the telling phrase of Albert Camus. Different from the self-destructive protagonist of Camus' last novel, *The Fall*, my emphasis is on "penitent," and who among us is not one of those or one who should admit to being one of those, thereby obviating the besetting sin of casting the stone. Moral outrage frequently masks systemic hypocrisy. See, for example, the official rhetoric during the war in Vietnam, in which the moral posturing on behalf of democracy was in fact a cover-up for jingoistic scapegoating. Try one closer to our time, that is, now, alas. Many ill veterans of the Gulf War have been accosted with the moralistic attitude that they are actually hypochondriacal and medical malingerers. Despite these bravado pronouncements from paragons of official dissemblement, with each passing day it becomes both startling and obvious that once again the public moral take is but a smokescreen, blocking us from the malodorous underbelly. Put directly, the word in question is not dissembling. It is lying. There is a difference and, once more, if you have lied, you know what I mean. (For every gloss here—I am just as aware as you, that there exist exceptions. They are just that, exceptions. Further they are used in the manipulative form of co-optation, namely, to throw us off track, off the scent. It is the bad faith of an appeal to boot-strapping by those who have no such experience.)

It goes something like this or with Kurt Vonnegut, "and so it goes." Hey there, John J., Have you ever done anything wrong? Have you ever flouted, flaunted, trashed, ignored or violated the moral law? First response: Who me? Not me? Second response, well, perhaps, a time or two. Third response, Yes, Big time. Now and only now can I suggest that there may be a better way. To sustain this proposal of the wounded moralist, you reach for St. Augustine who offers to the infinite God, that "if we had not sinned, you would not have loved us." Or you can appeal to the antique and deeply Christian moral tradition of the "felix culpa," the happy fault which sees sin as the way to grace. A more recent invocation would be that of John Dewey for whom we lived by the funded experiences of our personal and collective historical past, learning equally from the negative and damaging. Whatever, however, the paradox is that unless I say I am sorry, unless I apologize, I am not in any position to offer advice let alone wallow in moral outrage. Parenthetically, I trust that you have noticed this form of authorial confessional critique is noticeably absent in the long history of ethical theory.

So, having said that I am sorry on more than one occasion, I set forth on the text in hand.

The American Setting: A Tale

I was a young child in the bleak decade of the American 1930's. Three of my grandparents were dead. My paternal grandfather was buried on the nasty January day that I was born in 1932. My remaining grandparent was my maternal grandmother, known in our family as Nana. Widowed at an early age, with three young children, she made a living for them by scrubbing fire-house floors and sewing men's ties. She was a follower of the New York Giants of John McGraw and a whiz at pinochle. My entire extended family was shanty Irish. We had nothing, except the American dream, Irish style.

I correct myself, for I should not say "nothing." For the shanty Irish did manage to obtain, grab or perhaps even purloin one precious possession, lace curtains, to be had no doubt in defiance of our often offensive and patronizing peers, the lace-curtain Irish. My Nana had such a set of curtains. Each spring they would be ceremoniously washed, starched and tacked to a long, nail-pronged stretcher. For decades, I helped to do that. And then, as she failed in strength I did them for her. Some thirty years ago, when she was in her eighties, I said to her, "time for the curtains." Nana replied, not this year. What! Why not? They were *threadbare*. A stretch was beyond their reach. They would fray and the threads would unravel, spinning dizzily out of control, dangling, footless, homeless, anomic and pathetically lonely, each and all of them, lonely together.

Nana Kelly was dead within the year.

I think here of America, our "strand" of hope and I ask do we still have that long-standing, self-announcing confidence in our ability to meet and match our foes, of any and every stripe, political, economic, natural, and, above all, spiritual, arising from without and within our commonwealth? I do not ask this as a rhetorical question but rather one of direct, existential contemporaneity, the intention of which is to elicit an equally direct response. For most of my life, even through the turbulent and bewildering decade of the 1960's, I would answer, yes. Subsequently, my reply became halting and had the responding cloak of "maybe" about it. Of late, I carry with me, resonant of many others among us, a lamentable dubiety about whether, in fact, we are still able to tap that eros of community, which has served us so well for the past three centuries.

This dubiety does not trace to events so much as to mood. To be sure, events such as the Oklahoma City bombing and the escalating, precipitous rise in acts of violence as traceable to the increasing presence of estrangement, and ontological rather than functional frustration, is of central moment. The issue in question, however, cuts deeper and may presage our having lost the capacity to rework and reconstitute the viability of a pluralistic and mosaic communal fabric which, in truth, is simply quintessential if we are to survive as a nation.

Taking heed of botanical and physiological metaphors, far more helpful in telling us what is happening than is the language of logic and conceptual schemas, I hear the following conversations. After an ice storm, a flood, a fire or just the constant, searing sun of the Texas summer, one asks of the tree, the plant, the bush, or perhaps a tendril or two, can it come back, will it come back? I do not know. There exists a line of viability, for the most part invisible and even, despite modern science, mysterious. Cross that line and the leaves wither, announcing the death of the botanical life form.

So, also, with physiological metaphors. We speak of atrophy, as when a muscle loses its febrility. The common watch in our mediated society is for the rampant, destructive cell, as in cancer. Far more present, however, is the malodorous activity of inanition, wasting away, loss of tone, in short, he, she seems to be failing. In what, of what we ask? I do not know, just failing, in general. You can tell! The many diseases of the central nervous system carry on by *via negativa*. Neurons do not fire. Cellular messages are not sent or if sent are not received, or if received, not heeded, as in the biblical admonition, they who have eyes, but do not see, they who have ears, but do not hear. The terror of addiction and Alzheimer's disease is that we do not know how far to go with it until it is too late and we cannot turn back for a fresh start.

"Turning" Backward: The Erosion of Moral Sensibility

It is best to begin by glossing the title. The meaning of "turning" descends from the Jewish notion of *Teshuvah*, from the Hebrew, to recover, as being in recovery. It is a turn of the heart, not simply of the mind, even if there be such a phenomenon as mind, on its own. A "teshuvah" is not primarily an enlightenment as when John Dewey first read *The Principles of Psychology* by William James. Nor is it akin to the "dream" of Descartes or to the separate, but equivalent, intellectually shattering discovery of Kant's *Prolegomena* by Nicholas Berdyaev and Martin Buber. We come closer if we think of the *"tolle lege"* episode in Augustine's life or Kierkegaard's decision to "make trouble" as his *Point of View.* Further, we find proximity to a "teshuvah" in William James's reading of Charles Renouvier and patently in Josiah Royce's retrospective version of his defining moment in the mining camp of his California childhood.

Versions of this experience of turning abound in our lives, in yours I hope and trust. I could extemporaneously offer one or more of these "turnings" in the life of each of my children. These events, these explosive stories are transforming of our deepest sensibility and in Spinoza's version, they are constitutive of an "emendatione," a healing of the preternatural wounds that for some reason come with our coming to consciousness.

Lamentably, the "teshuvah" is not necessarily permanent. In the language of addiction recovery therapy, one can and often does, relapse. Further, a second turning is difficult to come by for disappointment, self-abnegation and skepticism dog the second effort. Still, even given these obstacles, a deep personal struggle can generate a return to the original turning.

At issue here, however, is an event, personal or culturally systemic, which is more foreboding by far and largely unsung, namely a "turn" backward. This baleful undoing of the moral fabric is unsung because it rarely, if ever, is accompanied by an announcement, a pronouncement or even an acknowledgment that it has taken place. Actually, the turn backward is a form of spiritual arteriosclerosis, accompanied by a hardening of the heart. The remonstrances of the "everyday" echo here in these "deading" walls of the chambers of the heart, as in, he has no heart, she is heartless, can't you find it in your heart to, don't you have a heart, please, please have a heart, they are hard of heart and as famously wailed by Bert Lahr in his lion persona, paraphrased as "if they only had a heart."

The downshot of this hardening of our hearts is the existential instantiation of amorality. This is the Pontius Pilate syndrome, made infamous by Adolph Eichmann and now found planetary-wide in response to one or the other frequenting atrocities that pollute the human landscape of our epoch. It is of baleful and sour note that even creative moral pedagogy is helpless when faced with amorality.

The "turn" backward is most often quite subtle and instead of being characterized by a decisive and personal-public event, its etiology reflects rather the post-colonic phrase in our title, namely, the erosion of moral affection. The word at issue here is erosion, not implosion or explosion. Erosion is subtle and masks its foreboding of catastrophe. By contemporary example, you can replace millions of coconut trees but you cannot replace any of the Pacific black coral now being foraged for commercial trinkets. In time the island-dwelling merchants of this egregious theft will be under water.

When the eroded is gone, it is gone. Forever? Hard to say for sure, but probably. We ask of others (rarely, of ourselves) will he ever "turn" around. She seems to have "turned" around, but I have my doubts. He, she, is hopeless. The recidivist rate in turns of *attitude* is constant, high and seemingly defiant of moral pedagogy, assuming that such a distinctively human effort still exists other than in isolated precincts of the culture. The present discussion is of moral sensibility and not of ethics. The latter, ethics, in our time has become bowdlerized of the patterns of human affectivity. The teaching of contemporary ethics features the use of wooden case studies often introduced by the hapless phrase, "let us suppose." Let us suppose she is pregnant—let us suppose you have end-stage renal failure—or pancreatic cancer, or you are HIV positive—positively. Or let us suppose that you are a clinical alcoholic—*Who me?* For those of us who have received one or more of these "announcements" among others extant, the use of "suppose" takes on the dull face of abstraction.

The absence of existential, experiential affections in these discussions wilts the eros of imagination and turns the moral question into a game of checkers, or for self-announced really smart philosophers, a game of chess. Antique ethics, of whatever culture, the *Analects*, the *Tao Te Ching*, the *Enchiridion* and Native American moral pedagogy have ethical prescriptions and proscriptions but they are entailed within a living and affective cultural setting. In the words of Jonathan Edwards, they have to do with "holy practice." One thinks here of the Stoic ethics as found in Book II of the *Meditations* by Marcus Aurelius. He tells us that no matter how long we live, even for thousands of years, we live only the life we live. And of that human life, he offers

the time is a point, and the substance is in a flux, and the perception dull, and the composition of the whole body subject to putrefaction, and the soul a whirl, and fortune hard to divine, and fame a thing devoid of judgment. And, to say all in a word, everything which belongs to the body is a stream, and what belongs to the soul is a dream and vapour, and life is a warfare and a stranger's sojourn, and after-fame is oblivion.

Well, what of the Aurelian "take" on being in, of and about the world? Is this an ethical position? I think not. Rather, it is a matter of attitude, of sensibility. The American apothegm tells us that you cannot legislate morality. Fair enough, but that phrasing is an emptying derivation from the far richer original line of the Roman, Horace: *"quid leges sine moribus vanae proficiunt."* That is, no use of idle laws in the absence of moral civics. What could be more enervating to a human life than to have little or no moral affections and at the same time to have parental, familial, societal and legislated moral dicta hanging around one's neck?

If we were to come clean on the issue, we could ask ourselves who among us makes ethical decisions? Who among us, when faced with the travails of living seek out ethical principles, weighs the options and then acts? I never did, I don't and I hope I never do. If we live shallow lives then we shall act shallowly. If we live deep lives in which the moral question is one of sensibility rather than one of rule, we shall act accordingly. You say, no way. Cannot happen. We have to rein in the instincts. We have to get this straight once and for all. It is said that moral attitudes are too murky. The affective life lacks objectivity.

Feelings are not to be trusted. It is said, as well, there is a clear right and clear wrong and that distinction must prevail in everyone's life. (Except in my own life.) The classic question is "can virtue be taught?" My question is "can compassion be taught?" The above approach is not an issue of moral pedagogy. To the contrary it is an issue of law and authority, a moral regulae. Yet, if you peel away this self-righteous rhetoric on behalf of getting things straight on the moral business, once and for all, you look directly into the underlying "attitude," one of cynicism about the possibility of moral sensibility, moral growth and, above all, moral transformation, that is, the possibility of a "turning." The erosion of this belief in the "turn" is of paramount importance in any diagnosis of contemporary American culture. How has this happened? Why has this happened? How could it be that collectively we seem to have lived the life of the fabled Mr. Jones of the Bob Dylan lyric, around whom the wind was blowing, but he did not know it. So, a word or two here, about the wind.

Losing Our Way

Over against the *modus vivendi* of affection and compassion, we seem to be slipping into a *modus moriendi*, willing victims of the virus of cynicism in what I think to be an obviating of our once deeply held commitment to the possibility of possibility.

If I were to ask the following question as I frequently do, "How is it with you, America?" or better, "How is it with me, America?", diagnostically I come up with a dolorous intake. It is very important to ask such questions, constantly, for one powerful characteristic of a culture awash in cynicism, is the abandonment of self-reflection, let alone self-critique. The need for our doing this intake was nailed to my forehead by a down-home, homely, brief story. While scouring America this last spring and summer, I found myself on Northern Boulevard in Nassau County of the State of New York. Not surprising, I had left my gas cap at the last filling station. So, in transit, I was delighted to find an old-fashioned autoparts, hardware store. In our transaction, I mentioned to "mister hardware" that last night some wise guy keyed the side of my rental car, a sort of rhetorical wonder about just what is happening here. He said, happens all the time and last week "they" (who, by the way, are they?) blew up the telephone booths on Northern Boulevard. I was leaving with the ironically cheering news that I was not alone, so to speak, when he opined, "Something has gone wrong along the way." Indeed! And just what has gone wrong such that the way is no longer a *Tao*, nor even a journey, so much as it is the pursuit of a basset hound for the mechanical rabbit. In short, no cigar!

If we were to scan the recent decades of this cluttered trip we are taking, a sort of spiritual MRI of how we have lost our way, I suggest that the following culturally palpable signs, in fact, are mis-directions, deceiving directions or no directions at all. Every *way*farer should take some time at a *way*side so as to reflect from whence they have come, where they are heading and, as they say, how is it going. Well then, how is it going?

First, I believe that we are witnessing the collapse of inherited expectations, especially those which were appropriate only as a shell game or three-card monte. And this holds, whether the expectation emerged from the religious motif, that all will go well for those who love God; the political motif, that democracy will bring both equity and peace; or the economic motif, that in time everyone will have their needs fulfilled. (This last motif now has escalated to having our wants fulfilled.) So penetrating in the American psyche were these expectations, they soon began to function as assumptions, or remarkably as eschatological redemptive clots to happen in our very own generation. Surely, however, even the casual observer, let alone those more reflective, cannot fail to see that these promises are bogus. For us, they are broken promises. The ensuing malady comes about in our inversion of the usual phrasing, that is, we see, yet we do not believe. In consequence, we become disconnected from our experiences, from our empirical, affective sensibilities and continue to chase a chimera. Sorry about this, but we are not going to live forever. More, it is not simply that we shall die. We are going to be zapped out of existence. Non-being awaits us. No, we are not going to be remembered beyond a generation or so, if that. No, America is not eternal. No, the planet Earth is not eternal. Worse, far worse, baseball is no longer a game. It is a business. Of equal pathos, or should we say bathos, the university is no longer a cathedral of learning, a birthing of sensibility. See it rather as a placement center with athletic teams.

And so it goes. How quaint now is the earlier refrain, "Where have all the flowers gone?" or more foreboding, "Where do the children play?". Think about that one. As we prep in "expectation" of the global economy for the twenty-first century, hard census data figures reveal that millions of American children do not have sufficient food to eat and are trapped in what can be appropriately called an ontological cycle of poverty.

Too strong? I think not. Take some substantial time and monitor all that advertising that comes your way, by print, by radio, by video, by billboard, by the Web and the Net, by whatever. Does it not promise more than most of us can have, ever? And does not this unctuous farrago of promises have as the thematic hook, that we deserve to have, to be, to experience the object of the pitch? Does not this mode of communication move from announcement to expectation and self-deceivingly to birthright?

The spiritual message here is crystal-clear. As the biblical admonition warns us, in time our foot will slide. Either we become totally consumed by the chase, thereby losing our bearings, our *way*, or we fail to be requited and turn bitter. Worse still, we become envious and jealous, the most destructive of the human vices.

Second, it is this *ressentiment*, in the language of Nietzsche, which feeds the media frenzy to expose cynically those who are successful in whatever way. If I can't have it, then you can't have it. Bring them down. The time-honored assumption that all of us have feet of clay, are penitents for one reason or another is now escalated to the judgment (in Journalism, I trust you note, there are few penitents) that anyone who steps forward has feet of rotting clay. These naked public figures are then judged retroactively and punished presently. Although a penitent in some areas of my life, I am basically a decent fellow and could conceivably be of some public help. Yet, if I were to announce for public office, it would not take longer than fifteen minutes and a few phone calls to obtain enough allegedly damaging information sufficient to destroy me, my family and those close to me. The cynicism here pertains to the erosion of belief in *penitence*, recovery and growth. The affectionate childhood phrase, give them another chance, has disappeared under the intentional onslaught on behalf of bringing everyone down.

A third source for this cynicism can be found in the fraying of even the bronze parachutes. We no longer trust the viability of those social programs constructed precisely to prevent our being subject to the catastrophic in our lives. I refer here to the post-hoc disappearing pension, the savage inequities in our health-care delivery system, the threat to both Medicare and Social Security and the terrifying future for an ever-increasing, exponentially, geriatric population. A word about the latter collective and widespread fear. Retirement homes, well appointed, are available to the very few who have substantial resources after retirement. We are speaking of at least $30,000 per year. Although there are exceptions, nursing homes are often a euphemism for warehouses. A battle taking place at present between operators of nursing homes and state regulatory officials is revealing. The state of Texas, for example, has banned the use of the anti-paranoid drug Haldol from use in nursing homes. The reason is simple and instructive. Haldol was being used, indiscriminately, to render the residents of the nursing home as zombies. This is convenient but cruel and clearly dehumanizing. Yet, without such a drug the trapped, often abandoned aged population, acts out and creates a situation of institutional dysfunction. One might ask, not rhetorically I trust, how did we get ourselves into this situation? Quite directly, it descends from the diagnosis sketched above. If a society is trapped in the chase, those who worked with us and for us are exiled as soon as they are no longer in harness. Most of us live lives as flotsam, carried by forces not of our own making, a sort of second-hand living. When aged, we find ourselves hooked, impaled or simply wrapped around one jutting stream branch or another, now only jetsam.

Listen to Mary Tyrone in O'Neill's *Long Days Journey Into Night*:

But I suppose life has made him like that, and he can't help it. None of us can help things life has done to us. They're done before you realize it, and once they're done they make you do other things until at last everything comes between you and what you'd like to be, and you've lost your true self forever.

We should not be surprised at any of this if we focus on the following, startling irony, one mentioned to me by dozens of persons from most walks of life. As we "downsize" personnel, tossing them out on the street, we are asked contemporaneously to celebrate the entailing fact that the stock market is consequently healthier, richer and dare I say it, more secure. If that does not generate cynicism, nothing will. For many among us, it does! What we indulge here is a Dow—not a *Tao*.

These signs have nefarious companions, which I have discussed elsewhere. One could consider the afflictions of public school education, the inequities, the frequent shabbiness, the embattled teachers, the de facto segregation, and the drop-out rate. Or, one could discuss the epidemic facts of mindless violence and, if I may, the bizarre move to legalizing concealed weapons. And riding well beneath the surface, yet perilous, nonetheless, is the decades-long failure to maintain our infrastructure: bridges, tunnels and water-quality. We seem to be heading, inexorably as it were, towards a bottom, in which we no longer care about the things we care about. One can never claim to care *about* something or someone if they do not care *for* that someone or something. We note a systemic state of personal depression hidden by a pasty smile. In his *Treatise Concerning Religious Affections*, Jonathan Edwards offers twelve signs of conversion. Forebodingly to the contrary, we are moving towards twelve signs of reversion to a form of moral acedia, an inner decay.

I tell you a story. When my son, David, was with the Peace Corps in the Kingdom of Tonga, a group of islands on the International Date Line in the Pacific Ocean, he had occasion to educate the children in matters environmental. At one point, with the children in the last remaining rain forest on Tongatapu, he told them that their trees had a disease. They were astonished and said how could that be, Tevita, for there is no industrial pollution of any kind in Tonga. Taking his vaunted knife, David slit open the bark of a tree to show them the fetid presence of disease. He then taught them about acid rain and global wind currents. The decay was hidden but, believe me, palpable and lethal.

At the Turning

What to do! Is it too late? Is this dew-line already hanging shards over a moral landscape which has undergone the tipping phenomenon, the algae of cynicism everywhere?

Recall your reading of the opening pages of *The Plague* by Albert Camus, pp. 7–10 to be exact. One rat appears and then three rats. The concierge, M. Michel, is adamant, "there weren't no rat here." So begins the plague of Oran. Do you remember that line from your childhood? *I smell a rat.* Think about that line, once again. Think about it. In the face of our denial, the rats revealed that something had gone wrong along the way!

Well, now let us make a turn ourselves. The above jeremiad is in place. What to do! First, I tell you a story from the life of Martin Buber. After speaking to a group of students in an adult education program held in Jerusalem in 1947, Buber is accosted by one listener, a tough guy, a warrior in those fractious, dangerous early days of the modern Israel. The man chided Buber for his seemingly ethereal thoughts and asked, aggressively, how could he possibly be expected to achieve that sensibility, that form of affectionate relations with nature, with persons, and especially with profound ideas. Buber heard this outcry of frustrated rage but did not respond in kind. To the accoster, Buber said simply and directly, "You are really able." You can do it for you have the strength.

Note that Buber did not chastise this man for his feelings of contempt. He had these feelings. They do not lie. They can, however, be turned around and for that turn, Buber believed him to be "*able.*" Clearly, the task here was to undergo a "teshuva" and the pedagogy was not one of admonition or instruction. The pedagogy was that of the midwife, a mediator, of one who appeals to the dormant but not dead energies and strength of the other. Martin Buber assumed to be so what Josiah Royce had written earlier, that "the popular mind is deep and means a thousand times more than it explicitly knows." Buber asks us to live pedagogically in the creative zone of the *zwischenmenschen*, that between each of us, free of manipulation, nominal authority and the patronizing. In effect, can I help you? How can I help? Let me try to help you. And, by the way, can you help me?

The "turn" I question here has to do with the awareness of human fragility, ontologically. Your fragility and my fragility. This gives rise to virtues not of the legalistic type, those falling under the rubric of justice, important though that be, but flowing from *caritas*, which I render as caring, for and about, with affection. The moral pedagogy would then direct itself to the nurturing of compassion, gratitude and loyalty. In so doing, we would drop, or at least mute the acquisitive chase and turn towards healing. The assumption here, as I have written elsewhere, is that by the very nature of being human, we are disconnected, personally and systemically lonely, *ontologically*. The pursuit of inherited, societally-driven expectations which now characterize most of our lives, mine included, is a journey without nectar and without an awareness, let alone a celebration of the sacrament of the moment. Proximate goals are necessary and can even be salutary as we forge our own version of being in the world, on this trip. Ultimate goals and goals beyond our reach, beyond our means, beyond our abilities, turn out to be manacles dragging us forward in a manner that causes us to be oblivious to the very experiences we are now having. Following Kafka, as we should, the "castle" of our dreams turns out to be a burrow in which we are self-entombed.

In *The Myth of Sisyphus* (no myth, that), Camus writes "I want to know whether I can live with what I know and with that alone." Subsequently, in *The Rebel*, he tells us that we are the only creatures who refuse to be what we are. What, then, are we? We are creatures in need, ever, always. Josiah Royce has it right. The most dangerous among us is the "detached individual," that person who comes to realize, to say to himself, to herself, "I have nowhere to turn." A person comes to have nowhere to turn if they have "lost the way to turn." Ironically, sadly, threateningly, these detached individuals, lacking a way to turn, then "turn on others." Why has she "turned on me?" He is "turning on" everyone around him. Why are they "turning so?" It is because they have "lost the *way* to turn."

And given our cultural penchant for obsolescence it is surprising that as with most of these depressing cultural trends, there is more here than meets our complaining eye. Although always somewhat characteristic of American society, the nefarious instantiation of obsolescence as a *modus vivendi* is now both rife and systemic. If I come to consciousness with the belief that if something is out of sync, toss it; or if I subscribe to the now common attitude that on the face of it, new is better; or if my puerile philosophy of history is of the linear vein by which the march forward is cannibalistic, eating its past and hopelessly naïve about its future, then I stand bereft of roots, aesthetic comparisons and, in short, become an "isolated individual" among hordes of *"isolated individuals."*

Now it is precisely the task of moral pedagogy to assist in having us "turn" toward compassion, affection, gratitude and loyalty and away from turning backward, scapegoating in response to our journey going sour, as if it must be derivative of false and second-hand expectations.

Centuries ago, Jean Jacques Rousseau told us that if you are not free, then I cannot be free. Recasting this admonition, if I am not compassionate, if I am not loyal, then I cannot expect others to so be. As ye sow, so shall "we" reap. Speaking in November of 1951, to a group of young persons in New York City, Martin Buber said that we were "at the turning." Buber asked:

> Where does the world stand? Is the ax laid to the roots of the trees—as the Jew on the Jordan once said, rightly and yet wrongly, that it was in his day—today, at another turn of the ages? And if it is, what is the condition of the roots themselves? Are they still healthy enough to send fresh sap into the remaining stump and to produce a fresh shoot from it? Can the roots be saved? How can they be saved? Who can save them? In whose charge are they?
>
> Let us recognize ourselves: we, in whom, and in whom alone, that mysterious affirmation and negation of civilization—affirmation and negation in one—was implanted at the origin of our existence, we are the keepers of the roots.
>
> We are? How can we become it? How can we become what we are?

My version of this turning was written some thirty years ago as a passage in which I still believe, only more so, with the scars to sustain that belief. Do not await salvation while the parade passes by. Surprise and mystery lurk in our experiencing the obvious, the ordinary. Salvation may be illusory, but salving experiences can occur day by day.

3

The Mission of the Military and the Question of "the Regime"

Hadley Arkes

I have taken it as a part of my mission in recent years to point up the critical connection between comedy and philosophy. It could be said that the comedians and the philosophers make their livings in the same way, by playing off the shades of meaning and logic contained in our language. Henny Youngman would say, "My wife will buy anything that's marked down. She brought home an escalator." I used to say that my favorite epistemologist was Lou Costello, because in one of his skits, when his partner, Bud Abbott, came up with an apt idea, Costello remarked, "That's an excellent thought—I was just going to think of it myself."

At times, the laughs mark contradictions that run to the core of what some people affect to regard as the anchoring principles of their lives. And so we recall, in this vein, Bertrand Russell's joke about Christine Franklyn-Ladd, who was a "solipsist." That is, she earnestly professed that she could not know for sure that there was anyone in the world apart from herself—though she lamented, at the same time, that she couldn't find other solipsists, to come to meetings.

That line elicits a laugh unfailingly, and I have suggested that if our ears were properly tuned, we would react in the same way to this line, which has become quite familiar to us—indeed, it has become one of the most widely traveled fallacies in what passes as our public discourse: "If there really were moral truths, grounded in logic, and therefore true in all places, then why aren't they acknowledged in all places? The fact that we find so much disagreement in the world, such a wide variety of opinions about right and wrong, would seem to argue powerfully in another direction: namely, that there are no such universal moral truths. It is more reasonable to assume that notions of right and wrong will vary from place to place, according to the opinions or the 'culture' that is dominant in any place."

As I say, this has become one of the most familiar lines in our public discourse, and yet it is also, quite simply and patently, a fallacy: It stands in the class of what the philosophers would call "self-refuting" propositions, and it collapses in contradiction in a matter of seconds. As I have tried to explain in another place,[1] the argument here reduces to this proposition: The presence of disagreement—the absence of consensus—on any question of moral consequence is sufficient to establish that there is no truth of the matter. Now, I would be obliged to record my own disagreement with *that proposition* (that the presence of disagreement indicates the absence of truth), and by its own terms, that should be quite enough to establish its falsity.

That refutation can be unfolded in about twelve seconds, and there is no trick here, no play on words. It is simply a matter of uncovering the self-contradiction. And when we are in the presence of propositions that can be contradicted only by propositions that are self-contradictory, that is a telling sign that we are in the presence of what the Founders understood as self-evident, or necessary, truths (or what Kant referred to as "apodictic," or logically necessary, truths). In this case, the proposition in question is that there are indeed "truths," true propositions, and that certain truths will indeed be true in all places. Once we understand, say, the truth of the Pythagorean theorem, no one supposes that the theorem refers only to "Greek triangles," or that it would be true only in Greece.

And yet a number of prominent people in the professions have been able to build whole careers on the simple fallacy that the presence of disagreement, on matters of moral consequence, indicates the absence of truth. Justice Harry Blackmun even managed to found a new branch of our jurisprudence on this vacuity. In the hands of Blackmun, in the famous case of *Roe v. Wade*, the proposition came out in this form:

> [There is no] need to resolve the difficult question of when life begins. When those trained in . . . medicine, philosophy, and theology are unable to arrive at any consensus, the judiciary, at this point in the development of man's knowledge, is not in a position to speculate as to the answer.[2]

On the strength of nothing more than this logical fallacy, Blackmun proclaimed nothing less than a "right to abortion," and the law would cease then to cast its protections over the lives of children in the womb. In the domain of foreign policy, Blackmun's cliché takes the form of the cultural relativist argument that we heard so often during the war in Vietnam: "Who are we to say just which form of government is better or worse for people in another place?" The question of what is the good or just regime is indeed a moral question, and in the standard refrain of the period, moral judgments must always be relative to the culture or the country in which they are held.

There is of course nothing novel in this argument, or this fallacy; it has been with us since the beginning of political philosophy and the beginning of our own republic. But it is a matter of persisting importance for us to recall the way in which this question had been posed to us during the gravest crisis in our political history, the crisis of our "house divided." This question was at the heart of the famous debates between Abraham Lincoln and Stephen Douglas, and the problem was framed in this way: When the Founders had proclaimed, in the Declaration of Independence, that "all men are created equal," did they in fact mean all men, black as well as white? Or did they really mean, as Douglas argued, "all white men"? Were they merely proclaiming the equal rights of Englishmen, or the rights of those people who shared a common, British culture? Lincoln thought that the Founders did in fact mean "all men," as an abstract, universal proposition; and indeed he managed to show that any other construction would fall into a kind of gibberish of incoherence. As Lincoln quickly explained, the Founders never argued that all men were equally intelligent, equally beautiful, equally virtuous. But as beings possessed of reason, they had a claim at least to be governed with their own consent; they did not deserve to be ruled in the way that men rule dogs and horses.

Lincoln argued, then, on the ground of "natural right." His contention in the debate with Douglas was that the rights mentioned in the Declaration of Independence had a "natural" foundation: they were grounded in the things that separated human beings from other animals, and those rights would remain the same in all places where human nature remained the same and men were still distinguishable from animals. If it were not right to rule human beings as though they were horses or cattle, slavery would be wrong wherever humans were still distinguishable from horses and cattle.

Lincoln left us, altogether, a masterful restatement of the understanding of the American Founders on natural rights and moral truths; and yet the irony in our own day is that the teaching in our schools of law has been far closer to the doctrines of Douglas. In fact, the cultural relativism of Douglas is far closer to the slogans of "multiculturalism" that now prevail on the campuses of America. But even beyond the law schools, Lincoln and the Founders would seem to stand now in an adversarial relation to the orthodoxies that have become dominant in American colleges and universities. In these new orthodoxies, there are no "natural rights" because there are no moral truths and, for that matter, no "nature." The proponents of "postmodernism" and "feminism" now insist that the doctrines of "natural rights" were merely an ideology to cover "patriarchalism" and the rule of white men. The postmodernists insist that there is no "nature," that even gender, or the difference between men and women, is "socially constructed" from one place to another according to the vagaries of the local culture. And since there are no rights grounded in nature, there is of course no basis for casting moral judgments across cultures or pronouncing on the rightness or wrongness of political regimes in other places.

And yet, the curious thing about the people offering these arguments is that they continue to cast such judgments, across cultures, on arrangements and regimes in other places. They condemned a regime of apartheid in South Africa, and the violation of "human rights" in countries such as China. In fact, these commentators seem able to detect the injustices done to women in all countries of the world, in cultures other than their own, and indeed they seem to betray no want of confidence in their ability to identify "women" in other cultures. And so, in our own time, we have arrived at this paradox: In the world of the Left on American campuses, there are "human rights" to be vindicated in all parts of the globe, but strictly speaking there are no "humans," for there is no distinctly "human nature." And since there are no truths, there are, strictly speaking, no "rights." There may be claims and arguments about rights, but no claims that are "rightful," because there are no claims to rights that are actually "true."

Now I would put all of this in place for the sake of understanding what was truly melancholy in a report that was offered to me several years ago by a friend who was teaching at the war college attached to one of our military services. His students were all seasoned veterans in their forties. They had all seen military action; but they were still, twenty years later, the people who had been students in college in the 1960s, and they had absorbed much of the secular religion that affected other young people in the '60s. They had served their country in the military, but they were far from clear that there was anything about the American republic that truly justified the risk of their lives. For they were, on the whole, skeptical of the notion of moral truths that held in all times and places. They could not really say, with Lincoln, that the right of human beings to govern themselves was a right that was "applicable to all men at all times." These soldiers of their country were more disposed to believe, with other people their age, that the understanding of what was right and wrong was always contingent, always "relative" to the "culture" or the country in which it is held. They would not claim, then, that the political regime in America was morally superior to the institutions in the Soviet Union or Vietnam. They would settle for the far more modest claim that our political way of life was at least "ours": It was consistent with our traditions—it was "right," we might say, *for us*, and on that basis, we were warranted in hazarding our lives to preserve it.

But in this construction, the principles that defined the character of the American republic would be no different from the rules that marked the character of a club or the rules that defined a regime of play: the rules of the American Constitution were hardly distinguishable then from the "rules of baseball" or the "rules of chess." In that event, I offered this proposition to my friend at the war college: The willingness of his students to risk their lives for the rules of the American republic apparently stood on the same moral plane as a willingness to risk one's life to preserve the infield fly rule or the institution of the designated hitter. My friend agreed that such was indeed their understanding. The only redeeming thing he might say in their defense is that it is "our" infield fly rule, and we are free to change it. And in any system of conventions, in any rules of the game, that is certainly true. We are free to decide that it will require *five* balls wide of the strike zone to constitute a base on balls. But are we really free, in the same way, to alter these axioms of the law: that people should not be held blameworthy or responsible for acts they were powerless to affect; that like cases should be treated in a like fashion; that people accused of a crime should be presumed innocent until proven guilty; that beings who are capable of understanding reasons deserve to be ruled only with their own consent? We would be far more reserved about "legislating" a change in propositions of this kind. For even the dimmest of us may suspect that these truths are not merely conventional: They are not ours because we have chosen to adopt them; rather, we have adopted them—we have made them "ours"—for the sovereign reason that they happen to be compellingly true.

In striking contrast, of course, the men who founded the American republic were not cultural relativists. And for that reason, the principles they set forth, in founding a new republic, they did not regard as distinctly, or exclusively, American. When they spoke of natural rights or the principles of justice, they were invoking principles that they respected because those principles could claim to be true of necessity in all places. And so, for example, the principle of "ex post facto laws" barred the practice of making something illegal after the fact or treating as criminal an act that was regarded as legal at the time it was committed. The Founders recognized that principle as one of the enduring "principles of law," which existed long before they came to shape the American Constitution. The provision on ex post facto laws would not depend for its validity on the fact that it was mentioned in the Constitution. Rather, it was mentioned in the Constitution because it was simply respected by the Founders as a principle of law that was true in its own terms, true in itself.[3]

I mentioned in passing, earlier, the Pythagorean theorem—that the square of the hypotenuse of the right triangle is equal to the sum of the squares of the two adjacent sides. This theorem had been articulated by Pythagoras, a Greek, and no doubt he was aided by a tradition of reflection on mathematics and philosophy in his own country. It could be said, I suppose, that Pythagoras's contribution was something that emerged more readily within Greece as an outgrowth of the Greek culture. And yet, as I remarked earlier, there seems to be no tendency to assume that it is a theorem about Greek triangles. We do not spring to that inference because we do not think for a moment that the postulates or axioms on which that theorem is founded could possibly be confined to Greece. And it would be silly to hear someone say that he "believed" in the Pythagorean theorem, for its truth does not depend in the slightest degree on what anyone happens to believe. But in the same way, the Founders would have regarded it as quite as ludicrous if someone declared that he "believed" that "all men are created equal" or that "human beings deserved to be ruled only within their own consent." The Founders would have regarded that report as ludicrous because they would have seen an attempt to reduce to a matter merely of opinion or personal belief what should have the standing of an axiom or a necessary truth. It was bizarre to think that beings who could give and understand reasons did not deserve to be ruled in a manner quite different from the manner in which we rule beings who were incapable of giving and understanding reasons. For the Founders, the principles that established the rightness or wrongness, the goodness or badness, of political regimes were as firmly grounded in the axioms of human understanding as the axioms of mathematics. Plato and Aristotle understood the matter in that way, and Alexander Hamilton made the point quite explicit and clear in his opening paragraph in *The Federalist* #31:

In disquisitions of every kind there are certain primary truths, or first principles, upon which all subsequent reasonings must depend. These contain an internal evidence which, antecedent to all reflection or combination, commands the assent of the mind. . . . Of this nature are the maxims in geometry that the whole is greater than its parts; that things equal to the same are equal to one another; that two straight lines cannot enclose a space; and that all right angles are equal to each other. Of the same nature are these other maxims in ethics and politics, that there cannot be an effect without a cause; that the means ought to be proportioned to the end; that every power ought to be commensurate with its object; that there ought to be no limitation of a power destined to effect a purpose which is itself incapable of limitation.[4]

I linger with this matter of axioms and the political regime because there seems to be a critical falling away these days, a critical act of forgetting, that the question of the "political regime" provides the central touchstone in estimating our national interests in foreign and military policy.[5] The concern for "the regime" summarizes the moral core of our interests in politics, and it provides the grounds of our practical judgment. After all, if the Nazis had taken over in this country during the Second World War, there would probably still be baseball and hotdogs and many of our familiar entertainments (though probably not jazz and swing music, fostered by black people, or the work of Jewish comedians). There probably would have been little loss of life, and certainly there would have been no danger to the lives of our Scandinavian population, or to those people with blond hair and blue eyes in Minnesota. The Jews and certain Slavic people might have been endangered, and yet if the matter were measured according to some utilitarian calculus, it could not have been in our interest to accept a war with about 30 million deaths for the sake of saving several million Jews and blacks and Slavs. As Michael Walzer once remarked, the danger represented by a Nazi victory ran well beyond the calculus of the lives risked and saved; it involved the resistance to an "immeasurable evil."[6] The fabric of daily life might have looked familiar in America under a Nazi puppet regime, but it would no longer have been a government based on free elections, with independent courts that could restrain the power of the government. And there would have been a noticeable absence of the many ways in which that principle of "all men are created equal" tends to diffuse itself and affect the manners and character of our people in our daily lives. To capture the matter in a phrase, what would have changed in America was our "way of life," or the notions summed up in the concept of the "political regime."[7]

As Aristotle said in the *Politics*, we do not have political life solely for the sake of preserving our lives, though that is one of the principal ends of the polity—to protect life from unjustified assaults. But we have polity or laws, as Aristotle taught, for the sake of cultivating in our people a good character of life.[8] Politics involves the capacity to make decisions that are binding on the population with the force of law. But politics never occurs merely in general. There is always a character to it. If we follow Aristotle again, that character is measured along two dimensions: first, in the distribution of power, whether it is dispersed widely among the people in a popular government with elections, or whether it is concentrated, say, in a single person acting without the restraints of law. The second dimension involves the character or the *ends* of government:

Is it a government that seeks to protect its people and enhance their well-being, or a government that seeks to satisfy the private interests of the rulers themselves?

Is it a government that respects zones of privacy, in the family or the church, beyond the reach of political power, or is it a totalitarian regime that seeks to control everything and suspects everything it does not control?

Is it a government that seeks to preserve the same laws or the same rules as the conditions of fairness or equity, or a government that is always trying to tilt the rules in order to benefit some people at the expense of others?

Is it a government more inclined then to keep itself at a wholesome remove through the discipline of uniform rules or principles, or is it more inclined to interfere in the private arrangements of our lives for the sake of trying to assure that the incomes of people are more and more the same?

These are the kinds of differences that matter profoundly in our daily lives, and they are the kinds of differences that we have associated with the nature of political regimes. Those differences are seen in the difference between Germany under Hitler and the constitutional government that has governed in Germany, especially in West Germany, since the end of the war. Or it is seen in the difference between the Soviet regime and the regime that emerged with the collapse of communism, the Russian republic with free elections and an economy with private ownership, a polity in which it is legitimate to make use of the press and the media and oppose the government in public.

If we did not understand what was morally significant about these differences, we could hardly understand the justification for any foreign or military policies that were built around these differences. The statesmen of the Founding generation could give an account of why a constitutional government, or a government by consent, was morally better than despotism. Lincoln could remark later that "the doctrine of self-government is right—absolutely and eternally right." But if we cannot summon that conviction and give that account, then we cannot explain, in principle, why the American regime is one that *deserves* to be preserved: Why would we be justified in taking the lives of our adversaries and sacrificing the lives of our own people for the sake of defending it?

This question was taken to the moral root by Plato in his dialogue the *Laches*, in which Socrates winds through a conversation with Laches, a famous general, about the nature of courage. There is a temptation for people to identify courage with bravery, in the sense of a willingness to court dangers or show a disregard for one's own safety. But lions or other animals may be ferocious, and we would not impute bravery or courage to them. "Courage" is not merely a descriptive term, a label used to describe a person who acts in a swashbuckling way with a heedlessness or contempt for his own safety. "Courage" is a moral term: To say that someone is courageous rather than cowardly is to *commend* that person, to hold him up for emulation, to suggest that the world would be a better place if other people acted on his example. But we cannot commend somebody as good or admirable if he does not understand what he is doing, or if he does not understand the ends that justify his acts. If a child runs up a hill braving the fire of an enemy, can we assume that the child knows why he is acting thus, any more than the lion, or the wild animal, would know? As the dialogue unfolds in the *Laches*, Socrates leads his interlocutors to see that courage cannot be defined through formulas that have nothing to do with moral purpose. For example, courage cannot inhere simply in staying at one's post, never running away, for that may involve only a "foolish endurance" that imperils one's men and oneself. And it cannot inhere simply in showing spiritedness in charging up a hill or charging into danger, for the commander who leads his men up a hill in a reckless charge without hope of success may merely be squandering their lives. As the inquiry moves on, it must move toward this end: Courage must involve an understanding of the ends that alone could justify the risk of one's life and the lives of one's men. As Nicias comes to say in the dialogue, courage must require an understanding of whether "suffering or non-suffering . . . will be best for a man."[9] Or to put it another way, it will have to encompass an understanding of the grounds on which sacrifice would be justified. It must depend finally on an understanding of just what ends are worthy of the commitment of decent people, and whether they would justify the risk of death.

As I noted in my book *First Things*, in the annals of warfare, few armies have fought with as much cohesion as the German Wehrmacht in the Second World War, and that cohesion was preserved largely through the commitment and leadership of German officers. Those men risked their lives and offered uncommon examples of dedication to their cause. Yet, can we regard them as courageous? As I have suggested, we cannot really regard them as courageous unless we are prepared to commend them, and we can hardly commend them unless we are prepared to commend the ends for which they fought. But how can we coherently commend people who have chosen to expend their valor, risk their lives, and inspire the sacrifice of others in the service of a regime of genocide, of ends that were thoroughly evil?

This understanding of the matter was borne out poignantly by General Grant, in his memoirs, when he recalled his meeting with General Lee at Appomatox. The two soldiers reminisced together about their service during the war with Mexico, though Grant, as a junior officer, had seen Lee only from afar and known this senior figure through his reputation. As Grant took in the full presence of Lee now at Appomatox—as he noted Lee's bearing and dignity—Grant's satisfaction was touched by sadness. There was a pity to be felt, as Grant said, for "the downfall of a foe who had fought so long and valiantly, and had suffered so much for a cause." But he was quick to add—"though that cause was, I believe, one of the worst for which a people ever fought, and one for which there was the least excuse."[10] Grant's respect for valor could not be detached from the principles of moral judgment on which respect was properly offered. He could not extend the final measure of his respect unless he had been willing to blind himself to those ends for which Lee was willing to expend his valor. Grant came closer to Plato's understanding in the *Laches*, for he reflected seriously on the ends that justified war and determined, as Plato had Nicias say, whether "suffering or non-suffering . . . will be best for a man."

In 1977, two years after American helicopters had lifted off the roof of the American embassy in Saigon and North Vietnamese troops had come rolling through the streets to finish the war, there appeared in American papers an "Appeal to the Government of North Vietnam." The appeal was made by a cast of some of the most celebrated opponents of the war in Vietnam: Joan Baez, the singer, and Aryeh Neier of the American Civil Liberties Union. But now these people, who presumably had some experience in the world, were affecting a certain naiveté and surprise. They sounded rather like the Claude Raines character in *Casablanca:* they professed to be "shocked—shocked" to discover that there was no political or religious freedom in communist Vietnam: There was no right to publish in a free press and no right of a political opposition to organize and run candidates, for of course there were no free elections. And people who persisted in their religious practice as Catholics or Buddhists ran the risk of being imprisoned, as religion was suppressed. The protesters announced gravely that this was not what they had been led to expect from a movement that had been aimed at national liberation.

But that movement had always been under the direction of communists in North Vietnam, and it was aided by fraternal parties in China and the Soviet Union. Did the protestors not understand that if that movement was victorious, the result would be a communist regime in Vietnam? To be sure, there would be certain flavorings, reflecting the local cuisine or the local culture, but the outcome was still bound to be a communist regime in its essential structure. And did the protestors know of any regime constituted on Marxist-Leninist principles that had free elections as part of its way of life? Or that contained serious, constitutional restraints on the government? Why had they expected things to be different in Vietnam?

As the protestors curiously, and strikingly, "explained" in their protest, they had been offered assurances by the leaders in North Vietnam that the Vietnam emerging from the war would be a free society, abounding in rights amply respected. But as the late Sam Goldwyn used to say, a verbal contract was not worth the paper it was written on. The protestors, as the children of America, should have known better. They should have known, that is, that the assurances they were receiving were merely personal assurances, emanating from the goodwill or the sentiments of the men who were offering these assurances. But as worldly children of America, they should have been asking more pointed questions and suggesting some tests far more precise, tied to the question of political institutions. If the leaders of Vietnam truly believed in freedom and equality or in human rights, then the visiting Americans should have suggested to them that they would be far more believable if they took some public steps at once to demonstrate their commitment to these things, in the manner of the American Founders. The rulers of Vietnam should have been asked to translate their promise of "rights" into institutional commitments that would not depend in the least on the dispositions or the feelings of the men who happened to be in office from time to time.

The curious thing here is that the visitors from America did not ask the leaders of Vietnam to take that modest first step or to draw at least the first inference drawn by the American Founders after they had declared that "all men are created equal" and endowed by their Creator with certain unalienable rights: that a rightful government over human beings draws its legitimate powers only from the consent of the governed. The American Founders translated the principles of the Declaration into a political-legal structure of government by consent. If we reduced that structure to its most elementary and defining parts, it would involve, in the first instance, free elections, and then a system of independent courts, in which the government of the day could actually lose cases. The Founders understood that the purpose animating this whole project was not the creation of new rights, but the securing of the rights we already possessed by nature, even before the advent of a government. As their understanding ran, even in the so-called State of Nature we never possessed a "right" to steal or to rape or to kill without justification. Or, to put it another way, even before the advent of a government, we had a right not to be assaulted or killed without justification. As the Founders understood, the government did not invent those rights. One of the Founders, James Wilson, explained that the purpose of the government was not to invent new rights, but to secure and enlarge the rights we already possessed by nature. And the government would do that through enforcing or protecting those rights with the power of law.[11]

But the principal instrument for the securing of those rights was not the listing of rights, in ever longer lists, on parchments, or in appendages tacked onto the Constitution as amendments or afterthoughts. The Founders thought that they were creating a *structure* for the securing of rights, and the principal ingredient in that structure was this: The people whose freedom and lives were most directly affected would have the means of protecting themselves through the vote, through the prospect of voting out of office any politicians who seemed to threaten their lives or their freedom. We apparently need to be reminded these days that the courts did not become active in applying the Bill of Rights to the states until 1922. We may ask, What preserved the freedom of the press or the freedom of speech in America up to that time? And the main answer is that these rights were preserved by a structure of politics in which the active participants had a strong interest in protecting their own freedom, including their freedom to publish and defend their interests in public.

Justice Antonin Scalia has pointed out, in this vein, that there have been few constitutions in the world with longer inventories of "rights" than the constitution of the former Soviet Union. But those "rights" were of course fictions, so much window dressing in a totalitarian regime, because there was no structure for the protection of those rights. What is curious, in turn, about the former protestors who were later appealing to the government of Vietnam with a sense of betrayal is that they could be so obtuse in overlooking the obvious. What they seemed to be expecting were the most refined rights that we associate with a "regime of law," but without a constitutional government as the structure that was needed to protect those rights: for there would be, in Vietnam, no elections, no independent courts, which support, and then extend those rights. For some reason, the former protestors had never thought it important to demand those institutions or structures from the rulers of Vietnam as the institutional support for all other rights.

But it is remarkable that even lawyers seem to have forgotten that we encountered another variant of this problem at the beginning of the republic in the argument over the Bill of Rights. What is forgotten is that the Bill of Rights was opposed by a number of federalists, not because they were hostile to the notion of rights, but because they thought that a bill of rights would actually narrow or truncate our rights. For one thing, it would foster the impression that the main rights we had were the ones that were written down. Or it would suggest to many people that the rights written down were far more important than the rights that were left unmentioned. And beyond that, a bill of rights could misinstruct the American people about the very ground of their rights: It might subtly persuade Americans that these critical rights were not natural rights, which they had even before the appearance of a government, but *positive* rights, rights that were there only because they were "posited" or set down in a legal enactment. And so we must ask ourselves earnestly: Have we not heard people commonly speak of those rights we possess *through* the First Amendment—as though in the absence of the First Amendment we would not have those rights to speak and publish? Alexander Hamilton posted a caution about the "intemperate partisans" who showed an "injudicious zeal for bills of rights." They did not realize just how much they were working to diminish, rather than expand, our rights. But carrying the matter closer to the core, they did not understand that the powerful device for securing rights was to be found in the Constitution itself as a structure of popular government. As Hamilton noted, the key was in the preamble to the Constitution: "We, the people of the United States, to secure the blessings of liberty to ourselves and our posterity, do ordain and establish this Constitution." In that passage alone, said Hamilton, was "a better recognition of popular rights, than volumes of those aphorisms which make the principal figure in several of our States bills of rights." For that preamble expressed, in itself, the understanding that made the American notion of government strikingly novel in its time: namely, that the government did not spring from nature as an entity quite separate from the rights of its members; that the very purpose of the government, the purpose that called it into existence, was that of securing the rights of its people. Those who sought their security and their rights in parchment lists did not understand, as Hamilton put it, that "the Constitution is itself, in every rational sense, and to every useful purpose, A BILL OF RIGHTS."[12]

And yet we commonly find people today who identify the Constitution, not with the body of the Constitution and its text, but with the amendments containing the Bill of Rights. The people who view the Constitution through this prism rather confirm Hamilton's warning, for these people do not seem to understand, as Hamilton said, that the Constitution itself was the most impressive achievement in the securing of *human rights*. What is overlooked is the thing that should be plainest in view, but precisely the same mistake is made today by human rights activists in foreign policy. For the most part, it is the same mistake made by the former protestors of the war in Vietnam. They conceive human rights in terms of the provisions of our Bill of Rights, on criminal procedures, on rights against unwarranted searches, and on rights of publication or religious worship. They will protest over the use of torture in another country or the use of preventive detention. But they will not take as the *central aim* of their policy the establishment in other countries of a regime of consent—a regime of free elections, and free migration, which offers but another way for free people to give and withhold their consent.

As I have suggested, the same state of mind accounts for the tendency of the Vietnam protestors to have missed what was at stake in Vietnam—and just which side in that conflict represented the cause of human rights. As grownups in their forties they should have had ample experience in their own lifetimes to know that no regime denies more fully the premises of government by consent than those regimes we have rightly called totalitarian. The protestors, advancing in their years, had ample reason to know that communist regimes began by denying, at the root, the very notion of natural rights or human rights—the rights that arise from the very nature of human beings and deserve to be respected in all places. We might offer an echo then of Hamilton in this way: What the protestors did not understand is that a military policy that sought to resist the extension in the world of communist regimes and their power was *itself nothing less than a policy of "human rights."* Or, to state the matter from the other side, they did not seem to understand that the most powerful policy of human rights was the policy that sought to preserve democratic regimes where they existed and to extend the blessings of that regime of freedom to other peoples.

We were often reproached, of course, for the fact that our allies did not seem to be as fully democratic as we ourselves prided ourselves on being. Indeed, we often found ourselves allied with weak authoritarian regimes, like the regime under Salazar in Portugal, or the regime that prevailed for a while in Greece in the 1960s under the military. But these regimes were nowhere near as repressive as totalitarian regimes, and as we should readily understand by now, there are times when we are compelled to use the allies who are available to us, as we were compelled to ally ourselves with Stalin's Russia during the Second World War as a means of defeating the Nazis. And yet, people may curiously overlook the logic and the effects of coalitions, even when they are thus fashioned out of prudence. It mattered profoundly that countries like Portugal and Greece were incorporated in a military alliance of democratic countries whose purpose was to resist the extension of totalitarian power in the world. These authoritarian regimes of the political Right were rather shaky and brittle; they were bound to suffer crises and come to an early end. And when they did, it turned out to make a notable difference that they were nestled in a coalition of free countries. When the government of Salazar fell in Portugal, or the regime of the colonels finally gave way in Greece, all of the pressures emanating from NATO, and from our allies, supported the move in these countries to restore constitutional government. Portugal and Greece were brought back then into the fold of the democracies, and those democratic regimes, restored, have been sustained now for over twenty years. But if Portugal and Greece had been incorporated in an alliance directed by the Soviet Union, they would have experienced none of the pressures to convert themselves into regimes of consent. And it should go without saying that the spread of free governments in Eastern Europe has come with the collapse of the Soviet Union—a collapse that was advanced through the policy of containment, sustained in America since the days of Harry Truman and sharpened in a decisive way by Ronald Reagan.

It could be said then in all strictness that the human rights policy that brought the most dramatic, even miraculous, results was the policy of sustaining the cold war and resisting, even with military force, the spread of communist regimes. And yet, the willingness to deploy our forces to stop the extension of communist regimes in Southeast Asia was denounced as a form of imperialism. Strangely, the same protestors would not regard as imperialism the willingness to use our leverage to shorten the life of the regime of racial apartheid in South Africa. But in spite of everything that has happened in the world, it appears that the people who opposed the war in Vietnam would make the same arguments today, overlaid now with the rhetoric of "multiculturalism."

The same obtuseness, then, is to be found all about us, even today, and it will still have its effects on foreign policy. We have recently marked the fiftieth anniversary of the United Nations Declaration of Human Rights. And it was fairly easy to anticipate that one faction in our politics would take the occasion to launch a campaign to use the United Nations as a means of pressing now, as global rights, some novel claims that reflect the fashions or sensibilities of our own day. "Reproductive rights" would be a likely candidate, along with other, more advanced constructions of "the rights of women," including certain protections against sexual harassment. One variant we are not likely to find, I suppose, is the right of a female not to be aborted or destroyed simply because she is a female, in cultures all too willing to rid themselves of female babies. But we can expect that these rights will be expansive in their reach, and that, one way or another, they will bring new levers into the hands of administrators in international organizations to force a certain brand of feminism on third-world countries. And all of this will be pushed along regardless of the popular sentiment in those countries or the willingness of voters to accept these kinds of policies. But the one thing we can probably bet on is that the people seeking to use the occasion in this way will not in fact credit the real logic of human rights or apply that notion in the most consequential way, in the style of the American Founders. That is, they are not likely to take it, as their first and primary mission, to extend and protect in the rest of the world the kinds of governments that arise from free elections.

In this obtuseness there is also a certain blindness on the issue of peace. For the record of experience reveals, in a striking way, that democratic countries do not tend to make war on one another. Their commercial interests may often conflict, but they do not conceive their interests in foreign affairs in terms that are threatening to one another because they have no interest in depriving other countries of a government by consent. In theory, one would suppose that governments responsive to the opinions of their publics would also be quite responsive when those publics are animated by a religious zeal or a passion for war. But something else, something very elementary, seems to be at work in the structure of democratic governments: It seems harder to initiate and sustain wars when the government depends on the consent of the people who will have to supply their sons and their money to support the war. As Pericles was supposed to have said in his famous funeral address, "[N]o man is fitted to give fair and honest advice in council if he has not, like his fellows, a family at stake in the hour of the city's danger."[13] Let no man, that is, hazard the lives of other men's sons when he is not willing to hazard the life of his own. That, too, is part of the logic of a government by consent, and it is part of its wholesome discipline.

We readily grasped the understanding contained in NATO, that a common program of defense was practicable precisely because the allies were agreed in their understanding of the kind of regime they were seeking to preserve. Almost all of them had one form or another of parliamentary democracy. And yet, one of the astonishing things to me was that our schemes for Europe, from the Monnet Plan to the Marshall Plan to NATO and European integration, never quite caught the central point of the American idea or the American Constitution, as I discovered when working on my book, years ago, on the Marshall Plan.[14] Whenever statesmen spoke of fostering integration in Europe or of taking America as an example, what they saw in America was merely the model of an integrated commercial market. What they seemed to forget was that the American Union, reflected in the Constitution, was, even more importantly, a union for the sake of preserving democratic government in all of its parts. The Constitution contains the so-called Guaranty Clause, namely, that we guarantee a republican form of government to each of the states (Art. IV, Sec. 4). As a consequence, there could not be, for example, a coup in Rhode Island or the sudden advent of a monarchy or a dictatorship that calls off elections. But in Europe, after the war, there was a sense that democratic government could indeed be hanging in the balance. The possibility was taken quite seriously by the political classes that democratic government would be imperiled if the devastating winter of 1946–47 brought starvation, and if people were moved then out of desperation to the side of the communist parties in Italy and France. Nor was it to be discounted in this reckoning that, in the midst of this crisis, with many things unsettled, the Soviet army might cross the frontier. To meet the crisis we brought forth the Marshall Plan and NATO, and yet even with this flexing of imagination, this willingness to think anew, the idea never seemed to take hold that the very purpose of the alliance in Europe was to preserve democratic governments *within the separate states.*

That would seem, on its surface, a rather implausible claim, yet I think the point was confirmed in a telling way by the crisis that arose in Italy in the mid-1970s. There was a live prospect, and a serious danger, that the government in Italy would bring the Communist Party into its coalition as a major partner. An earnest debate then ensued as to how much the Communist Party had really changed: Did it still see itself as a party committed to Marxist-Leninist principles? If it did not, it might no longer be a threat to democratic government in Italy. But if the party had not changed in its essential character, it was hard to see how the military plans of NATO could be shared with a ruling party that had ties to the Soviet Union. The point I would underline, though, is that almost none of these vexing questions would have been problems if the understanding had been established that NATO had as one of its principal missions the preservation of an elected government in each of the separate countries. In that event, it would have been understood that units of NATO would have been deployed at once if any government in Italy had sought to stage a coup and call off elections. Under those conditions, there would have been no particular danger to national security in the Italian communists' coming to power, for they could not have come to power as real communists, committed to establishing a communist regime. And in fact, if this understanding had been established as part of the structure of the alliance, it might have encouraged the Italian communists to do even earlier what many of us had urged them to do: to break their affiliation with the Soviet Communist Party and mark the break by changing their name. Until they did that, the inference would have to persist that the communists in Italy looked upon the regime in the Soviet Union as one plausible or legitimate version of a "socialist regime." And if the Italian communists professed to see in the Soviet Union a legitimate brand of a socialist regime, why should anyone have supposed that they would have thought it illegitimate to establish the same kind of regime in Italy as well?[15]

But again, these worries over the Italian communists simply confirmed the fact that integration in Western Europe was never understood to be anything more than an economic union, and there may be a serious question of whether it is understood in any different way today. I would pose this as a question to people who have studied the moves toward the European Community: Is there anything in the current charter of the European Community that would authorize the central authorities to engage troops of the community and intervene in a member state if there were a coup in that country or if the electorate decided to vote out democratic government?

The question is really a simple one, and yet we realize that we would have to pass through several layers of understanding and commitment before we would arrive at anything as firm as the understanding contained in the American Constitution: that our purpose in this union is to secure that form of government that begins with the notion of natural rights and the right of people to be governed with their own consent.

As it turns out, that is not quite as easy a thing to preserve as we had imagined. In our own case, it helps immeasurably that the forms of a government by consent have been woven by now into the fabric of our daily lives. We have had national elections every two years since the republic began, and it is now virtually impossible to think of calling off those elections, even if some people no longer remember just why, in principle, we have elections. And yet, as with many things buried in convention, the original reasons have become lost, and Americans in our own day seem less able to explain why we have elections and the rule of the majority. Is it because that is the form of government that most people in this country prefer? Would it cease being a good, then, if most people ceased to prefer it? Or do we have free elections and government by consent because there is something good in principle about that arrangement? But if it is good in principle, we could not be free to vote it away. Would Americans recognize any longer what we are saying if we said, in the accents of the Founders, that the case for this form of government is grounded in something in our natures that we are not free to efface or deny, even for ourselves?

It should be clear that most people in this country cannot explain these things any more, which brings us to an older and graver problem, which may be put in this way: Is it possible that the outward forms of this regime may remain the same while the inner substance is changed and the regime is converted, in substance, into something else? In that event, might we cease to be a democratic people even while the forms seem on the surface the same and the people who exercise power hold familiar titles (such as justice of the Supreme Court, congressman, president)? Even now we do not have a sense of how serious or how subtle the problem may be or how deep it may run. It becomes hard, then, to capture Lincoln's sense of the gravity of the situation when he referred to Senator Pettit of Indiana, who insisted that the self-evident truth of the Declaration of Independence was a "self-evident lie." That central truth of the Declaration was that "all men are created equal," and as I have already noted, that proposition was never understood by Lincoln or the Founders to mean that all men were equally virtuous or intelligent or that they all deserved the same rewards and punishments. It meant that all men had a claim to be governed with their own consent, that it was not right to rule human beings in the way that men ruled dogs and horses.

Lincoln described that central truth of the Declaration in the way Madison described it, as an "absolute" truth. At Gettysburg, Lincoln said that the nation was founded "four score and seven years ago" on that "proposition" that all men were created equal. If we count back four score and seven from 1863, we do not arrive at 1787 but 1776. That is to say, as Lincoln understood, the American republic did not begin with the Constitution, nor was it made for the Constitution. The Constitution was made to enhance and protect the union, but the union began in 1776, with the articulation of the principle that defined the character of the American regime. The country, he said, brought forth by "our fathers," was dedicated to the proposition that "all men are created equal," and anyone who would change the regime, anyone who would convert this country into an oligarchy or something other than a republic, would have to strike at the Declaration. In that respect, as Lincoln said, they would have a "hard nut to crack," because the Declaration still elicited a powerful reverence on the part of the people. And it stirred that reverence because the people at large still grasped the point that the proposition contained in the Declaration was the key, or the first principle, of their citizenship, or their standing as Americans. And that is why Pettit's line was so disturbing or portentous: It indicated that respect for that principle had been eroding among a portion of the American "political class," from those men who held office and exercised the levers of authority. And that erosion would show up before long in places where it counted. A country that could enslave black people could begin restricting the franchise of whites. The republican features in the regime could become muted, and the authoritarian aspects could become more pronounced. In its outward forms, the regime might still appear to be democratic, but behind the facade of its forms, its substance would have been decisively altered. The regime would have been turned into something else. Hence the crisis of "the house divided," as Lincoln described it: the country could not endure if half-slave and half-free. Lincoln did not deny that the country could survive in some form, but he insisted that it would cease to be divided, that it would become all of one thing or all of the other.

These shifts in understanding may be quite subtle, but their cumulative effects may be momentous. And those shifts in understanding may express themselves where people are least aware of them. After the Battle of Gettysburg, President Lincoln urged General Meade to press the attack on Lee's army before the Southern troops could make it back across the Potomac River into Virginia. But Meade held back with a certain caution, for he was still absorbing the massive casualties suffered by his army; and in holding back, the moment was lost. The tide in the Potomac receded, the river lowered; Lee and his army made it safely back to their home ground. Meade telegraphed the president that at least the Union side could take satisfaction in "driving the invader from our soil." That dispatch merely deepened the frustration of the president. As Lincoln remarked to his secretaries, "Will our generals never get that idea out of their heads? The whole country is our soil."[16]

It must be one of the most exasperating things in politics when people on one's own side begin to absorb, subtly but deeply, the premises of their adversaries. In another incident, the year before, Lincoln had his secretary, John Hay, deliver by hand a summons to an officer in the Union army, Major John Key. Lincoln directed Key to establish, within twenty-four hours, the truth or falsity of an incident reported to him in this way: Major Levi C. Turner, a Judge Advocate, had put the question to Key, "Why was not the rebel army bagged immediately after the battle near Sharpsburg?" And according to Turner, Key had replied, "That is not the game." What he apparently meant by that was that the "game" was to have both sides skirmish, put on a good show, until they were exhausted. At that point, the political leadership would reach a settlement that dissolved the crisis without overturning the institution of slavery.

The next day, Key and Turner appeared before the president. Neither one denied that these things were said, but Turner thought that this much could be said on behalf of Key: He had heard Key on other occasions conversing about the current troubles, but he had "never heard him utter a sentiment unfavorable to the maintenance of the Union. He has never uttered anything which he Major T[urner] would call disloyalty." Lincoln, however, insisted that it was "wholly inadmissible for any gentleman holding a military commission from the United States to utter such sentiments," and he ordered that Key be "forthwith dismissed from the Military service of the United States."

Lincoln's secretary noted that Key had said nothing to controvert the account. Instead, he had sought to prove that "he was true to the Union." But as the secretary recorded, the "substance of the President's reply was that if there was a 'game' ever among Union men, to have our army not take an advantage of the enemy when it could, it was his object to break up that game."[17]

For Lincoln, everything was connected, and he was not to be taken in—as we ourselves might be taken in—by the assurances offered on the surface of things. Major Key was playing a different "game," as he put it, because he evidently did not think it worth fighting for the sake of removing slavery. Nor, apparently, would he have fought for the moderate policy set forth by Lincoln, namely, to put slavery in the course of ultimate extinction. Key might have been quite earnest in professing his loyalty to the Union, but what did the "Union" mean to him? Not, evidently, the Union described by Lincoln, the Union that was founded on the proposition that "all men are created equal," or the right of human beings to the ownership of themselves. The Civil War,

said Lincoln, was a test of the question of whether any government so dedicated, and so consecrated, could long endure. But clearly that was not a proposition at stake for Major Key at any point. Key might have been loyal to some
notion of a community, a population, in this territory, but whether the political order established in this territory was based on the premise of freedom or
of slavery was for him a matter of moral indifference. That is to say, he was
attached to his country, but he was indifferent to the principle on which the
common life of that country was constituted. He was indifferent, then, to the
character of the regime.

But in the same way, we must put the question honestly to ourselves: Do we
not face precisely the same problem with those people in the government or in
the military service who claim to serve their country but who are evidently incapable of offering any account of the ground of that commitment? They may be
loyal to their friends and their service, but they cannot quite explain the grounds
on which this regime in America could be regarded as good in principle for anyone but themselves. And even for themselves, they cannot explain why this regime should command their loyalty on any ground other than that it is the form
of government they prefer because it happens to be familiar. It happens to be
"theirs," not for any compelling reason but because they have grown up with it.
In their affable haze, they are apparently far from recognizing the depth of the
problem before them. For if they cannot supply that moral account, they cannot
explain the ground of principle on which that government has a claim to their
respect or their loyalty. In that case, they cannot really explain why they could
be justified in using deadly force in defense of this country—or why they would
then be justified in risking their own lives to defend it.

I have approached this question in an indirect way, but I trust that my point
has been clear. I hope that you, as cadets, would put these demanding questions
to yourselves, as people who have entered the military life and taken the defense
of the country as their vocation. If we have trouble in giving that moral account,
I hope that the problem will encourage us to engage in earnest reflection and
serious conversation. As we have already seen, it is no longer a surprise to find
people, even in the military, who profess to a certain skepticism, or even relativism, when a question arises about the grounds of moral judgment. But a commitment grounded in that moral skepticism is a commitment with no
grounding at all; and we should hardly be astonished to find that, for some people, that commitment dissolves into nothingness when it is tested. After all, if
there is no morally compelling reason to preserve this republic—if it does not
command our loyalty on grounds of principle—then the whole matter of loyalty

may be thrown up to the most prosaic calculation: Why not then sell a few pieces of military information if we can make a bit of something for ourselves and our own families?

It is idle to think that this philosophic emptiness, or this moral puzzlement, is simply an abstraction that produces no effect. As Lincoln understood, those subtle moral shifts produce the most emphatic, and even thunderous, results. Lincoln is still celebrated in this country, even by people who do not yet appreciate how deeply his example runs. But what is passed over is one of the most elementary things he exemplifies: that one cannot really fight for this country—one cannot even begin to fight as one should fight—unless one understands the moral ends that justify that fight and that sacrifice. People cannot understand why Lincoln was so vigorous in suspending the writ of habeas corpus and prosecuting the war unless they can understand, as Harry Jaffa observed, how deeply wrong it was, for Lincoln, to make war on the United States. For Lincoln, as Jaffa reminds us, the wrong of slavery and the wrong of rebellion were in point of principle the same.[18] In one of his first messages to Congress Lincoln put it in this way:

> This is essentially a People's contest. On the side of the Union, it is a struggle for maintaining in the world that form, and substance of government, whose leading object is, to elevate the condition of men—to lift artificial weights from all shoulders—to clear the paths of laudable pursuit for all—to afford all, an unfettered start, and a fair chance, in the race of life. . . . [This] is the leading object of the government for whose existence we contend.[19]

In a recent book, *What They Fought For, 1861–65,* James McPherson offered strands drawn from the letters written home by Union soldiers, several in response to letters from their wives pleading for their return. The husbands had already risked their lives in the service of their country, and some had been wounded. The gist of the pleas, offered by their wives, was that their families, too, had a claim to their loyalty. There were at home wives and children who desperately missed their presence, their care and support. One soldier, a lieutenant from Ohio, wrote back to his wife:

> Our Fathers made this country, we their children are to save it. . . . Why denounce the war when the interest at stake is so vital? Without Union & peace our freedom is worthless . . . our children would have no warrant of liberty. . . . [I]f our Country be numbered among the things that were but are not, of what value will be house, family, and friends?[20]

A sergeant from Minnesota, thirty-three years old, father of three children, wrote home from an army hospital where he was recovering from exhaustion:

> My grandfather fought and risked his life to bequeath to his posterity . . . the glorious institutions [now threatened by this] infernal rebellion. . . . It is not for you and I, or us & our dear little ones, alone, that I was and am willing to risk the fortunes of the battlefield, but also for the sake of the country's millions who are to come after us.[21]

What is one to say in the presence of that kind of generosity? We encounter here, quite plainly, a man who was willing to give his life in order to make a gift to the next generation, to us, as though we were his own offspring. How does one respond to that with an adequate sense of gratitude, except perhaps through a willingness to match the gift and bear the same risks?

When Lincoln was twenty-nine, in 1838, he delivered a speech to the Young Men's Lyceum in Springfield, Illinois, about the breakdown of law. In this remarkable speech, Lincoln prefigured his own mission in politics—and even his own assassination. He talked about certain rare men who would gain distinction and rise to power either by freeing slaves or enslaving free men. He pointed out that the people who rise to the highest office in a republic do not necessarily become, in that rise, ever more committed to republican government. Caesar and Napoleon rose to prominence and came to power under republics, but they soon replaced the regime with another, built around themselves. As Lincoln said, these men were part of "the tribe of the eagle." They soared above others. They could not be fitted into the laws made for people in the bulk. They could not find their satisfaction merely in treading along the paths trod by others before them or in simply preserving for the next generation what had been handed down to them.[22] They had to create something new, a regime arranged around themselves and their own, personal power.

Lincoln recognized here, as Aristotle had recognized, certain figures who were, in truth, naturally superior men. But Lincoln also suggested that there were two kinds of superior men: One rose above the law for the sake of becoming the destroyer of a republic, and the other rose above the law for the sake of becoming the savior of a republic.[23] During the crisis of the Civil War, Lincoln was compelled to suspend the writ of habeas corpus for the sake of striking at the rebellion. The procedure was contemplated under the Constitution, and yet there was no getting away from the fact that in this situation, someone in executive authority might have to go beyond the law for the sake of preserving the law. He might have to move, for the moment, beyond the restraints of the law for the sake of returning the regime to the regime as it was. Of the two kinds of men who go beyond the law, it may be argued that the one who goes beyond the law to become the savior of a republic is a man even more superior yet. For at a critical moment, when he is not restrained by the law, he shows a supreme level of self-restraint. He could create something new, but instead he returns the regime to what it was—he restores a regime of popular government. And when he shows, at the edge of that law, that supreme level of self-restraint, what he shows also, and quite dramatically, is his respect for a law outside himself.

On more than one occasion, we have seen that the security of the country may have to repose in the hands of men in positions of executive authority, who will have the freedom to act without any practicable restraint of the law. There is no security here that the law may provide or fashion. That is a hard truth we would prefer not to face directly, and yet we come here to the real limit of our capacity to contrive a remedy by creating a new structure, spinning out an ingenious new form of checks and balances. At the end, we come to the sober recognition that there is only one surety we have that the regime will be returned to the regime as it was, and that surety lies in the character of the man who makes that decision. With Lincoln, we had a man whose loyalty to the regime ran to the deepest levels of his sense of himself and his place. He said on one occasion that this was the only country in the world in which a man of his origins could come to the highest office in the land. But again, other people had risen to power under republics only to defect, to withdraw their loyalty.

The difference with Lincoln is that he had become utterly clear about that central proposition—or the central idea, as he called it—that lay at the heart of the American regime. He knew why it compelled his respect and the respect of any other man and why he was not free, in any moral sense, to abandon that regime. What made him so tenacious in fighting the war accounted, then, at the same time, for his deepest loyalty. Everything was contained, finally, in the point he made when he explained the ground and the justification for the war: What was at stake in the war, as he said—and at stake for us now, and at all times—was that simple right of a people to govern itself.

Notes

1. See my book *First Things* (Princeton, N.J.: Princeton University Press, 1986), 51–52, 134–36.

2. *Roe v. Wade*, 403 US. 113, 159.

3. See, as a notable and elegant instruction on this point, the opinion by Chief Justice John Marshall in *Fletcher v. Peck*, 6 Cranch 87 (1810). In his separate, concurring opinion Justice Johnson remarked that, in applying the principle of ex post facto laws, he was not merely relying on the text of the Constitution. He was relying, he said, on "a principle which will impose laws even on the Deity." Even God did not have the authority to revoke the principle of ex post facto laws. See ibid., 143.

4. *The Federalist* (#31) (New York: Random House, n.d.), 188.

5. To this cardinal point I once devoted a book; see Arkes, *Bureaucracy, the Marshall Plan and the National Interest* (Princeton, N.J.: Princeton University Press, 1972).

6. See Michael Walzer, "World War II: Why Was This War Different?" *Philosophy and Public Affairs* (Fall 1971): 19.

7. It is always appropriate to remind ourselves of that telling line of Leo Strauss's: "When the classics were chiefly concerned with the different regimes, and especially with the best regime, they implied that the paramount social phenomenon, or that social phenomenon than which only the natural phenomena are more fundamental, is the regime." *Natural Right and History* (Chicago: University of Chicago Press, 1953), p. 137.

8. Aristotle, *Politics*, 1252b.

9. Plato, *Laches*, trans. Benjamin Jowett, in *The Collected Dialogues of Plato*, ed. Edith Hamilton and Huntington Cairns (New York: Pantheon Books, 1961), 185e–196a; see also 190d–e, 192b–d, 197a–b. See also my treatment of this problem in *First Things*, 304–6.

10. See *Personal Memoirs of US. Grant* (New York: Charles Websster & Co., 1894), 629–30.

11. See James Wilson, "Of the Natural Rights of Individuals," in *The Works of James Wilson* (Cambridge: Harvard University Press, 1967; originally published, as the Lectures in Jurisprudence, in 1804), 2:585. These lectures of Wilson were delivered in 1790–91, when he was a member of the first Supreme Court.

12. Hamilton in *The Federalist* #84, 560–61; see also 558.

13. Thucydides, *History of the Peloponnesian War*, ed. and trans. Richard Livingstone (New York: Oxford University Press, 1960; originally published in 1943), Bk. II, p. 116.

14. *Bureaucracy, the Marshall Plan, and the National Interest.*

15. I considered this problem at length in a piece I wrote during the height of the crisis, and in retrospect I think the argument in that piece holds up fairly well. See "Democracy and European Communism," *Commentary* (May 1976): 38–47.

16. John G. Nicolay and John Hay, *Abraham Lincoln: A History* (New York: The Century Co., 1909; originally published 1886), 7:278.

17. *Abraham Lincoln: Speeches and Writings, 1859–1865* (New York: Library of America, 1989), 373–74.

18. See Harry Jaffa, "The Emancipation Proclamation," in his *Equality and Lib-*

erty (Oxford Press, 1965; republished in 1999 by the Claremont Institute), pp. 140–68, at 144: ". . . [T]here has been an underestimation of how wrong, from Lincoln's point of view, it was to rebel against the United States. For Lincoln . . . the wrong of rebellion and the wrong of slavery were in point of principle identical."

19. Speech of July 4, 1861, in ibid., 259.

20. Quoted in James M. McPherson, *What They Fought For, 1861–65* (New York: Anchor Books, 1994), 29.

21. Ibid., 29–30.

22. See Lincoln, Address to the Young Men's Lyceum of Springfield, Illinois (January 27, 1838), in the *Collected Works of Abraham Lincoln*, ed. Roy P. Basler (New Brunswick, N.J.: Rutgers University Press, 1953), 1:108–15.

23. Harry Jaffa offers a compelling analysis of Lincoln's Lyceum Speech along these lines in *Crisis of the House Divided* (New York: Doubleday, 1959), 236–72.

4

Why Serve the State?

Moral Foundations of Military Officership

Martin L. Cook

Moral Talk and Military Virtue

I want to address what I think is the single most serious moral question any military officer needs to be clear about in her or his mind: the moral foundation of the enterprise of military service itself. Morally serious and thoughtful military officers feel a deep tension in the moral basis of their profession. On the one hand, there are very few places in our society where the concepts of duty and service above self have such currency. On the other hand, there is the reality that the military exists to serve the will of the political leadership of a particular state and will, at times, be employed for less-than-grand purposes.

The language of nobility, of honor, and of sacrifice are used by military officers in ways that, for most of the rest of the society, might well sound quaint or outmoded. One hears talk about discipline and sacrifice of self for the good of others that made even a pacifist such as William James seek some "moral equivalent of war" that could instill those values in civilian life![1]

There is, to some extent, cynical talk in the military about this appeal to values and character. I think much of that is caused by inevitable tension between the reality of those values and the inherent limitations of a bureaucratic military system that tries to make those values real in practice. But I would remind you of the remark of a wise person who observed that "hypocrisy is the tribute that vice pays to virtue." Or, seen in another light, in the context of discussing the use of moral vocabulary by political leaders, the philosopher Michael Walzer observes that even if what they say are lies, the fact that they feel *obligated to tell lies*, and more importantly *to tell those particular lies*, is probably a testament of the importance to all of us of the values that their rhetoric expresses.[2]

Cynicism, then, is grounded in aspiration. That is to say, I think that what drives cynicism is *disappointed* love. It seems to me that most of the young people who come to the military are full of the highest ideals. They are often disappointed to find that reality falls short of those ideals. To some degree this is just frustration with the inherent limitations of human institutions. Disappointment with the discovery of those limitations is a perennial characteristic of young people in all areas of life—and one to be cherished. It is the idealism of each new generation that gives us hope and makes human progress possible. Of course, some of the frustration also flows from aspects of the system that are not as good as they could be in trying to implement its values in institutional form. But rather than focus on the cynicism, it is important to acknowledge the deep longing for the values that underlie the disappointments.

My point is simple: The military profession's rhetoric of a unique moral basis should be taken as a testimony to real and powerful aspirations—aspirations to be deeply valued in our society. The value of those aspirations remains and should be honored, however far short of them we sometimes fall in experience. These aspirations are the foundation of the military virtues which preserve and sustain some of the noblest of human values: to serve others even at the cost of personal sacrifice, to discipline one's mind and body so that it serves a purpose larger than self and the pursuit of pleasure.

Having said all that, however, I want to note that there is a tension between these ideals and another important reality of the military system. That other reality is that the military exists as the servant of particular states and of their political leadership. If we believe Karl von Clausewitz that "War . . . is an act of policy,"[3] the military exists not to serve grand and universal moral principles but simply to sacrifice itself for the political ends of the state. To put it bluntly, on Clausewitz's account, the real purpose of military leadership is simply to serve the national interest as that interest is defined by political leadership. Viewed from this perspective, all the rhetoric about the high moral purposes of military service constitutes a verbal smoke screen behind which lurks a very unpleasant truth. If this perspective were the final word, then the truth would be that it is *functional* to persuade individuals to think about service in such moral terms, but only to make it psychologically easier for them to evade the true reality—that they and their organizations exist only to serve the tribal interests of their state. And since states, on Clausewitz's analysis, are engaged in a constant struggle to advance their interests and to diminish those of other states, there is little here to be seen as truly morally grand.

Of course, if we were to think about the military this way, we would probably disguise that reality by invoking ideas of the "self-defense" of the state. But such talk is vague. We know the core meaning of "self-defense"—self-defense is when someone is attacking us personally, or when extended to the state, when we resist a border incursion or protect the lives of fellow citizens in peril. In that narrow and relatively precise sense, all but absolute pacifists grant there is a right to self-defense. But it requires considerable conceptual sleight of hand to extend the concept of self-defense to foreign interventions—whether humanitarian or imperial—and to balance-of-power wars. In short, only rarely do militaries—perhaps especially the U.S. military—fight in wars which are genuinely defensive of political sovereignty and territorial integrity. More typically our wars serve something considerably broader and vaguer than strict self-defense would imply—something expressed with claims to vital national interests or important national values.

So we are now prepared to focus the fundamental question: What is the moral basis of states themselves that justifies our fighting to advance their interests? Certainly, one might say, it is only human individuals who make moral claims on us, and the use of force and violence might be justified in the defense of such individuals. But apart from conflicts of this type, where individuals are really being threatened, why should anyone be willing to kill and die for the state—an entity which, after all, is a relatively artificial construct, built on its own morally ambiguous foundation of conquest, domination, and destruction of other cultures?

What States Are and Why We Value Them

Our question was posed most sharply by St. Augustine, arguably the most important influence on Western intellectual culture. He writes at one of those few real crossroads of history, literally watching as the Roman Empire is collapsing around him, sensing that a new age of darkness is descending on the Western world. In his great work, *The City of God*, Augustine reflects on the ruins of the Roman Empire. Romans of the old school have a ready explanation for the collapse of their civilization: the fall of Rome is the fault of the

Christians. For centuries, they reasoned, Rome was secure in its political and military strength because it worshipped the civic gods of Rome. In return, those gods protected the empire and sustained its armies. Indeed, for the Romans, much of religion had a primarily practical and civic function, and from the beginning Christians' appeal to universal and transcendent values that embraced all of humanity seemed politically dangerous and profoundly "un-Roman." From this pagan Roman perspective, a century of Christian rule had undermined those civic virtues and hence undermined Roman character and will to fight.

It is Augustine's task, as he sees it, to refute the pagan charge. And in the course of doing it, he ranges widely across Roman history, political philosophy, and the philosophy of history. Augustine's ideas become quite literally the intellectual foundation of the Western Christian church and of Western political philosophy for the next thousand years. His influence is by no means absent even today. His point of departure is to question Roman assumptions about the glorious character of the state itself. With *painstaking* and—to Roman audiences, anyway—*painful* detail, he recounts the legends of the founding of Rome. Were not the legendary founders of the state, Romulus and Remus, suckled by wolves? Was the state not founded on murder and treachery?

Then, in one of the most famous passages in the entire work, Augustine offers his own view of the glory that was Rome:

> Remove justice, and what are kingdoms but gangs of criminals on a large scale? What are criminal gangs but petty kingdoms? A gang is a group of men under the command of a leader, bound by a compact of association, in which plunder is divided according to an agreed convention. If this villainy wins so many recruits from the ranks of the demoralized that it acquires territory, establishes a base, captures cities and subdues peoples, it then openly arrogates to itself the title of kingdom, which is conferred on it in the eyes of the world, not by the renouncing of aggression but by the attainment of impunity. For it was a witty and truthful rejoinder which was given by a captured pirate to Alexander the Great. The king asked the fellow, "What is your idea, in infesting the sea?" And the pirate answered . . . "The same as yours, in infesting the earth! But because I do it with a tiny craft, I'm called a pirate: because you have a mighty navy, you're called an emperor."[4]

On Augustine's view there simply is no moral difference between states and bands of pirates. There is only the difference of scale, which can make the state seem grand while the robber band is simply evil. Both depend for their success on a kind of internal harmony and organization (what we might call "military virtues"), and both measure success by their ability to take and destroy the lives and property of others.

Augustine thus counsels Christians to look to their true home not in the City of Man or the Earthly City, as he calls it, but in the City of God—a "city" of universal and transcendent value. Only in such a city can human beings find spiritual and moral rest: as he wrote in another work, "God, you have made us for yourself, and our hearts are restless until they find their rest in Thee."[5]

But for the time being we live in both cities. In this life, and in this history, we must struggle amid the shades of gray of the state, of warfare, and of injustice, doing what we can to make things better and more peaceful than they would otherwise be, but not hoping for or expecting purity. We are to live, then, "between the times"—aware of the City of God, but not trying "before its time"[6] to live as if we were its citizens exclusively.

It may be necessary to go to war in service of the *relatively good* state, which is all that stands between us and complete political and moral chaos— a chaos Augustine quite literally sees on the horizon as Rome falls and barbarian armies advance on his own city in Africa. But we are to enter into such wars "mournfully," justified by the aggression of others' disruption of the peace but free of false hopes of creating a City of God amid the shadows of the City of Man.

This Augustinian line of thinking laid the foundation for the classic Christian and, later, secular international-legal justification for participation in warfare: the just (or justified) war theory. This theory worked out a place for the moral conduct of soldiers intermediate between the pacifism of the early church and the amoralism of the nihilist's denial that moral categories apply to war at all.

Of course this tradition underwent enormous elaboration and qualification as it wended its way through Western intellectual history and through the changing political contexts in which it was worked out. For most of the thousand years after Augustine, the Western world was a relative backwater compared to the stronger and more sophisticated civilizations of the East—first of the Eastern Roman Empire and then of the new Islamic civilization centered in Baghdad. In the West, the ideal was a unified Christian civilization centered in Rome and under the authority of the bishop of Rome, the pope. On this understanding, wars were justified, at least theoretically, as responses to disruptions of the order of that civilization.

It is important in our thinking about fighting in defense of *states* to remind ourselves that the state as we know it is a fairly modern invention. For much of history, and for many cultures, *the state as we think about it* does not exist at all, or its existence is highly relativized by other forms of human organization. In the West it was not until the period after the Reformation that the nation-state, with its claims to sovereignty and territorial integrity, became the dominant institution. Prior to that, European nations and political leaders were subordinate in principle, and often in fact, to the ideal of a universal Christendom. Similarly, to this day, the Islamic world affirms in principle the unity of all Muslim peoples and the ideal of gathering all these peoples into a single political order with a single political head. This Muslim civilization as a unified entity is set in contrast to the *dar al harb*, the world of conflict, which lies outside the order of Islamic civilization. And in many parts of the post-colonial world—in Rwanda, Bosnia, Ethiopia, to name only a few examples— we daily discover horrible evidence that the boundaries of states on the map correspond poorly if at all with the ways in which the inhabitants believe their society to be organized in tribes and clans.

The development of the concept of states with rights to territorial integrity and political sovereignty and the evolution of a world system that takes that form of organization as fundamental are attempts to give a moral shape and definition to the realities of post-Reformation Europe. It became obvious as Europe exhausted itself in the religious wars following the Reformation that the last illusions of a unified Christian empire were no longer thinkable. In place of the earlier ideal, laws and customs of international relations evolved to deal with those new realities, and particularly to put an end to perennial war over religious differences. At the end of the Thirty Years' War, the European states, accepting the futility of restoring political and religious unity by force, crafted the Peace of Westphalia in 1648. In this new Westphalian international system, religion would no longer be a factor in determining alliances or granting or withholding citizenship. Nor would it be a cause of war. What resulted was a system in which Europe was organized into nation-states of differing religious systems. Here the "rules of the game" were that the internal matters of states were their own business. It is from this that we get the modern international system, in which a state's political sovereignty and territorial integrity are the highest values. The whole body of international law is founded on this idea of the sovereign state as an entity closely analogous to John Stuart Mill's idea of the free individual, able to do as he or she sees fit in matters that affect only individual welfare. And correlatively, each free individual is at liberty to pursue the life and beliefs which seem to him or her most likely to lead to happiness, free from the interference of others.

The whole body of Christian and medieval thought about the just war is transposed in this new environment into a secular version of the theory. Here *jus ad bellum*, the reasons for going to war, are increasingly defined in terms of the defense of the twin principles of the new international system: territorial integrity and political sovereignty of states.

In developing the moral foundations of military service, the military, too, comes to have a rather different conceptual framework in this model than it had in medieval Europe or in the Islamic world. Naturally, I don't mean to defend the Crusades or the military aspects of the Islamic concept of *jihad* (religious struggle) to expand the realm of Islam. But I do want to note that those notions of military struggle place the activities of the warrior in a supposedly universal moral and religious frame; *in principle* the soldier fights not for the local interests of a particular ruler or state but in the name of values believed to be universal and transcendent.

With the rise of the nation-state, the role of the military is set in a much smaller, and probably more realistic, context: that of defending a particular political and social order in the face of threats to it by other militaries in the service of similarly particular states. It is an axiom of this new model of the international order that all states *have equal moral claims* to territorial integrity and political sovereignty, and that *each state* has the right to be free of aggression by others and to use its military in defense of those rights. Although occasionally the rhetoric is more grandiose, perhaps especially in American political discourse (the "war to end all wars," defending democracy or civilization, defeating communism), the "official rules" of the international system were built on the idea of the fundamental equality and internal sovereignty of all states.

There is an implication here for the morality of the military: in the Westphalian international system, military officers are moral equals, regardless of the state they serve. This is the classical modern European understanding of the moral foundation of officership—that all military officers are morally co-equal members of the profession of arms. Even though they may be called upon by their political leadership to fight each other, and to fight in wars of unequal moral worth, this is not strictly an issue for the military professional. On this model, the moral demands on the military profession are great, but they are also delimited. The officer is obliged to serve the state with integrity and to conduct military operations in a professional manner, disciplining subordinates and ensuring that they conduct themselves within the bounds of the laws and customs of war. But it is *not* the responsibility of the officer to assess the moral worth of the state itself or, in all but the most extreme cases, the justice of the war the officer is ordered to conduct.

But with this Westphalian model, one may still ask our fundamental question: What is the moral basis on which officers of these particular states can justify killing and dying for their interests? Such states are, after all, hardly bearers of universal moral, religious, or political truth. This is a hard case to make, but it is important to make it. Let's look only at our own history. Suppose someone said that the United States is built on the morally very questionable foundation of conquest or the destruction of indigenous civilization by disease and war, of dishonorable and dishonest dealings with both Native American peoples and with Mexico; and that its current territory is the product of those complex forces and trends which rather arbitrarily interacted to make the United States have the borders it now has. Suppose that person went on to say that racism is alive and well in American life, and that the relations between the sexes are far from fair and equal. To that litany of charges, what can any well-informed and educated American say but "true"?

Admiral James Stockdale has written a fine essay in which he discussed his observations on education and the prisoner-of-war experience.[7] He pointed out the dangers of a POW with so little education or such a misguided understanding of patriotism that the realities of a less-than-perfect American society could be presented by an enemy as something he or she did not know. Stockdale's point, I think, is profound: If one is to serve the state as a thinking military officer, one must serve the state *as it is*, not the fantasy state of America's highest ideals and ambitions. In this regard, Augustine's somber estimate of the state—of any state—is far closer to reality than the "alabaster cities" whose gleam is "undimmed by human tears" of our best national song. Of course the above litany of injustice, with only appropriate regional variations, would be the story behind every other state in the world, too—except the even worse cases of Middle Eastern and African states whose borders are even more unnatural, imposed as they were by departing colonial powers.

I believe, however, that we are in a phase of human history where this Westphalian state system and the model of military officership it generated are undergoing profound change. Symbolically the change was marked by General Dwight Eisenhower's conduct at the end of World War II. When German General Jürgen von Arnim was captured, he requested a meeting with Eisenhower—a request completely reasonable on the Westphalian model. Eisenhower refused, however, saying,

The tradition that all professional soldiers are comrades in arms has . . . persisted to this day. For me, World War II was far too personal a thing to entertain such feelings. Daily as it progressed there grew within me the conviction that, as never before . . . the forces that stood for human good and men's rights were . . . confronted by a completely evil conspiracy with which no compromise could be tolerated.[8]

The Changing Character of State Sovereignty: Implications for Military Officership

Clearly, Eisenhower's attitude marks a change from the idea of morally equal military professionals to one of military service set once again in the framework of universal moral questions about the nature of the states that officers serve. And even in cases where that model applied less clearly (Vietnam or the Korean War, for example) American political discourse has tended to follow that trend in the post–World War II environment, speaking of each engagement as a battle of moral and human good against unalloyed human evil. Of course, insofar as military power and determent were *actually* (rather than simply *rhetorically*) in the service of the resistance to communism, those claims made considerable sense. At the very least, it was true that the form that communist states took were affronts to human dignity and liberty on a scale comparable to that of the Nazis.

But as everyone now knows and no one fully understands, we are now in a "post–cold war world," or, as we have come to call it, "a new world order." There is much that only time can tell us about what this means, but I wish to note at least a few of the trends it implies, and then to return to our central question concerning the moral foundation of military officership. Of course much of what I'm about to say is common knowledge. Nevertheless, I think it important and necessary to rehearse these considerations.

The first and most dramatic change in our new environment is that it is no longer bipolar, either conceptually or militarily. For the entire post–World War II period, the important military and political power in the world was effectively divided into the two spheres of superpower influence. But we do not yet know what will replace that system. Will it be a monopolar world, with the United States dominating as the sole remaining superpower? While theoretically a possibility, I do not think such an option is likely to materialize. There are too many strong non-superpowers that have their own claims and agendas in this world, and the United States lacks the will and desire (fortunately, in my opinion) to impose on the world a *pax Americana* by the same brutal means that the Romans needed to impose the Roman Peace in Augustine's time.

If that is so, then we look forward to a much more complex and multipolar world than we have experienced in our recent history. We see this tension in all our recent military deployments, and it appears as a kind of national schizophrenia about the uses of military power, and therefore also about the moral foundations of military officership. Let me say, too, that while I have clear opinions about the prudence and desirability of both of the examples I'm going to use, I shall not comment on those opinions here. Rather I choose these examples as illustrations of what seem to be our confusions in thinking about the moral basis for the use of military power.

Take the Gulf War as an example. No war since World War II has so clearly matched the Westphalian paradigm: A sovereign state, internationally recognized, has its territorial integrity and politically sovereignty directly and unambiguously attacked. That state requests help from the international community to restore it among the nations of the world. States respond; aggression is rolled back; Kuwaiti sovereignty is restored. This is the classic Westphalian story with a happy ending.

But, say the critics, the moral basis of the Gulf War is tainted. Despite all the rhetoric of international law and multinational coalitions, so the argument goes, *really* the war was about oil and economics. The implication seems to be that *because* there were important international economic interests involved in that war, the presence of such interests makes the motives impure. "No blood for oil!" went the chant. But would "blood for Kuwaiti sovereignty"—in the absence of oil—rally the enthusiasm of the critics?

For the sake of contrast, let us briefly examine the Haiti deployment. Here, in extreme contrast to the Gulf War, it is very hard to make a case for a crucial U.S. interest in Haiti. True, here there was a clear and unmistakable violation of human rights, of respect for law and international diplomacy, and there was real repression of the smallest stirrings of internal resistance. Yet here the criticism is the opposite to that of the Gulf War; the cry, I suppose, would be "No blood for the rights of foreigners when there is no national interest involved!"

These examples seem to me to point to the horns of the Westphalian dilemma in its post–cold war form: Is military power to be used in the service of national interests, wherever they are? If so, then claims to higher moral justifications are unnecessary and misguided. In other words, Clausewitz's word is the final word, and war really is just politics by other means.

Alternatively, is military power, freed from the fairly artificial and historically abnormal framework of the bipolar superpower world, now at last at liberty to serve the universal moral ends of promoting democracy, supporting human rights, and removing oppressors to the cheers of the oppressed? If so, how and why should national political leaders be willing to spend the blood and treasure of their individual nations in the service of the lives and rights of foreign nationals?

I believe we are deeply ambivalent about these alternatives, and much of our national confusion about the role of U.S. foreign policy generally, and about the purposes of military power specifically, results from this conflicting pair of models for thinking about force projection. As I said, I think only time will provide some of these answers, but let me sketch two models for the moral basis of officership in this changing environment.

The first accepts the Westphalian model of international organization, but with modification. Michael Walzer, in his fine book *Just and Unjust Wars*, attempts to work out why national loyalties should matter to people. His argument is that even though existing states and their boundaries result from utterly irrational patterns of arbitrary map-making and histories of conquest, still in reasonably good states, the nation with its twin rights of territorial integrity and political sovereignty creates a "space" (both literal and metaphorical) where a group of people can attempt to work out a "common life." He explains this concept of common life as follows:

> Over a long period of time, shared experiences and cooperative activity of many different kinds shape a common life. "Contract" is a metaphor for a process of association and mutuality, the on-going character of which the state claims to protect against external encroachment. The protection extends not only to the lives and liberties of individuals but also to their shared life and liberty, the independent community they have made, for which individuals are sometimes sacrificed.[9]

On this model, therefore, one serves the state in order to protect the "common life" that the officer shares with fellow citizens. One recognizes the complexity and often the moral ambiguity of the processes that give rise to that common life. But one recognizes as well that the persistence and flourishing of that common life is a condition for human welfare and goods less tangible than life and property—the goods of shared memory, common symbols, and history and culture. It provides a language to try to articulate why, in reasonably good states, it matters to be an American or a Haitian, over and above the good of individual survival.

The foundation of this idea of "common life" is Westphalian, and applicable to every society possessed of sufficient historical continuity through time. It is here, I think, that General Eisenhower's perspective weighs in. If the moral basis of states is that they create and maintain the "space" within which a common life can flourish, it is obvious that states succeed in doing this to widely varying degrees. Walzer continues his argument:

> The moral standing of any particular state depends upon the reality of the common life it protects and the extent to which the sacrifices required by that protection are willingly accepted and thought worthwhile. If no common life exists, or if the state doesn't defend the common life that does exist, its own defense may have no moral justification.[10]

It is this reality, I submit, that we encounter with ever greater frequency in the new world order—of "states" with borders on maps and seats of government that correspond poorly, if at all, to the common life (and often common *lives* of multiple communities) contained within their borders. When we survey the horrors of Bosnia and Somalia, to name only two examples, we clearly see states of this type—states that contain no clear common life and fail to protect even the individual lives and rights of their inhabitants, let alone this grander concept of common life. These situations call to the sympathies of all of us and cry out for "someone" to do something to remedy the situation. Yet it is here that the moral tug collides with the Westphalian reality: What individual states are willing to sacrifice their citizens' lives in such a cause?

It may prove to be utopian, but is it too far-fetched to imagine that the new world order, premised not only on the collapse of a bipolar world, but also on the growing world culture of communication and global awareness, may also work a change in the moral foundation of military officership? If Walzer is right, and states are worth defending for the common life they protect, may we not be witnessing the painful, but inevitable, birth of a truly global common life? As we watched the failure of international institutions to deal effectively with Somalia and Bosnia, were we perhaps realizing the inadequacy of existing international mechanisms to deal with the problems of states that do not protect a genuine common life? As the United Nations was founded on a clear realization of the need for effective mechanisms for collective security, so too, I think, we are entering a period where farsighted leadership would see the need for a military dedicated to the high moral purpose of defending fellow citizens of the global common life.

In a profound speech to a joint session of the United States Congress, South African president Nelson Mandela said the following:

> In an age such as this, when the fissures of the great oceans shall, in the face of human genius, be reduced to the narrowness of a forest path, much revision will have to be done of ideas that have seemed as stable as the rocks, including such concepts as sovereignty and the national interest. . . .
>
> If what we say is true, that manifestly, the world is one stage and the actions of all its inhabitants part of the same drama, does it not then follow that each of us . . . should begin to define the national interest to include the genuine happiness of others, however distant in time and space their domicile might be?[11]

Mandela's vision of the new world order has much to commend it. To a large degree, it seems to reflect accurately the global convergence we daily witness around us. It reflects, too, the growing sense that the existing structures of international relations are increasingly inadequate to the tasks now facing them in the post–cold war world.

But it leaves much unresolved at the practical level. Are the armed forces and leaders of individual nation-states prepared to enlist in the service of such a vision? Can we ask the military of our state to fight and die in the name of such a global vision of our interests?

Clearly, it is too early to tell. But it is equally clear that the moral foundation of military officership is showing all the signs of a fundamental revision. The world of the Peace of Westphalia is passing from the scene, and we only begin to glimpse what will take its place. Young officers enter a military full of challenges, different in kind from those of any of their predecessors. It is theirs to take the lead, not only in command, *but in thought*, about what that future will be.

Notes

1. William James, "The Moral Equivalent of War," in Richard Wasserstrom, *War and Morality* (Belmont, Calif.: Wadsworth Publishing Co., 1970), 7.

2. Michael Walzer, *Just and Unjust Wars: A Moral Argument with Historical Illustrations*, 2nd ed. (New York: Basic Books, 1992), 12.

3. Karl von Clausewitz, *On War*, book 1, chap. 1, sect. 23.

4. Augustine, *The City of God*, vol. 2 of *Basic Writings of St. Augustine*, ed. Whitney J. Oates (New York: Random House, 1948), book 4, sect. 4.

5. Augustine, *Confessions*, vol. 1 of *Basic Writings of St. Augustine*, ed. Whitney J. Oates (New York: Random House, 1948), book 1, 1(1).

6. Augustine, "Letter to Count Boniface." In this fascinating letter, Augustine counsels a Roman general, tired of war and thinking of entering the monastic life, to remain in the field against the barbarian armies advancing upon his forces. In this struggle, forced upon him, Boniface plays out the role of the biblical "peacemaker," Augustine argues. Among many other places, this letter can be found in Arthur F. Holmes, ed., *War and Christian Ethics* (Grand Rapids, Mich.: Baker Book House, 1975), 61–63.

7. Stockdale, "The World of Epictetus: Reflections on Survival and Leadership," in *War, Morality and the Military Profession*, ed. Malham M. Wakin, 2nd ed. (Boulder, Colo.: Westview Press, 1986), 16–22.

8. Dwight D. Eisenhower, *Crusade in Europe* (Garden City, N.Y.: Doubleday, 1948), 156–57, quoted in Walzer, 37.

9. Walzer, 54.

10. Ibid.

11. Nelson Mandela, "Address by Nelson Mandela, President of the Republic of South Africa, Before a Joint Meeting of the United States Congress," Oct. 6, 1994. *Congressional Record—House*, H11008.

INTEGRITY

5

Some Personal Reflections on Integrity

General George Lee Butler

A s a 1961 graduate of the United States Air Force Academy, I have had over thirty-two years to reflect on my experience as a cadet. If I had to single out one thing that I took away from the Academy that is most worth reflecting on, it would be the honor code. You see, it has been the entire foundation of my military career. It has been with me every step of the way. It is still with me, every day of my life.

In order to appreciate how I can say that, you need to understand a little bit about me. I'm from a small rural town in northern Mississippi. My dad was in the Army for forty years. He started out as a private and retired as a colonel. I grew up with small-town values. I went to a school with 240 kids—there were 21 people in my class. A low point in my young life involved Mrs. Criss, my English teacher, who was one of those wonderful, wonderful women who devote their entire lives to teaching students like myself the principles of English. She caught me one day helping one of my less intellectually gifted classmates with a book report. To this day I will never forget the look on her face or the words that she said to me when she realized what I was doing. She said, "Lee, your friend Joe was only in danger of failing this report. You have failed me, and worse, you have failed yourself." I failed myself! Those words are seared into my brain. I shall never forget them as long as I live. It is an episode that will always be part of me, and that I carried into my Academy experience.

It is a painful story. But I must be square with you. This is a painful essay for me to write, because it forces me to walk back over the mental broken glass

73

of a dozen traumatic episodes, as a cadet and at intervals throughout my career as a young officer and even as a senior leader. In every one of those episodes, the honor code had a tremendous impact on me. I took it completely to heart. I took it into my career, and I vowed to be true to its precepts every moment that I wore the uniform.

Let me tell another story. This one is from late April 1961. I was a senior cadet, five or six weeks from graduation. I was a cadet squadron commander, an honor student, and an honor cadet with four years on the superintendent's merit list. Late one evening, I turned to my roommate, who was an honor representative, and said, "Oleg, there is something I have to say to you. I want to report myself for an honor violation." I was absolutely sure in my heart that I would be leaving the Academy. Oleg listened patiently to my dissertation about an event that had occurred my third class year and had tormented me for all of the ensuing time. It had to do with whether or not I had been true to my signature when I had signed a report. He went to the other honor representatives that night, and they convened at midnight. It was a long night for me, but I shall never forget when Oleg came back and said, "The committee reviewed your case and concluded that this was an extraordinarily minor incident; it has no honor implications and they are amazed that you would have agonized over it for so long."

Why do I tell this story? It's one of my early experiences with the honor code, and it also helps me to convey a message. The first message I want convey, as an old grad reflecting back on a full career, is that the demands of my profession far, far transcend the simple precepts of the cadet honor code. That is an absolutely minimum standard for behavior in the Air Force. If you struggle with the honor code, you will strike out in the Air Force and the profession. But the honor code is not sufficient. So again, and especially for anyone who is about to step into the crucible of life in the military, here is the heart and soul of my message, which thirty-two years of military service have driven home with absolutely crystal clarity: The singular distinguishing, defining value of the military profession is a priceless quality called integrity. Integrity—here is the touchstone upon which everything depends. If I could change one thing at the Air Force Academy, I would modify the exhortation affixed to our granite wall, "Bring Me Men." I would write, "Bring Me Men . . . of Integrity."

Why do I feel so strongly about this? Why do I write this essay from a sense of professional obligation to share with whoever will read it? It is because I have seen the price of ethical collapse time and again in my career. And I have been terribly disheartened and dismayed by the consequences. I have been around long enough. I have been responsible for people and I have been accountable for missions, so I fully appreciate what is at stake. Without integrity, we lose first and foremost public trust and confidence—the willingness of the American people to allot hundreds of billions of dollars of the national treasury to our missions; to send their sons and daughters into the military ranks, perhaps to fight and to die on foreign soil; to accord us pride and respect, even though most people only dimly perceive the details of what we do; to take us on faith; to *trust* us. It is also our credibility as leaders. It is the moral authority that we must earn and sustain if subordinates are to entrust us with their lives and fortunes and their sense of worth. It is the dignity of all the people who come into our care and our sway, not just subordinates, but their spouses and their children as well, and the quality of their lives at work and at home.

We are talking about the first great measure of a professional, the singular quality that preserves public trust in who we are and what we do. It is the sine qua non, the spirit of open and honest communication, of teamwork, on a staff, in the field, or among crew members. It is the wellspring of leadership. It is the basis of earned authority, of unswerving loyalty and disciplined obedience to orders.

So integrity is our most important asset as professionals. It is to be cherished and guarded against all assaults, temptations, snares, and illusions. When integrity fails, everything fails. There is no sense of outrage equal to that of a public shocked by scandal in high places; or of a unit whose mission and reputation are soiled by an incompetent or unscrupulous leader; or of a subordinate abused by a trusted boss or of a spouse betrayed by an unfaithful wife or husband; or of an Academy awash in honor violations. That is why we witness such a visceral rejection of the hypocrisy, the greed, the grasping for power, and the distorted values of public officials who violate their oaths and trample on the most common standards of human behavior. It is because they have committed the cardinal sin for a professional—they have proved unworthy of their trust, of their influence, of their access to privileged information or to the public treasury. Avoiding this is the root of the high expectations and demands of the military profession, the crucial import of its first commandment, "Thou shalt not violate thine integrity lest public trust be lost."

But how do you grapple with a subject like this? First I want to talk about the elements of integrity and what they mean to me, the elements that form the framework of my personal code of behavior. It is the measuring rod that I use to gauge both myself and the people who work for me. It is the way I decide whether or not to promote them or even to retain them. Then I want to talk about why integrity fails, why people of high station stoop to low deeds, why they throw away reputations and careers and families for trivial ends and forsake the public trust for momentary personal convenience or gain. Then I want to share some thoughts on how you can preserve integrity. I want to give some advice on how to protect and shield your sense of propriety, of right and wrong, against the assaults of careerism, the lure of monetary gain, the euphoria of power, the fear of failure, or the darker sides of human nature, which can overwhelm our commitment to decent, honest behavior. Finally, I am going to share with you the simple code that I have hammered out in thirty-two years of trial and personal temptation and disappointment. But it is a code that also comes from living in the company of great people, whose ironclad standards, high expectations, and towering strength helped build and reinforce my own sense of integrity and why it is so important.

Integrity

What is integrity? Of what does it consist? What are the standards of behavior that form an alarm system that insures an unfailing sensitivity to ethical issues? My first thought is that the ethical standards that characterize integrity begin with the same principles that are contained in the cadet honor code. I have court-martialed only three officers in my career: one for lying—he falsified a leave slip. Another for cheating—he tried to copy off of a crew member on an inspector general examination. And a third—believe it or not—shoplifted a pair of sunglasses in the base exchange. Lying, cheating, and stealing. But the standards of integrity don't end with a strict reading of the cadet honor code.

Falsifying a leave slip is very obvious dishonesty. But for the ethical officer, what else does lying encompass? What other standards does it entail? How about misleading or misrepresenting statements, or half-truths? How about when a young person uses a false identification card? Does that fall within the bounds of lying? If there is any doubt in someone's mind about the propriety of that, I think that person has failed to grasp the concept of integrity. Surely one must accept that a modified piece of plastic—substituting for a direct answer to the question, "Are you old enough to drink?"—is a lie just as much as if the words had come from your lips. What about quibbling or fudging or covering up for subordinates; or gossiping or rumormongering or maligning the reputation of peers or seniors; or not speaking up to correct the facts? Or co-ordinating on documents you have not read or signing off on maintenance forms without doing the appropriate checks? None of these things is permissible for a person of integrity.

And what about cheating? A pretty straightforward concept, right? But what about being disloyal to your boss? Or just doing lazy, sloppy work on government time? Not giving your best effort on the job or in school, or being unfaithful to your wife or your husband or your congregation or your city or your constituents or your unit? Using a friendship to get an edge on a contract? Do those sorts of things constitute cheating according to your sense of integrity? I think they had better.

And stealing—we don't take things that don't belong to us. Pretty simple, right? But what about taking office supplies home or using government phones for personal calls or padding travel vouchers or using the office computer for personal use? Are these forbidden by your definition of integrity? What does your own code tolerate for yourself and for others? Let me say it again. The principles in the cadet honor code are a beginning for understanding integrity, an absolutely minimum standard. But a simple reading of it does not encompass all the kinds of situations that confront one daily in the military and which we must resolve properly.

A second element of integrity for me is competence. Professor Sam Huntington gave the best definition of a profession that I am aware of. He concluded that three values distinguish a profession: corporateness, expertise, and responsibility. Corporateness—what that means for the military should be obvious: a sense of common identity, the same sorts of uniforms, shared values and principles, the same heroes. Expertise—being a professional in the military means mastering a demanding range of knowledge. But most important is responsibility—being responsible for people, for units, for millions of dollars' worth of equipment. What is our bottom line? In the business world it is profit. For professionals it is public safety and security, the lives and fortunes of others. For the *military* professional it is much more than even that. It is the survival of the nation. It is freedom and preserving a way of life. It is the lives of coworkers and subordinates. It is unit missions and reputations. It is knowing and doing a job with great competence, not for making money or setting records or for personal gratification, but because we have been entrusted with a great responsibility. So this responsibility makes competence a crucial ethical concern.

Let me tell a story about another low point in my career. I was standing on a stage much like this, giving a welcoming speech to new members of my bomb wing at 8 o'clock in the morning. Suddenly the door on the side swung open and the brilliant sunlight came in and I was momentarily blinded. But as my eyes cleared and I peered out the door, my heart sank, because I saw a towering pillar of smoke off the end of the runway, and then I saw the ashen face of my deputy commander for operations. He didn't have to say a word. I knew it. A B-52 with ten crew members had just crashed. When the accident was investigated, it became apparent that two senior, experienced instructor pilots knowingly conducted an unauthorized version of a minimum-interval takeoff, putting the faster airplane behind the slower one. When the second airplane got airborne and began to overtake the first, the panicked student pilot, who was on his first such mission, snatched back the power. The instructor pilot pushed it back in, flooding the engines on the right side and creating a flying coffin. It staggered for thirty seconds and then ten lives were snuffed out. Why? Because of a lapse in professionalism of two senior instructor pilots who had the lives of other people in their hands.

The third element of integrity for me is moral respect for others. By this I mean the behavioral norms toward fellow human beings that spring from attitudes at the very core of our belief systems. These are the key qualities that condition and define the worthiness of leadership, qualities that encompass all the values of the leader. Respect separates the tyrants from the beloved, the abusive from the even-handed, the charlatans from the towering giants of integrity. I think of the men for whom I worked throughout my career, who were my role models, who set examples for me, men who got the job done while maintaining high standards of personal and professional conduct. They treated their people with unswerving dignity, decency, equality, and impartiality. They reserved their outrage for the lowlifes who demean our profession with their racist or sexist or religious bias or their bullying, arrogant attitudes

Let me dwell on this point for a moment, because the failures of respect that I have experienced and witnessed account for some of my most challenging and disillusioning experiences. I saw some of those failure as early as my Academy days. As a new cadet I was absolutely appalled by the brand of so-called leadership that I encountered. I never expected it; I never accepted it; and I have fought against it my entire career. In its worst form it is "leadership by decibel." There were far too many shouting, posturing, and abusive upperclassmen who, for lack of personal stature and character, or worse, for sheer malicious fun, stripped new cadets of their dignity and their self-confidence. That is contrary to every principle of human decency and totally foreign to the high standards of conduct in today's military. Make no mistake; leading by fear and threat and intimidation is neither toughness nor an acceptable expedient.

It is a personality disorder. It represents the worst flaws of character in a leadership position. It's abusive authority rooted in excessive ego and ambition. It creates a corrosive working environment. It breeds dysfunctional tension, anxiety, and uncertainty in people. And it takes a terrible human toll, both on the job and in spilling over into peoples' family environments.

You may be familiar with the leadership model called total quality management. It is a style that first and foremost values people. Pretty fancy. People have earned lots of money teaching a principle that really is ages old and says, "Do unto others as you would have them do unto you." It is a principle that creates an environment where talent, training, and dedication are nurtured and enhanced. That does not mean that poor performers are tolerated; far from it. If you can't meet standards, then you are identified and retrained, or out you go—swiftly, but humanely. Does that sort of leadership work? You bet it does.

It is exactly the kind of leadership that I exercised as the commander of the 13th Cadet Squadron for an entire year, from 1960 to 1961. It was superb leadership training. I had a cardinal rule—any upperclassman that I caught demeaning or abusing a fourth classman was out—out of my squadron, and if I could get it done, out of the Academy. The rule was that we would treat each other with decency and respect. How did we come out? The 13th Cadet Squadron was the outstanding squadron in 1961 and for four of the next five years. The tradition carried on. I think that is a record that still stands at the Academy.

The next time I was privileged to wear the title "commander" after my name was in 1982, almost twenty-one years later, when I became the commander of the 320th Bomb Wing. It was the first time I had commanded anything since I left the Academy. I ran that wing exactly as I had run the 13th Cadet Squadron, and it served me very well. It also worked for me in two bomb wings in Strategic Air Command and it worked for me in United States Strategic Command. I give a lecture to every person who came into my headquarters. I made it crystal clear: the cardinal rule in Strategic Command is integrity, and as a part of that we treat each other with dignity and respect. And I made that stick both by my behavior and by swiftly removing supervisors who failed to live by those standards.

I dwell on this point because integrity is defined in terms of relationships with and among human beings—and because we human beings have such a sad history of finding cause to hate and to demean and to diminish. I learned about that early in life as a boy in rural Mississippi, living in a town where black people went to different schools and churches and lived in tumbledown shacks and drank from separate water fountains and worked for slave wages and even died at the hands of bigots. I saw the slurs of racism scrawled on the rest-room walls and dormitories at an Air Force base I once commanded (a base where I became legendary for a year-long campaign to stamp out the attitudes and the slogans that spread racial fear and hatred). Finally, I insist on this point because of the lingering, debilitating, and intolerable sexism that still permeates our society and, worse, our own profession. "Tailhook" was only the most recent and visible manifestation of sexism in the ranks of the armed forces.

But the problem is far more pervasive and deeply rooted. It is bred in a terrible double standard whose origin goes back to antiquity. It is the horrific notion that the female of the species is a sexual object for the male. This leads to tolerating, justifying, or rationalizing virtually any form of abuse, from leering looks and dirty jokes to physical harassment or rape and, in some societies, even murder. The price for this kind of behavior is unimaginable, incalculable. In my first six months as the commander of Strategic Air Command, now STRAT-COM, I relieved and had retired two general officers for sexual misconduct. As a wing commander I had investigated, and subsequently relieved, a colonel for making a pass at the wife of a noncommissioned officer in my wing. He was an Air Force Academy graduate, and a three-time early promotee. He left a scar on my soul and on my profession that I will never recover from.

How can such things happen? How can they happen in our noble profession, where trustworthy leaders are the cornerstone of mission accomplishment? How is it that a female cadet can be raped at the Academy, an institution whose sole justification is to produce leaders with ironclad standards of integrity? Its *sole justification* — so if we don't train leaders at the academies, if we don't insist upon high standards of conduct, if integrity is not the core value taught, then shut them down. We can get smart folks—people of integrity—from a host of academic institutions across America.

Why Integrity Fails

Why, then, does integrity fail? Why is it that people of great reputation and talent lose their way and risk a lifetime of work and achievement? Why do leaders abuse their authority and their people through an exaggerated sense of importance and power? Why do officers tarnish and destroy careers for a few dollars or momentary convenience? Why do crew members and technicians risk their own or others' lives by disregarding directives and procedures? Let me give some personal observations on this score, taken from years of coming to grips with the shock of fallen heroes and shattered trust.

First of all, I think integrity fails because of a fundamental character flaw, a flaw that I term "confusing who you are with what you are." The historian Lord Acton once said, "Power corrupts and absolute power corrupts absolutely." He got that right. He understood what ambition, ego, and greed can do. I have watched people become enamored with their position and their perks and watched as it fostered a meanness of spirit and abusiveness. Let me give you some words to live by. Words that are carved in my brain and on my heart: "Great men seek power to do, not to be."

Second, I think integrity fails because of a human frailty—simple fear. Sometimes it's fear of failure. The trauma of taking examinations and being evaluated leads to an overwhelming temptation to cheat. We also fail because we fear embarrassment or taking responsibility for mistakes. Lying is often meant to cover up, to shift the blame, to avoid confrontation, to not accept responsibility as a supervisor or leader. We fail because we want to condone, to look the other way, to pass on our bad apples. Or in the words of the honor code I hold so dear, we can fail by tolerating behavior in others that we know to be wrong. If you think that the toleration clause in the code means "ratting" on your friends, I'm afraid you have failed to appreciate properly the core standards and institutional values of leadership in the Air Force.

Third, I think integrity fails because of a sheer lack of competence. Some people are inadequate to their tasks and duties. They come face to face with the "Peter Principle," having been promoted to a level of incompetence. Or it may simply be a matter of poor discipline or lack of application or bad training or supervision, the failure to deal with a lack of intelligence or misassignment of subordinates. In any of these cases, incompetence constitutes a lack of integrity for those with great responsibility.

Fourth, I think integrity fails because of weak moral reasoning. Sometimes we handle moral dilemmas and conflicts (with their competing values and priorities) badly, using poor judgment. Sometimes we suffer from a kind of moral blindness. Think of our society, shot through with racism and sexism; or an institution like the United States Navy, where debauchery becomes common practice among carrier aviators; or a unit where lying, cover-ups, and fraternization become a way of life. It takes a clear head to see the moral problems. Integrity fails because people fail to recognize that they are dealing with moral issues, because they lack education and a personal code, because they fail to keep their minds on what education and a moral code require.

How to Preserve Your Integrity

That brings me to my final point. How do we nourish and reinforce integrity? First and foremost, it is absolutely imperative to develop an understanding of what is at stake, a sense of personal responsibility and accountability. That means reading and studying ethics, reflecting on consequences, and thinking about implications and outcomes. It means grasping the wrongdoings of senators who sexually harass aides, Wall Street schemers, scoundrels in the pulpit, contractors who overcharge, consultants who trade on friendships, mayors who do crack cocaine, or archbishops who develop intimate relationships with members of their flock.

Second, it means developing mental toughness. Mental toughness is absolutely essential to being in charge of others, to accepting responsibility and holding subordinates accountable and not tolerating a diminishment of standards. It means never making excuses, never rationalizing mistakes. It means brutal self-assessment and introspection. It means being an inward- rather than an outward-directed person. It means focusing on the mission rather than yourself and your career.

Third, it means keeping a sense of perspective, remembering that those of us in uniform should be engaged in public service, not making money, not seeking power or status. We will always have greater responsibilities to our God, to our country, to right living, to our family, and to ourselves.

This personal code of mine, derived from the cadet honor code and hammered out in the crucible of thirty-two years in the Air Force, is very simple. First, "Always do and say the right thing." Don't lie or cheat or steal or quibble or look for excuses. Don't worry about consequences, and remember that no one has ever improved on the Golden Rule as a basic guide for dealing with other people. Second, "Work hard, but for the right reasons"—to fulfill the mission, not for personal advancement. Third, "Live your life as if someday you will have to account for every moment, every thought, and every deed, public or private." That's not only a good rule of thumb, it's smart—someday you might have to.

Let me conclude with a wonderful story about a wonderful woman named Babe Didrikson Zaharias. I took this from a book called *Taking Charge* by

Major General Perry Smith, one of my great heroes. The "Babe" was one of the greatest athletes of all times. She was a legend in the 1932 Olympics and was one of the best women professional golfers of her age. One day, she walked into the scorer's tent, having apparently just won a tournament. She checked her card, signed off on it, and turned it in after having assessed herself a two-stroke penalty. She thereby lost the tournament by a stroke. The scorekeeper, who was absolutely astonished, said, "What in the world is this all about?" She replied, "As I played the last hole out of the rough I realized that I had somehow played the wrong ball; that's a two stroke penalty." "But," he said, "no one would have ever known."

"Oh, yes," she said, "I would have known."

Whether integrity works ultimately comes down to you—in your day-to-day life as a professional. Your integrity (or lack of it) is shown in what you do when no one is watching or listening. It's what it means to you in the kind of penalty that you assess yourself, according to your values and standards; what it means to you when the chips are down, when values conflict, and when things go wrong; what it means to you when temptation beckons, when easy money or small misrepresentations offer quick profits at the expense of your integrity. Ultimately your integrity is the best asset that you will bring to the unit that you will command; to the office you will supervise; to the table where you will bargain and debate with your peers; to the boss who will depend on you for open and honest presentation of facts; to the Air Force, whose quality is founded on the integrity of its people; and to the nation, whose survival depends on the rock-solid values and unfailing competence of its military professionals.

6

Decisions of Leaders and Commanders — Ethics Counts

LIEUTENANT GENERAL BRADLEY C. HOSMER

T he military is a profession of hard choices. Choices in our profession have a way of coming along suddenly and unexpectedly. Choices in our profession may involve painful decisions, and it can be especially painful to make the *right* decisions. Choices and decisions in our profession also involve, on occasion, expensive mistakes. Making ethics count in hard choices like these is crucial.

Three Examples

I want to start with a few examples that will carry us through this discussion. All three are real events. The first involves a lieutenant who lent his new car to his fiancée. One Friday morning, someone bumped into the car from behind while she was stopped in traffic. She, along with the driver who bumped into her, examined the car. They didn't see anything seriously wrong, just one small scratch, so they parted company amicably. Still a little uneasy, when she got back to the base she reported to her fiancé what had happened. He looked the car over carefully and saw that the rear bumper had been pushed in one-half inch. He thought there may have been a couple of hundred dollars' worth of damage.

He took the car to the local dealer, and the damage turned out to be $1,500. This was a big problem. He didn't have a police report, and he believed his insurance company was going to want a police report to file the claim.

It occurred to him that he could go to the Security Police and say, "My car was in the Officers' Club parking lot, and I found it afterwards with this damage." Then he could get a police report from the Security Police and use it to make his claim. The insurance company then would pay his claim, as they should anyway. No harm, no foul; it all comes out the same. So this was the decision he faced. Why not go to the Security Police with his story to get his police report?

Now for a second example. Two students were in pilot training, flying the T-37. They were not doing well. Because they were having trouble, they were assigned to a strong instructor. They proceeded in their training towards their first solo flight. Their progress was good on some days, and not so good on some days. The instructor worked with them, moved by the fact that they were diligent, worked hard, and paid close attention.

As they approached the point of flying solo, the instructor was faced with a tough choice. He was confident enough of his own abilities as an instructor that he felt the students could solo and solo safely. But he had doubts about their prospects for fully completing pilot training. Perhaps if he could get them through solo and watch them a little while longer, as they accumulated more flying time, then he could make a better decision about whether they would ultimately finish and be decent pilots. That is the decision he faced. Should he let the students solo?

The third example comes from the Vietnam War, in 1971. The war in the North was not going well. At that time, we were not bombing in the North, but we were flying reconnaissance missions and taking careful note of the developments in the enemy's logistics. Our rules of engagement required that we could not fire, not bomb, not attack, unless we were first attacked by the North Vietnamese. That meant that a reconnaissance mission, with its escorts, could not take any action until the surface-to-air missile site or anti-aircraft artillery site had let fly. We were losing pilots because of this. No matter how big the escort packages were, it still cost us both reconnaissance and escort pilots. The four-star commander, the air commander in Vietnam, was, as you might imagine, quite frustrated by this situation. He didn't know what to do about it. About this time, the commander received direct oral guidance from the Joint Chiefs of Staff that said, "We really think you should find ways to be more inventive to put more pressure on the North Vietnamese. Do your best, be inventive."

The commander knew ways to be more aggressive, but those ways would violate the rules of engagement. In fact, to use those ways he would need to falsify the combat action reports. But he could save aircrews' lives and be more effective in what they were doing in the North. His question was, of course, Should he do that?

The Character of Leaders

I hope to convince you that anyone who has a *reflex* for honorable action would find that reflex a very powerful ally in dealing with situations like these. The military officer's world is exposed, full of temptations, ambiguous, and in many ways, morally unforgiving. For an officer, ethical failure is failure of the worst kind and can be disastrous. On the other hand, the rewards for ethical conduct, both personally and professionally, are very great.

Now what do I mean by ethical conduct? At the very minimum, I mean conduct that is in accordance with the basic principles in the honor code we teach cadets at the Air Force Academy. But I also mean more than that. So let us assume the basic elements of not lying, cheating, or stealing and then elaborate on that "something more" that I'm talking about. Together, they should give us some guiding principles for determining ethical conduct.

One extra component is, I believe, the character trait that's of the most value to an officer. When you need advice, to whom do you go? I think it's fair to say that most of you go to someone you trust. If you're in a position to distribute responsibility, to whom do you give it? I think you would most often give the same answer—someone you trust.

Edgar Puryear made a lengthy study of what makes for effective military leadership by interviewing key World War II leaders and people who worked with them. He asked them all, "What are the key ingredients?" The results were published in his classic book, *Nineteen Stars*. Let me quote a few of the points made by those he interviewed. General Eisenhower said that "character in many ways is everything in leadership. It is made up of many things, but I would say character is really integrity."[1] General Lawton Collins stated, "I would place character as the absolutely number one requirement in leadership. By character, I mean primarily integrity. A good leader is a person whose superiors and, even more importantly, whose subordinates can depend upon that leader taking action based on honesty and good judgment. If he does not base his actions on honor, he is worthless as a leader."[2]

These sentiments are pointing to the issue of trust. My summary of them would be that actions and judgments that can be trusted completely are based on total honesty, putting mission ahead of self. These seem to me to be the characteristics that bring trust. So why is trust, and the integrity that leads us to give it, so valuable? I'll sketch a few reasons.

One simple reason is that they lead, by reflex, to right action, and thus keep us out of trouble. Let's go back to that example of the young officer with his damaged new car. What do you suppose happened? He did in fact go to the Security Police and said that his car must have been damaged in the Officers' Club parking lot. He asked for a police report so that he could use it for his insurance claim. The Security Police, trying to help him with his problem, started an investigation of what might have happened. In the course of the investigation they discovered that he had cooked up the story and lied about it. The lieutenant was given nonjudicial punishment under Article 15 and was dismissed from the Air Force for lying. The saddest part of the story is that his insurance company did not require a police report. They would have taken the officer's word as accurate and truthful. So that's one reason, at the very simple level, that the integrity reflex is important: In leading to the right action, it will keep you out of trouble.

But I don't think that's the most important reason. Another reason is that integrity satisfies public expectations about you. Yet another reason is that character and integrity bring the loyalty and trust of those who work for and with you. As a commander or leader, you can order these things, but the hard practical fact is that normally you earn them only by encouragement and example—and no other way. Another reason that character and integrity are valuable is that they bring much larger responsibilities. The reason I am wearing this uniform is because there is something I want to do, there is some service I want to contribute, there is something I wish to achieve. The larger the responsibilities that come your way, the more you can accomplish. Ethical conduct, integrity in your conduct, leads to trust; and trust tends to bring bigger opportunities to serve— to serve a purpose—which is the best reason for being in uniform.

Integrity and Decision-Making

I have mentioned some reasons that integrity and a commitment to right conduct are important. But the most important reason is this: Leaders and commanders who have character—who have that integrity reflex—make better decisions. This is the core of my message. I'll tell you why I think so.

First, I think that bringing an ethical approach into a decision helps ensure that you use a long-term, big-picture perspective. That is, it helps to keep your ego from getting in the way of a good decision. In 1944, after the Allies had made the cross-Channel assault and were established in Europe, General George Marshall made a tour of the battleground with General Eisenhower. At one point, he turned to the Supreme Commander and said, "Eisenhower, you've chosen all these commanders or accepted the ones I suggested. What's the principal quality you look for?" Eisenhower responded, "selflessness."[3] Selflessness. I think this is another way of saying that ego must not interfere with command decisions.

Let's go back to that second example, the one with two students in T-37 training who weren't doing very well, but were doing just well enough to solo. The instructor had to decide whether to send them solo and then have them get more experience so that he could make a better decision about their prospects. As it turned out, he did let them solo, they did all right, and they came back.

But not long after their initial solo, at Laughlin Air Force Base in Del Rio, Texas, there was a typical bad-weather day. The winter scud came up the river valley and created a low ceiling over the base, but not too low—they could still fly traffic patterns. So it was a traffic-pattern-only morning. These two students still needed all the practice they could get, so their instructor sent them out solo. The traffic pattern became very full, as you would expect. At one point, one of these two students saw a conflict with another aircraft in the crosswind leg, and he broke out of the pattern, as he should. He set himself up to re-enter at the correct place, as he should, and he commenced to re-enter the pattern on downwind leg.

Both of the students were having difficulty, and it took almost all of their attention to fly correctly. That meant that they didn't have much attention left for looking around. The student who re-entered flew directly into the other student on downwind leg. I was in the runway supervisory unit as senior controller, and I watched one aircraft disintegrate, and the other one crash into a nearby hill. We learned later that the student in that second T-37 was frozen on the controls, apparently completely taken by panic, and the radios had been carved out of the airplane by impact, so he couldn't hear us calling to him to eject.

Looking back on it, could it be that their instructor's ego got in the way of a good decision? The instructor's desire to solo the students and confidence in his own ability to see them through perhaps caused him not to weigh as heavily as he could, or should, the long-term prospects of those students. To me, this is an example of how ego can get in the way of a good decision.

One of the best stories I know about selflessness, or lack of ego, again involves General Marshall. During our preparations for the invasion of Europe, many of our leaders knew that Marshall would be the supreme commander of the Allied forces in Europe. The president and the secretary of war had discussed it, and Prime Minister Churchill had in fact recommended it to Roosevelt. It was, as we say today, a done deal. Marshall probably knew these things; I don't know what the record shows but I can't believe he didn't have some inkling. It was also known that Marshall had his heart set on it. Marshall's heroes had been the great field commanders, and I think that we can all be sure that he did not want to finish his nation's great war from an office in the Pentagon.

As the time came close, it seemed that Marshall's role in Washington was also vital, and in that role he may have been irreplaceable. As the president weighed this decision—whether he should send Marshall forward to become the supreme commander of the Allied invasion or keep him in his vital role in Washington—he couldn't make up his mind. To resolve the issue, he invited General Marshall to lunch. He described the quandary, put the problem to Marshall, and asked his advice. As best we know, he would have followed Marshall's advice. So here is a case where Marshall could have had the job of his dreams if only he would ask for it.

General Marshall declined to give the president any advice. He said, "Mr. President, you must decide." In the end the president decided he needed the comfort of knowing that the best man was in charge of organizing the entire effort in Washington at the military level, so he kept Marshall there, and General Eisenhower became the supreme commander.

Of course, truly ethical behavior will be costly from time to time; can you imagine what General Marshall's self-restraint cost him, keeping his ego buried in his pocket while the president asked for his advice? But Marshall kept his ego and his short-term benefit out of the decision. Integrity forced him to consider the big picture and the long term, and hence led him to a better decision. That to me is a vivid example of why and how Marshall was such a great man, and why he was able to make one balanced decision after another throughout that very difficult crisis.

The next reason why ethical decisions are better decisions is well demonstrated by the third case I discussed above, the quandary of how to pursue the air war in North Vietnam in 1971. The point here is that ethical decisions are more certain to keep you aligned with your leadership; that is, they are more certain to keep you in the role you are counted on to play in the overall plan. This keeps you part of the national strategic solution, instead of being part of the problem.

The air commander in Vietnam in 1971 resolved his dilemma by yielding to the pressure that he had received from the Joint Chiefs of Staff to go beyond the approved rules of engagement. To avoid reporting violations of the rules in his combat reports, he built a double reporting system. One set of true reports was kept for records at the bases, and a second set with altered facts was sent to Washington.

Of course, this practice meant that no one in Washington had a true picture of events in North Vietnam. This turned out to be very costly, because at the same time, we had secret talks going on in Paris between Henry Kissinger and Le Duc Tho, the foreign minister of North Vietnam. These two diplomats were feeling their way toward some possibility of disengagement, and unfortunately each had a different set of facts about events in North Vietnam.

The assertions made by Kissinger, based on his incorrect data but known by Le Duc Tho to be inaccurate, led the North Vietnamese minister to conclude that Kissinger was either dishonest or negotiating in bad faith. So he lost confidence, and the talks went nowhere. We don't know what the full cost of that failure really was. But we do know that a successful conclusion of those talks might have shortened the war. So the air commander's decision in North Vietnam may have saved a few lives in the short term, but probably cost much more in the long term. I believe that a more ethically based decision on the part of the air commander—one that refused to contemplate false reporting—might at a minimum have prevented that misunderstanding between Washington and North Vietnam and therefore prevented the breakdown in the talks.

One silver nugget emerged from that sad example. After the dust settled, the chief of staff at that time, General Jack Ryan, issued a personal message for every Air Force individual that explains why integrity in reporting is absolutely essential:

Integrity—which includes full and accurate disclosure—is the keystone of military service. Integrity binds us together into an Air Force serving the country. Integrity in reporting, for example, is the link that connects each flight crew, each specialist and each administrator to the Commander-in-Chief. In any crisis, decisions and risks taken by the highest national authorities depend, in large part, on reported military capabilities and achievements. In the same way, every commander depends on accurate reporting from his forces. Unless he is positive of the integrity of his people, a commander cannot have confidence in his forces. Without integrity, the Commander-in-Chief cannot have confidence in us.

Therefore, we may not compromise our integrity—our truthfulness. To do so is not only unlawful but also degrading. False reporting is a clear example of a failure of integrity. Any order to compromise integrity is not a lawful order.

Integrity is the most important responsibility of command. Commanders are dependent on the integrity of those reporting to them in every decision they make. Integrity can be ordered, but it can only be achieved by encouragement and example.

I expect these points to be disseminated to every individual in the Air Force—every individual. I trust they help to clarify a standard we can continue to expect, and will receive, from one another.

Ethically based decisions are also better decisions because they lead to stronger commands. In my experience, commands that are led by such decisions tend to be tight, enthusiastic commands that have a focus on common purpose. These commands have in their ranks people with higher expectations of each other and themselves, and they also have more fun on the flight line, on the shop floor, in the offices, and in the air. They tend to work better.

I don't know why this is. It may have to do with the fact that every unit reflects the standards of its leader. I expect everyone has good examples of the way standards ripple down through a unit and how high standards can inspire better performance than anyone ever thought possible. It is remarkable to watch.

For example, an incident took place in 1981 at a two-wing Tactical Air Command (TAC) fighter base out west where attitudes were known to be sour. Both wings had heavy responsibilities, and the troops had been working very, very hard for a number of years. Commanders were consequently quite understanding and lenient about the demands of the workplace. Small infractions of discipline or shortfalls in performance were not really noted carefully. Poor performance did prevail in many units. Even though forgiveness was common, performance of the wings on that base was average to below average. Police blotters revealed that many of the people in trouble had been in trouble before, sometimes many times. The commanders responded to infractions only with oral counseling, even for repeat offenders.

All these indicators show a challenging situation. An indication of poor morale was that reenlistment rates at that base, compared to all the bases in the TAC, were at the bottom or next to the bottom. If you looked at the actions taken by commanders (Article 15's, courts-martial, letters of reprimand, unfavorable information files), once again you found that among TAC bases that base was at the bottom, or next to the bottom, on every indicator.

There was a meeting of all the commanders who reviewed the data. When they saw the data, the squadron and wing commanders decided that they needed to raise their standards of discipline and what they required in duty performance. Two things happened almost immediately. One was predictable, and the other a real surprise, a surprise to me particularly.

The predictable one was that there was a real spike in Article 15's, courts-martial, and letters of reprimand. In effect, we were cleaning up backlogged business that had just been deferred. The second result surprised me because it happened so fast: Within six weeks, that air division became a tuned-up, tightly focused, happy command. And it was much more effective.

Now I don't believe in fast fixes. As a commander, my impression is that fast fixes are usually forced, and when the individual who forces them leaves, the fixes come unglued and don't last. But, in this case, though the fixes were fast, they appeared to be very deep throughout the units.

It didn't take long to find out why. Conversations with first sergeants, supervisors, troops on the line, and officers made it fairly obvious. First, at that base there was the normal sprinkling of top people. They had been trying to uphold high standards all along. When they saw their commanders beginning to take action against the people who weren't holding the high standards, they finally felt they were getting support from their bosses. Second, as the below-average performers began to leave, the workload actually got lighter. And of course, the good workers who were left behind began to feel that for the first time their bosses were available to work with them. The commanders, the first sergeants, and the supervisors now had more time to spend with the good people instead of working with the problem people. It was a positive step forward, and the effect was very powerful.

So I see this as a case where supporting high ethical standards was the best thing to do—not only because high ethical standards are inherently right, but also because they lead to a much stronger command with far happier people. The impact is not trivial. In the military profession, when things go right, lives are saved, national treasure is conserved, and national strategic purposes are carried out more effectively, and sometimes carried out when otherwise they would not be. We should all take great satisfaction in our profession, where doing the right thing, for the right reason, can also produce such satisfying results for our units and for the country.

Encouraging Ethical Conduct

While I was superintendent of the Air Force Academy, I observed some very interesting trends. In the four-year period from 1988 through 1991, officers from sources other than the Academy received Article 15's at the rate of three per thousand officers per year. They also got about one court-martial per two thousand officers per year. Graduate courts-martial, however, ran about 56 percent of nongraduates, and Article 15's about 46 percent of nongraduates. I think this difference is due to the fact that the graduates, from the very beginning, understood that high ethical standards are essential to this profession. They took their training with the honor code, and the principles of integrity that go beyond the literal code, and then reflexively made highly ethical decisions as junior officers.

Their example will help the whole organization. Academy graduates will comprise only about 20 percent of the new line officers that enter the Air Force every year. As officers from each of the principal sources of commissioning—also including Reserve Officer Training Corps and Officer Training School—enter the Air Force, they each bring their own specific strengths. One of the specific strengths that Academy graduates bring is recent experience with a demanding high ethical standard. As new officers associate with their colleagues in the Air Force, they will look to each other and learn from each other, and those from each source will tend to look at officers from other sources for those strengths in which those other sources are thought to be expert. The Academy graduates will be considered experts in high ethical standards, and their colleagues will look to them to set the standards in the Air Force with high ethical conduct.

After a few years and a few assignments, the graduates' particular strengths will diffuse across the entire officer corps. That's why their role, as the bearers of the high ethical standard, is so critical. After a few years have gone by, their actions, as exemplars, will set the ethical character of the officer corps across the entire force. I think a process like this can happen in any large organization and is probably the best way to encourage the integrity we need in leaders everywhere.

Conclusion

Leading and commanding is great work. Few people will face the challenges faced by military leaders and commanders. But we must not forget that in our decisions, ethics counts, and in a big way. Few are able to take the satisfaction we can take from doing the right thing, not only because it's right, but also because the decisions we make will come out better because of ethical standards. Ethical decisions will have a powerful and productive effect on our units, and our nation.

Notes

1. General Dwight D. Eisenhower, interview, 2 May 1963, in Edgar F. Puryear, Jr., *Nineteen Stars* (Washington, D.C.: Coiner Publications, Ltd., 1971), 289.

2. General J. Lawton Collins, interview, 20 September 1962, in *Nineteen Stars*, 290–91.

3. *Nineteen Stars*, 336.

7

Professional Integrity

Brigadier General Malham M. Wakin

Some years ago one of the students in my medical ethics class approached me after the major research paper had been graded (it was worth 40 percent of the grade in the course). This student had worked hard during the course and had also worked hard on this 20-page paper, but it was clearly a solid B paper and there was tragic disappointment on the face of this student. "I need an A on this paper to keep my A in the course," he said. "Please, you must raise my paper grade or you'll jeopardize my chance to be admitted to medical school."

Now I was very much interested in helping this student achieve admission to medical school because I believed he had the potential to be an excellent physician, and I had said as much in the strong letter of reference I had written for him and sent to several schools. But raise his grade on the basis of this request? My immediate, almost automatic response was "I *can't* do that."

What I want to discuss is bound up with that answer—"I can't do that." When I gave that answer, I didn't mean that I wasn't able to do that or that I didn't have the authority to do that. Physically and from the perspective of being the only instructor in the course, I could have raised that grade. And I didn't mean that fear of external consequences prevented me from changing that grade, such as fear that I might get caught and possibly lose my job. No, what I meant was that I can't change that grade because it would be wrong to do so for a number of good reasons. It would be *unfair* because the work really was not A work; it would be inappropriate to base a student's grade on his need to get into medical school rather than on the quality of his work; it would be unfair to other students whose work was graded on the basis of qualitative merit—all of these are certainly good reasons why "I can't do that." But perhaps what I also meant was that changing that grade to one I did not believe was earned would be a violation of my own integrity. My personal integrity, my self-respect, my ability to live with myself if I knowingly chose to do what I believed to be morally wrong, was probably a good part of the meaning of the sentence "I can't do that."

But personal integrity is not the end of the story here. It seems to me there is also such a thing as *professional* integrity, which is related to, perhaps dependent upon, and certainly compatible with but different from, personal integrity. There are communal or corporate values associated with the teaching profession that place role-specific constraints on my behavior, in addition to the normal moral values that I have as an ordinary moral agent. One thinks immediately of the special obligation to be competent in the subject matter and in teaching techniques. Proper preparation; special concern for each student's intellectual and, yes, character development; fair and timely evaluation of student work—all of these and more constitute special obligations of teaching professionals. And the teacher, who is literally in front of the students constantly, must be totally conscious of the example which he or she sets for students—we teach by what we are and do, perhaps even more than by what we say. Maybe all of this was what was constraining me; maybe this is what I meant when I said, "I can't do that." I have special responsibilities to the institution, to my professional colleagues, and to the community I serve in this profession, which really do matter to the well-being of our community, and they *trust* me.

Consider a more complicated case, this time from the medical profession. As a general practitioner, I've just received the results of blood tests on my 23-year-old male patient, and he is HIV positive. He is also engaged to be married. I point out to him his responsibility to inform his fiancée because she has a right to know about the danger to her and to any future children they might have. He reacts very emotionally to my suggestion because he believes she will refuse to marry him if she learns he has the AIDS virus. He says to me, "You must keep my condition a secret from her and from everyone. You're bound by the principle of patient confidentiality."

Upon reflection, I reply, "*I can't do that.*"

What I mean when I say "I can't do that" is that the moral principles that guide me as a medical professional require me to act, but in this case their guidance is not unambiguous. The principle of respect for my patient's privacy by observing confidentiality is a very important one, and it does indeed constrain my conduct. But the competing obligation I have to prevent harm is also very relevant in this case, and if I cannot persuade my patient to tell his fiancée himself, then I may judge that my duty to prevent harm overrides my duty to observe confidentiality in this case. My professional integrity is bound up in these competing moral principles, and although my decision may be extremely controversial, I tell my patient, "I can't do that."

It's the spring of 1968, and I'm a young sergeant in a combat infantry company in South Vietnam. My platoon has captured an entire village of suspected Viet Cong sympathizers: 400 people, women, old people, children, and babies. We found no weapons in the village. My lieutenant orders us to herd them all over to a roadside ditch and shoot them. I say to him, "I can't do that." What I mean is, *we* can't do that—no one can do that. I know that I have a duty to obey the orders of my superiors, but I know that this order is in direct conflict with both my country's laws and with the fundamental moral law against harming the innocent. Several years earlier, in confirming the Yamashita death sentence, General MacArthur said: "The soldier, be he friend or foe, is charged with the protection of the weak and unarmed. It is the very essence and reason of his being. When he violates this sacred trust, he not only profanes his entire cult but threatens the fabric of international society."[1] In this case of conflicting duties, my professional integrity tells me that my higher duty is to avoid harming the innocent, and when I'm ordered to kill babies—I can't do that.

These examples from education, medicine, and the military may help us to focus on this fuzzy notion of professional integrity. "Integrity" itself is a much used term but very much in need of analysis. When we use the word "integrity" in a moral context, we refer to the *whole* moral character of a person and we most frequently allude to one's personal integrity. When we say to someone, "Don't compromise your integrity," we usually mean, "Act in accordance with your moral principles within your value system. Be consistent." There is a real sense in which integrity encompasses our personal identity. As Polonius has it, "To thine own self be true." But we must be very careful here. Following principles is not all there is to personal integrity. There is little merit in being consistent with your principles if "thine own self" is egoistic, treacherous, criminal, and abusive. This is why integrity has to do with "wholeness," with one's entire character, and what that moral character is like is what counts. And subscribing to decent moral principles is not enough; we must *act* on decent principles— consistently. Others have noted accurately that integrity is the bridge between character and conduct.

Aristotle pointed out that moral credit is not automatic when right actions are done, nor is it enough to know what is right or to say what is right. He suggested that we are morally praiseworthy when we do a right action if we, first of all, *know* that the action is right; secondly, *choose* the act for its own sake because we know it is right; and thirdly, do the action from a firm and unchangeable character—from the *habit* of doing that kind of action consistently. For Aristotle, it was very important that we develop the moral virtues through habit and practice, doing right actions so that they become part of our identity, our character. "Integrity" is the modern term we use to describe the actions of those persons who consistently act from a firmly established character pattern, doing the right thing. We especially stress the concepts of integrity when there is temptation to diverge from what good character demands. Persons of integrity do not stray from acting in accordance with strong moral principle even when it is expedient or personally advantageous to do so. Persons of integrity act like the ideal persons they are trying to be. This is perhaps what the ancient Taoist has in mind when he says, "The way to do, is to be."[2] Thus the wholeness of the good person, the total identity, is what we mean when we refer to his or her integrity. When we say, "Don't sacrifice your integrity," we really mean, "Don't stop being who you ought to be."

If I'm a member of one of the professions, then "who I ought to be" must also involve my social role as a practicing professional. My professional integrity will include the role-specific obligations and responsibilities of my particular profession. I stress here the social character of professional integrity because the community is involved at every stage of professional development.

First of all, the very existence of the professions results from some fundamental need that society has, and it is likely to be an eternal need. The need that we have for health care, for example, is unlikely to go away, and that need over time has generated what we know today as the medical profession. (It may come as a surprise to some to learn that the health-care professions do not exist for the sole purpose of providing employment to health-care professionals or profits for health-care organizations.) It is because of societal need that our communities develop and maintain medical schools and nursing schools. Similarly, every organized society will express its need for laws by providing some variation of a judicial system and a legal profession. We need an ordered society, we want to be treated fairly, so we seek justice. We train our judges and our lawyers in law schools supported by the community because of the value that we place on justice. Similarly, we know how crucial education is to our society, so we provide for the training of teachers; we know how important security is to our nation-state, so we provide military academies and military training for the members of the military profession.

No member of the professions can escape these ties to the community, because the community constitutes the very reason for the existence of the professions. Thus, professional integrity begins with this necessary responsibility to serve the fundamental need of the community. Note that the community makes possible the opportunity for one to become qualified in a given profession and usually allows the professionals the authority to set the standards of competence and conduct of its members. Doctors control the licensing and certifying of doctors, lawyers do the same for members of the legal profession, and military officers certify and control the commissioning process for leaders of the military profession.

Members of the public professions are thus educated and supported by the society because of the critical services these professions provide. In the case of teachers in public institutions and in the case of the military profession, practitioners are supported from the public coffers during their entire careers. Clearly, some of the role-specific obligations are based on this relationship and on the authority to act on behalf of the entire society, which is literally bestowed on these professionals. With that authority to act goes the public trust, and violations of that trust are serious breaches of professional integrity. For example, there were instances recently in the local public-school systems where two male high-school teachers engaged in sexual intimacies with teen-aged female students. These teachers violated the trust they had been given, they violated their professional integrity.

Let us now direct our attention to the elements of professional integrity in the military profession to see if that will illuminate our responsibilities as military practitioners and the relationships between professional and personal integrity.

Professional integrity derives its substance from the fundamental goals or mission of the profession. For the military profession we might broadly describe that mission as the preservation and protection of a way of life deemed worth preserving. Just as in medicine one violates professional integrity by performing surgical procedures that are not medically indicated in order to increase the surgeon's income, so too engaging in operations that are not militarily necessary in order to reflect glory on the commander would be a breach of professional integrity. Killing unarmed prisoners or executing the elderly and babies who are not engaged in the attempt to destroy you is surely inconsistent with the goals of the military and hence is a breach of professional integrity.

In the military, as in all of the professions, the issue of competence is directly relevant to professional integrity. Because human life, national security, and expenditures from the national treasury are so frequently at issue when the military acts, the obligation to be competent is not merely prudential. That obligation is a moral one, and culpable incompetence here is clearly a violation of professional integrity. When a B-52 pilot is known to engage in unsafe practices, when he frequently endangers the lives of other aircrew members and people on the ground by performing forbidden flying maneuvers, not only he violates professional integrity—so do those colleagues and superiors who tolerate this conduct and take no action to prevent it. This aspect of professional integrity is worth noting.

Part of the social aspect of professional integrity involves the joint responsibility for conduct and competence shared by all members of the profession. When fellow surgeons bury the mistakes of their incompetent colleagues rather than expose these colleagues and remove their licenses to practice, they fall short of their responsibilities to the goals of the profession—they sin against professional integrity. Only fellow professionals are capable of evaluating competence in some instances, and hence, fellow professionals must accept the responsibility of upholding the standards of the profession. Fellow officers can spot derelictions of duty, failures of leadership, failures of competence, and the venalities of conduct that interfere with the goals of the military mission. The wing commanders of that B-52 pilot who knew of his repeated safety violations and failed to ground him before he killed himself and others failed in their responsibilities—they violated their professional integrity. Often the obligations of professional integrity may be pitted against personal loyalties or friendships, and where the stakes for society are so high, professional integrity should win out.

These lessons seem obvious in theory but are most difficult to put into practice, especially in the preprofessional training which takes place in military academies, medical schools, and law schools. Nontoleration of failures of professional integrity does not seem so crucial in training situations, where the stakes are not very high. Thus the penalties for tolerating lapses of integrity are light in training situations, and then often seem sensationally tragic when enforced in the professional context. But preprofessionals must learn the importance of the social elements of professional integrity and the responsibility they inherit to maintain standards of competence and conduct in the entire profession and not just for themselves. Society provides the training opportunities, the resources necessary for carrying out the professional function, and the authority to act on its behalf. With this authority to act and the autonomy that usually accompanies it, breaches of professional integrity must be viewed as a serious failure of the societal trust. For example, when a cadet at the Air Force Academy knows that a fellow cadet has plagiarized a paper to meet a deadline and takes no action to correct this behavior, he or she has violated societal trust in a fashion analogous to the colleagues who took no action to correct the unsafe B-52 pilot. If our preprofessional preparation does not inculcate the habits of professional integrity, can we have confidence that those habits will be practiced by these same individuals when they become licensed professionals?

We identify other aspects of professional integrity from examining the basic functions of each profession. If in preserving our way of life we must use the military instrument, then members of the military profession must sometimes go to war. If combat occurs, then professional soldiers must fight. To refuse a combat assignment is to break faith with all other members of the profession and is a first-order violation of professional integrity. It would be the equivalent of a teacher refusing to teach, a doctor abandoning patients, a judge refusing to hear crucial cases. Because the stakes are so high in the military case, this breach of professional integrity could be devastating to society.

There are varying opinions about the relationship between personal integrity and professional integrity. Some people believe that one can live up to high standards of competence and conduct in one's professional role but live an entirely different kind of moral life in one's private life. Some think they may be required to do things in their roles as professionals that they would never do as private people. Some instances of this dichotomy are obvious. As a private person I would normally not even contemplate harming other persons, yet as a military professional I am licensed to kill (under specified conditions) for reasons of state. A variation of this concern surfaced during an annual meeting of the Colorado Bar Association in the fall of 1995. One of the topics offered for discussion was the statement: "I would never do many of the things in my personal life that I have to do as a lawyer." At the heart of this matter is the issue of client advocacy. Lawyers are enjoined to act in their clients' interests and to do so zealously. In defending my rapist client, whom I know to be guilty, I may cross-examine the innocent rape victim in such a fashion as to totally discredit her, even though I know she is telling the truth. If it is legal and will help my client, it would seem that the standards of the profession require me to do it, even though in ordinary morality I would judge it to be wrong to harm an innocent person.[3] This sort of example really is problematic, for it appears to reveal a direct conflict between personal integrity and professional integrity.

There are similar examples in medicine. Abortion for convenience is legally permitted in most U.S. hospitals, but some obstetricians believe that convenience abortions are immoral, so they might face a conflict between professional integrity and personal integrity. (In most such situations, doctors and nurses may refuse to participate on moral grounds, even though the action itself is legally permitted. Perhaps this is one key to resolving integrity dilemmas—recognizing that what is legally permitted is not always, or even usually, morally obligatory.) I mention possible clashes between professional integrity and personal integrity because I wish to minimize them. I wish to support the view that the two types of integrity are generally compatible and even interdependent. What I wish to argue is that since professions exist to serve society's need for important values (education, health, justice, security, etc.), the means used to provide those values and services should be morally decent means and the persons in the professions who provide them should be morally decent persons.

Put in more direct terms, good teachers ought to be good persons, good doctors ought to be good persons, good lawyers ought to be good persons, and good military professionals ought to be good persons. We want to live in a world where the duties of a competent professional can be carried out by a good person with a clear and confident conscience. That means that professional practices must always be constrained by basic moral principles. That this is not always the case now is obvious: Several of the attorneys at the previously mentioned convention pointed out that they had left large law firms because they were being asked to do things that violated their personal integrity. In the best of all possible worlds, the personal moral restraints on professional functions would make those actions inimical to professional integrity as well. And this is the proper order of things. When professions go beyond their essential service function to society and distort their purpose toward profits, power, or greed, then they lose the trust and respect of their communities—they stop being professions. "Militarism," for example, refers to a society or a military gone bad, one that distorts the essential goals and function of the military profession. The two sets of guidelines we use to hold militarism in check are the just-war theories and the laws of war. These guides are related in an essential way to professional integrity—they represent, in the broadest terms, when and how the military instrument ought to be used.

Well-established professions often spell out the role-specific principles which support that profession's conception of professional integrity. The codes of conduct promulgated by the American Medical Association and the American Bar Association and state and local chapters of these groups are well known. The military profession has many codes, regulations, mottoes, and traditions that combine to form a military ethic on which professional integrity is based. At the Air Force Academy we have our honor code, our honor oath, and our specific list of core values, which is now identical with the official list of core values of the Air Force. When we say that we value integrity first, service before self, and excellence in all that we do, we acknowledge that the essential nature of the military profession is to serve our parent society. We make specific our commitment to the conception that good soldiers are good persons. What we should mean when we commit ourselves to "integrity first" is that we understand the importance of both personal integrity and professional integrity, and through our efforts to keep them compatible, we will best provide the crucial military function to our society.

Notes

The idea for a paper on professional integrity was suggested to me by a very thoughtful article written by F. G. Miller and Howard Brady which appeared in the *Hastings Center Report*, May–June 1995. The Miller-Brady article, "Professional Integrity and Physician Assisted Death," pursued the thesis that under carefully delineated circumstances "voluntary physician-assisted death as a last resort . . . does not violate physicians' professional integrity."

1. MacArthur quoted in Telford Taylor, *Nuremberg and Vietnam: An American Tragedy* (New York: Bantam Books, 1970), ii. General Yamashita was the Japanese commander in the Philippines in World War II. Japanese troops committed horrible atrocities in that theater. Yamashita was the first "war criminal" tried in the Far East after the war. He was convicted in a Manila court-martial and sentenced to death, even though it was not proven that he had himself committed atrocities or ordered any.

2. Lao Tzu in the *Tao Teh Ching*, trans. Witter Bynner (New York: Capricorn Books, 1944), verse 47.

3. I am indebted to F. A. Elliston's *Ethics and the Legal Profession* 1983 for this example as quoted in T. L. Shaffer's *American Legal Ethics: Text, Readings, and Discussion Topics* (New York: Matthew Bender, 1985), 335.

ETHICAL PROBLEMS OF WARFARE

8

The Just-War Idea and the Ethics of Intervention

James Turner Johnson

I ntervention across national borders by use of military force has long been a source of controversy and strong opinions. In this essay I address the question of intervention from three perspectives. The first section examines the use of power, including military power, in the context of statecraft and the role of moral debate in shaping policy for such use of power. The second section examines the just-war tradition of Western culture as a source of moral criteria for judging appropriate interventionary use of military power, comparing the classic ethical understanding of the just-war concepts with those contained in international law. Finally, the third section takes up the implications of this ethical tradition for a particularly pressing contemporary question, that of interventionary use of military force to protect and support humanitarian relief efforts.

Intervention: The Use of Power and the Role of Moral Debate

As with all uses of power, the question of intervention is not simply a political or military matter or one to be decided by appeal to international or domestic law or to calculations of the proportion between costs and benefits, though it is all of these together. But it is also a question that should be addressed from the perspective of ethical values, principles, and traditions of right action by means of a vigorous and informed moral debate that engages the political, military, legal, prudential, and other aspects of the larger issue, the right use of power. The ethical debate cannot be reduced to making sure that the people involved in these other aspects of the policy- or decision-making process are themselves morally upright people, though this is an important component. It must go beyond this, for what is right or wrong for the individual in terms of his or her own moral responsibilities to family, friends, or nation does not always translate directly into what is right or wrong for the political community, which naturally has a broader and more complicated set of responsibilities.

The ethical debate should proceed by identifying and clarifying relevant ethical wisdom and particular principles to provide ethical guidance and illuminate decision-making throughout the spheres of social responsibility affected. In the case of the use of military power these spheres include the moral life of the individual citizen, the individual in military service, military commanders, contributors to the making of policy, and the head of state and commander-in-chief. To make such guidance concrete, and more generally to make a contribution to living responsibly in a democratic and free society, such ethical debate must engage politics; yet this engagement should take place at the level of application, without the ethical debate itself being driven by political allegiances, ideologies, and commitments. That is, the ethical debate should proceed on its own terms, seeking to rise above the categories through which public argument often takes place: such categories as hawks versus doves, conservatives versus liberals, realists versus idealists. Good ethical reflection on the uses of power may be perceived as now hawkish, now dovish; now politically conservative, now liberal; now realist, now idealist. In itself, though, it is none of these.

The use of power itself, as Paul Ramsey has put it, "is of the *esse* of politics";[1] that is, it is part of the very nature of any political community. The right question is not whether the political community should exercise power but what kind of power it should exercise, when, and for what reasons. Military power is not, of course, the only expression of this characteristic of political communities, but it is an important part of the whole. Rightly used, military force may back up policies or behaviors whose principal expression is not military. Under particular circumstances, direct commitment of military force may be the only means by which a given end may be achieved. So understood, the right use of military force is part of the larger question of the right use of power by the political community and is inseparable from it. Its moral quality in any given case depends in the first place on the answer to this larger question. In this context, military intervention across national boundaries is not an issue to be addressed in isolation but only in the larger forum of the life of the political community, the nation.

To what degree, though, should the ethical debate reach even farther? The nation, after all, does not exist in isolation but interacts with others. Military intervention is one form of such interaction, but so are alliances and efforts at achieving a world order such as the United Nations. Unless one is a thoroughgoing relativist, moreover, ethical values and the principles that express them have a universal claim; they do not stop at the nation's border, or even at the border of one's own culture.

We can see the implications of this vividly in the contemporary context. Traditionally American military interventionary actions have been justified by consideration of our particular national interests or concerns to protect American nationals or in support of American law. The incursions into Grenada and Panama are the most recent cases in which such traditional reasons have been invoked to justify intervention. The case of the Gulf War exemplifies a different kind of reasoning. While U.S. interests were clearly at stake, the Bush administration relied most heavily on two other kinds of justification: first, the violation of Kuwait's sovereignty by Iraq's invasion and the continuing state of "armed attack" resulting from the occupation and annexation of Kuwait, together constituting a threat to international peace; and second, the depredations inflicted by the Iraqi forces against Kuwaiti civilians and the civilian infrastructure, including hospitals, schools, and museums. The former was an argument from the perspective of international law and, in particular, an appeal to the Charter of the United Nations; we may term it an internationalist argument. The latter was an appeal to universal considerations of human rights and common humanity; we may term it a humanitarian argument. The two arguments reinforced each other and together negated the claim of critics of U.S. military action that this was nothing more than an action of naked national interest aimed at protecting the supply of Persian Gulf oil.

The cases of Haiti, Somalia, and Bosnia exemplify a further extension of the internationalist and humanitarian arguments for interventionary use of U.S. military forces. In none of these cases—even that of Haiti, which is within the traditional sphere of interest of the United States and has been the object of American military intervention before—was a sustained national-interest argument advanced as the principal focus of efforts to justify the American military commitment. This is not to say that such an argument could not have been made; indeed, it would have been an important contribution to the ongoing public debate in these cases. The absence of such an argument tends to support the implication that the United States has no interests at stake in such cases as these. Without a national-interest argument, other sorts of justifications, those invoking the global responsibilities of the United States, were put first in the public debate: responsibilities following from membership in the United Nations; responsibilities as a rich, prestigious, and militarily powerful nation; responsibilities as a defender of human rights and a foe of starvation, privation, and the other harms suffered by the civilian populations of the three countries as a result of ongoing strife, which the interventions were intended to ameliorate.

It is important to note the particular moral element in these latter arguments. The internationalist argument appeals to responsibilities incurred as a result of the United States' commitment to maintaining world order and to the United Nations as a framework for multilateral action to respond to localized disasters and to threats to international peace. The humanitarian argument appeals to American ideals and values as such, then extends our responsibility to support and protect those values and ideals wherever they are threatened. Both sorts of arguments are altruistic; both play on some of the best in what this nation stands for. Neither is easily subject to the criticisms most commonly directed against national-interest arguments for military intervention these days—that they are racist or militarist or justification for economic exploitation or misguided relics of the Cold War. Indeed, the internationalist and humanitarian justifications for intervention may implicitly challenge justifications based on national interest. Yet the opposite is also true: reasoning based on national interest may challenge that of internationalist and humanitarian arguments and may lead to contradictory judgments on the commitment of U.S. military forces. We have seen internationalist and humanitarian criticism focused against national-interest reasoning for intervention in the cases of Grenada and Panama, and the tables were turned in the debates over intervention in Haiti, Somalia, and Bosnia.

At the same time, it needs to be stated strongly that national-interest arguments, at their best, also are influenced by ethical concerns, concerns that are embodied in the definition of national interest in the first place. This is the meaning of political realism properly understood. The debate among national interest, internationalism, and humanitarianism is not, then, a debate between ethical considerations and concerns that are devoid of ethical content; rather what is at issue with these three perspectives is the nature, source, and relative strength of the ethical values and principles embodied in each.

Ethical analysis, at its best, provides a way to critique such competing justifications and claims and to reach judgments that avoid the particular criticisms each directs at the other: that national interest is inherently selfish; that international order is more of an ideal than a reality; that the United Nations structure is ill suited to be a focus for decisions about military intervention and its nature and scope; that appeals to humanity are often extremely vague and open-ended. At the same time, ethical analysis should be framed in terms inclusive enough so that it can recognize the strengths and potential of each such approach, and particular enough so that it can provide useful guidance for policy and for specific decisions.

Collectively, these criteria constitute a tall order. Yet I will argue, together with other recent theorists of ethics and the use of force, that just-war tradition can meet them. In recent ethical writing on war such a claim has been made from a variety of perspectives. James F. Childress and Michael Walzer have advanced this same argument in a form suited to their own understanding of the nature and role of moral reasoning.[2] For Childress, just-war ideas are *prima facie* categories of ethical judgment, functionally universal within Western culture. That is, these categories represent the way people in our culture naturally think about war and set up a series of tests that any use of force must pass to be morally right. Walzer, in *Just and Unjust Wars*, writes, "I want to recapture the just war for political and moral theory" (p. xiv). Then he undertakes to do so by means of a systematic examination of cases that present the fundamental just-war ideas as having both historical and cross-cultural depth and by a philosophical argument that such standards are universal. Elsewhere, the U.S. Catholic bishops and such authors as William V. O'Brien[3] have argued for an understanding of just war rooted in natural law and hence universally valid. The prominent Protestant theologian Paul Ramsey, as noted earlier, finds in the idea of just war a general theory of statecraft, a perspective on the use of power in any political community anywhere.

My own approach is to understand the idea of just war as the product of a broad and inclusive historical tradition of experience, thought, and practice whose lasting relevance and power lies precisely in its having been shaped by contributions from many cultural sources and dialogues over time in many different contexts. In the following section I outline this approach to understanding just-war reasoning and to ethical analysis of uses of military force from a just-war perspective.

The Just-War Tradition as a Resource for Ethical Analysis of the Use of Military Force

The just-war tradition in Western culture is best understood as a broad river of ideas and practice moving through history, with specific streams now combining in various ways, now separating and moving along their own paths. This tradition is ethical not in the narrow sense of being a product of philosophical or theological reasoning but in a broader sense of collecting and systematically joining a range of ethical wisdom from many other contexts as well. To be sure, religious and philosophical efforts to define and shape morality have provided major contributions to the tradition as a whole. Yet along with the stream defined by Christian thought and practice and that of philosophical reasoning, there are others, also of major importance: those defined by secular law, both domestic and international; by the traditions of military life and the experience of war; and by the experience and customs of statecraft. Philosophy has helped to shape just-war tradition not only as a distinct stream of thought but as a mode of reasoning attached to religious, legal, military, and political discourse. Dialogue and mutual influence among the various streams has also been important in shaping the tradition as a whole. At times the Christian just-war doctrine developed in interaction with one or more of the other streams of the developing tradition, either influencing or being influenced or both; at other times it developed mainly in dialogue with its own internal concerns.

The development of just-war tradition is accordingly complex (see figure 1). But recognizing this complexity is a way to keep in mind that international law, military guides to conduct in war, and political conceptions of the appropriate use of force are all historically and thematically part of the broad just-war tradition, alongside more specifically moral and religious elements. Just-war reasoning about the use of force is not something alien that is imposed on political judgments or military thinking from outside. By its very nature this approach to the ethics of the use of force is already in dialogue with them. That there are differences of content and emphasis and tensions among these various approaches is, however, also the case, and this points at the necessity of an ongoing and sustained dialogue as the means of spelling out the contemporary implications of just-war tradition. This tradition as a whole reflects the totality of such interaction over history up to our own time.

The purposes of just-war reasoning have been defined by three levels of practical moral concern: the needs of statecraft, of the responsibilities of command, and of the individual moral agent (see figure 2). In the first of these respects it provides, as Paul Ramsey has argued,[4] a theory of statecraft that takes account of the connection between force and politics, establishing criteria for determining when the use of force for social good is justified and when it is not, and setting limits beyond which the justified use of force ought not to go. In the second respect, just-war tradition provides guidance to military commanders,

Figure 1. Sources and Development of the Just-War Tradition	

Late Classical Era:
  Deep Roots, Early
  Expressions
	The Bible (Old and New Testaments)
	Roman law and practice
	Christian theology: writers such as Clement of
	  Alexandria, Ambrose, Augustine

Medieval Era:
  Coalescence of a Cul-
  tural Consensus
	Canon law: Gratian's *Decretum*, writings of the
	  Decretists and Decretalists
	Scholastic theology
	The code and customs of chivalry
	Customary rights and practices of sovereigns
	The inherited idea of *jus gentium* (law of peoples or
	  nations)

16th to 18th Centuries:
  Consolidation,
  Transformation,
  Differentiation
	Transformation to natural-law base: Victoria,
	  Suarez, Grotius, others
	Theory of international law: Grotius, Pufendorf,
	  Vattel, others
	Military codes of discipline replacing chivalric code
	Limited-war theory and practice: "sovereigns' wars"

19th Century:
  Further Definition
  within Distinct
  Streams
	Customary international law
	First Hague Conference
	Origin of Geneva Conventions
	Military manuals on the law of war
	Popular, philosophical, and religious efforts to
	  restrain or end war

20th Century:
  Elaboration and Grow-
  ing Interaction
	Positive international law
	Jus ad bellum: League of Nations Covenant, Pact of
	  Paris, UN Charter
	Jus in bello: arms limitation treaties and conven-
	  tions, growth of humanitarian international law
	Military manuals on law of war, rules of engage-
	  ment
	Religious and philosophical recovery of just-war
	  concepts
	Public debate over war, its meaning and effects

Figure 2. Purposes of the Just-War Tradition	
A Guide to Statecraft:	Theory of the use of force by the political community Understanding of the moral qualities of political leadership Protection of fundamental rights and values Relation of ends to means in political life
A Guide to Commanders:	Relation of military command to authority/ purposes of political community Understanding of the moral qualities of military leadership Protection of fundamental rights and values in situations of armed conflict Moral limits on means and methods in conflict situations
A Guide to Individuals:	Claims on moral consciousness of individuals at all levels of political and military life Definition of responsibility in relation to the use of force by the political community Definition of the individual's rights and responsibilities in the use of force

placing their role and responsibilities in a larger context of value to be served by the forces at their command and locating their right to apply such force in relation to the ends rightly sought and the destruction of values to be avoided. Finally, at the level of the individual moral agent, just-war tradition offers moral guidance for conscientiously weighing the question of participation in the use of force and the degree of such participation.

Looked at as a whole, just-war tradition has two major thematic branches, classically denoted by the terms *jus ad bellum* and *jus in bello*. These have to do, respectively, with when it is just to resort to military force and what actions are justified in the use of such force (see figure 3).

Historically the *jus ad bellum* has developed around a set of seven principles on how to justify resorting to war: the requirement that a war must have a *just cause*, be waged by *proper authority* and with a *right intention*, be undertaken only if there is *reasonable hope of success* and if the total good outweighs the total evil expected (overall *proportionality*), be a *last resort*, and be waged for *the end of peace*. Each of these criteria has a particular meaning as shaped and transmitted by the tradition.

Figure 3. The Just-War Tradition as a Source of Criteria for Ethical Judgment

The *Jus ad Bellum*: Criteria Defining the Right to Resort to Force

Just Cause: The protection and preservation of value
> *Classic Statement:* Defense of the innocent against armed attack; retaking persons, property, or other values wrongly taken; punishment of evil

Right Authority: The person or body authorizing the use of force must be the duly authorized representative of a sovereign political entity. The authorization to use force implies the ability to control and cease that use—that is, a well-constituted and efficient chain of command.
> *Classic Statement:* Reservation of the right to employ force to persons or communities with no political superior

Right Intention: The intent must be in accord with the just cause and not territorial aggrandizement, intimidation, or coercion.
> *Classic Statement:* Evils to be avoided in war, including hatred of the enemy, "implacable animosity," "lust for vengeance," desire to dominate.

Proportionality of Ends: The overall good achieved by the use of force must be greater than the harm done. The levels and means of using force must be appropriate to the just ends sought.

Last Resort: Determination at the time of the decision to employ force that no other means will achieve the justified ends sought. Interacts with other *jus ad bellum* criteria to determine level, type, and duration of force employed.

Reasonable Hope of Success: Prudential calculation of the likelihood that the means used will bring the justified ends sought. Interacts with other *jus ad bellum* criteria to determine level, type, and duration of force employed.

The Aim of Peace: Establishment of international stability, security, and peaceful interaction. May include nation-building, disarmament, other measures to promote peace.

The *Jus in Bello*: Criteria Defining the Employment of Force

Proportionality of Means: Means causing gratuitous or otherwise unnecessary harm are to be avoided. Prohibition of torture, means *mala in se*.
> *Classic Statement:* Attempts to limit weapons, days of fighting, persons who should fight.

Noncombatant Protection/Immunity: Definition of noncombatancy, avoidance of direct, intentional harm to noncombatants, efforts to protect them.
> *Classic Statement:* Lists of classes of persons (clergy, merchants, peasants on the land, other people in activities not related to the prosecution of war) to be spared the harm of war.

I noted earlier, however, that there are differences and tensions among the various component streams of the larger tradition and between each of them and the thrust of the tradition taken as a whole. In the context of considering the justification and limits of the national or international interventionary use of force, it is especially important to consider the tensions between international law, one of the main component streams of just-war tradition, and just-war ideas in their broadest form as classically defined (see figure 4).

The requirement of *just cause* classically meant one or more of three possibilities: that the use of force in question was for defense against wrongful attack, retaking something wrongly taken, or punishment of evil. Contemporary international law views defense as the only justifying cause for use of force— either defense by one nation or group of nations against an attack from another, or internationally sanctioned defense against a breach of international peace. Yet a closer look suggests that the other two classic ideas have simply been absorbed into a broadened concept of defense. A retaliatory second strike,

---

Figure 4. The Just-War Criteria in Positive International Law

Jus ad Bellum:

Just Cause: National or regional self-defense against armed attack; retaliation for armed attack; international response to threats to international peace

Right Authority: Compétence de guerre possessed by states; some right to authorize force given to UN Security Counsel; some recognition of insurgency rights

Right Intention: Not explicitly addressed; implicit in above items.

Proportionality of Ends: In the twentieth century, a tendency to treat the first use of force as the greatest evil, always disproportionate.

Last Resort: Emphasis on international arbitration and/or adjudication; tendency to allow only responsive or "second" use of force after armed attack.

Reasonable Hope of Success: Not explicitly treated.

The Aim of Peace: Greatly stressed. Limits on just causes for going to war, emphasis on *jus in bello* restraints, preference for stability over other values. Currently in process of some reevaluation.

Jus in Bello:

Proportionality of Means: "Hague law," arms limits, bans on means *mala in se.*

Noncombatant Protection/Immunity: Greatly stressed. "Geneva law," various other provisions regarding noncombatants, POWS, "protected persons." Not treated: injury to noncombatants received due to proximity to legitimate targets, long-term damages due to persisting effects of otherwise legitimate means of war.

for example, would classically have been called "punishment of evil": today it is categorized as "defense." The use of force to retake Kuwait from Iraq would have classically been called "retaking something wrongly taken"; in the language of contemporary international law, however, it was "defense" against an "armed attack" that remained in progress so long as Iraq occupied Kuwait. (The Falklands war provides a second recent example of this reasoning.)

So the underlying ideas remain, though the vocabulary has changed to reflect the modern sentiment that the first use of force is morally suspect, while the second use is not. It is not entirely clear whether this contemporary sentiment raises possible problems with the interventionary use of force across national borders for humanitarian reasons; the *prima facie* thrust of classic just-war reasoning is more favorable to such uses of force, not only as properly defending the rights of the innocent but also as "punishment of evil."

The requirement of *proper authority* limits the right to authorize force to sovereign political entities, that is, those with no superior. Classically this was a way to deny the right to resort to force to local strongmen and to individuals bearing arms. It was not intended to restrain legitimate sovereigns, who, because authorized to use force, could employ it against such local strongmen and marauders. This also has the *prima facie* effect of favoring certain kinds of interventionary uses of force: for example, in combating international terrorism, other forms of international lawlessness such as the traffic in illicit drugs, or systematic and sustained violations of universally recognized human rights. In positive international law, however, the limitation tends to flow the other way: aimed at limiting the right of states to resort to war with other states, it also limits the states' right of intervention. States have nonetheless continued to reserve that right for themselves and to practice it, and so customary international law is somewhat at variance with the black-letter law. Debate over national authority for intervention in the present context, accordingly, is somewhat confused.

The requirement of right authority also raises questions about intervention under international auspices. International organizations up to and including the United Nations lack sovereignty in the traditional sense. Lacking sovereignty, does such an organization have any right to authorize force? Classic just-war doctrine would say no, reserving that right for sovereign states. Yet in contemporary debate, international authorization for interventionary use of military force is often claimed, though on the basis of consensus (as in the Security Council resolutions relating to the Gulf War and to the United Nations protective force in Somalia) rather than sovereignty.

Right intention classically referred to the motivation of the individual soldier and meant that he should avoid lust for battle, hatred for the enemy, and other such attitudes. Well into the Middle Ages, for example, soldiers after combat were required to do penance in case, during the heat of battle, they had fought with the wrong intention. In contemporary usage this just-war criterion is closely linked to the idea of *the end of peace*, where it refers not to the individual soldier but to the purpose of the state in employing military force. In this context it requires that this purpose not serve some aggressive end but establish or reestablish such goals as international order and respect for human rights. International law has no explicitly specified notion of right intention, though arguably one can be deduced from other principles expressed there.

Reasonable hope of success, overall proportionality, and *last resort* are, for just-war tradition in its classic form, all prudential tests to be applied as additional checks when the above deontological requirements have been met. All are derived historically from Roman practice, and they refer to political prudence at any time and in any culture. International law does not specifically address them, and religious just-war theorists historically have paid little attention to them. Yet they have come to figure prominently in what Paul Ramsey called the *bellum contra bellum justum*[5] in Cold War–era ethical debate: the use of just-war categories to deny the very possibility of a just war. In this reasoning the destructive capabilities of contemporary weapons form the core of an argument that any use of force today must necessarily be disproportionate and hence unjust. It follows that there can be no reasonable hope of success, and that contemporary war can never reasonably be a last resort for serving justice, order, and peace, because it will by its nature create injustice, disorder, and more war. The *bellum contra bellum justum*, then, though sometimes called "just-war pacifism," is really just pacifism. It begins with a presumption against war, and it employs certain dogmatic assumptions about modern weapons to attempt to undercut the possibility of any contemporary just use of force on the grounds of the just-war principle of proportionality.

There are two important problems in this reasoning. First, there is nothing inherently disproportionately destructive in contemporary weaponry. Indeed, sophisticated contemporary guidance mechanisms today allow military targets to be destroyed with far less collateral damage than was the case in earlier conflicts. Second, the concept of proportionality in just-war tradition means the overall balancing of the good (and evil) that a use of force will create against the evil of not resorting to force. It begins with the recognition that a loss of value has already occurred (the just cause) prior to the consideration whether force is justified to restore that value. Rather than implicitly ruling out recourse to force, then, the moral requirements of reasonable hope of success, overall proportionality, and last resort continue to be useful tests of the wise use of military power in given contexts.

The moral understanding of justified recourse to the use of force in contemporary American culture takes place in a historical context as reflected in just-war tradition. In general, given a world continuing to be beset by the presence of evil, moral reflection on how best to serve the ends of good statecraft is a perennial need. Yet for much of this century the focus of moral debate has been on a particular form of the use of military force, and sometimes focus has been on war between sovereign states itself as the evil to be countered. During the Cold War the focus narrowed even further to the possibility of nuclear war between the superpowers. In the present historical context, though, the issues have shifted, and with that shift comes a renewed need to clarify how ethical principles on the use of force apply to military intervention across national borders. In short, what is needed is not only to understand these ethical principles themselves, but to reach an understanding of how they might be translated into the somewhat different language of practical national policy.

The Language of Ethics and the Formation of Policy: Intervention for Humanitarian Reasons

Where the interventionary use of force is at stake, policy language must be developed to put in practical terms the broader, more theoretical concerns of the just-war principles. For the sake of illustration I draw attention to one recent policy statement on the use of force, interesting in the present context because of its close adherence to just-war categories (see figure 5). This statement, former Secretary of Defense Caspar Weinberger's "six conditions for committing United States military forces" (the "Weinberger doctrine"), emerged in the context of a debate over the interventionary use of military force to combat international terrorism, but the cautions it laid down bore implications for other sorts of potential interventionary uses of US. military power as well, up through Operation Desert Storm. It is, in my judgment, an unusually good example of how the tradition of just war may be translated into the language of policy, and in the contexts where it was employed, it served well as a guide to the commitment of US. military forces. Yet it has real limitations as well, and in the present historical context, renewed attention needs to be given in policy

---

**Figure 5. The Just-War Criteria in Policy Language:
The "Weinberger Doctrine" of 1984**

Jus ad Bellum: "Six Conditions for Committing United States Military Forces"

Just Cause: 1. When it is vital to the defense of national or allied interests.

Reasonable Hope of Success: 2. With the intention of winning.
  • Sole object of winning
  • Forces and resources sufficient to achieve objectives or not at all

Right Intention: 3. For clearly defined political and military objectives.
  • Determine objectives
  • Decide strategy

Proportionality of Ends: 4. With correlation between objectives and forces.
  • If national interests require us to fight, then we must win.
  • Assess and adjust force size and composition as necessary.

Right Authority: 5. With public/congressional concurrence.
  • Commit American public before American forces

Last Resort: 6. As last resort.
  • Only when other means have failed or have no prospect for success.
  • Military force not a substitute for diplomacy.

Aim of Peace: Not explicitly stated but implicit in 1 and 6.

---

language to expressing the implications of the moral criteria carried by just-war tradition.

It is important to note first that the context has indeed changed. In the debate over use of military force against international terrorism, against the international traffic in drugs, or even against Iraq after its takeover of Kuwait, a cogent case could be made that national interests were centrally at stake, and the question whether to commit forces or not and how much force to commit hinged on other issues.

Today, though, the interventionary use of military force for humanitarian purposes has moved to center focus, and in such cases national or allied interests may not be directly at stake or of pressing urgency. One is reminded that even in 1984, as his contribution to the debate that produced the Weinberger "six conditions," then Secretary of State George Shultz was framing the issue of just cause much more broadly, in terms of the need "to further the cause of freedom and enhance international security and stability."[7] There is no doubt that many Americans think of this nation's responsibilities abroad in terms of altruism and a high sense of moral purpose for America in the world. As a people we are strong defenders of human rights who are revolted by the abuse of these rights; we believe deeply in freedom and wish its blessings to extend to victims of tyranny; possessed by an optimism that sickness and hunger can be subdued, we are moved by the plight of victims of famine and disease. Theologian H. Richard Niebuhr, commenting on the missionary spread of American culture throughout the globe in the nineteenth century, described it as an effort "to bring light to the gentiles by means of lamps manufactured in America."[8] Where humanitarian impulses arise, such sentiment still surges: We can right the wrongs from which other peoples suffer, it says to us, and thus we ought to do so.

In seeking appropriate policy language for the concept of just cause, then, there is a *prima facie* case that such altruism and idealism should be taken into account. I also believe that such a broader understanding of the possible justifications for use of force better expresses the core moral purpose of the just-cause concept: defense of the innocent, retaking that which has been wrongly taken, punishing evil. What makes the case of intervention by force for humanitarian purposes so hard is that such moral justifications may be greatly compelling, and yet we still, in a given case, should not intervene by military force. There may not be the necessary authority to do so; there may be no reasonable hope of success; military intervention may produce more harm than good; other means of dealing with the crisis at hand may be more effective; and some forms of military intervention may hinder the cause of peace rather than serve it.

I have already suggested that the concept of right authority for the use of force is today confused by the somewhat contradictory implications of the historical ethical tradition, positive international law, and customary conceptions of the rights of sovereignty. As a result almost any imaginable argument for or against intervention that depends on only one of these rationales is open to challenge on the basis of the others, and the strongest authority for intervention comes from adding them together. This was in fact done quite successfully in the case of the Gulf War, where ethical argument, international law, and sovereign decisions by the nations taking part in the coalition against Iraq reinforced one another and established a claim to right authority well beyond what any one of them could have produced alone. Other contemporary cases are not characterized by such strong consensus, and authority for intervention suffers accordingly.

Right authority, though, does not refer simply to the decisions taken at the top; it also requires that the authority over the use of force extend downward through a well-constituted and effective chain of command, so that the forces in the field are genuinely directed by that responsible authority. In the present context, when much argument is being advanced that the United Nations should be regarded as the sole legitimate authority for interventionary projections of force in cases of humanitarian necessity or threats to international peace, it is essential to note that whatever the merits of this argument may be regarding the decisions at the top (a subject of hot debate), the United Nations does not now possess the intermediate structures necessary to project its authority downward to the level of directing the military forces in the field. On my reading of just-war tradition, then, it lacks right authority for commitment of interventionary forces unless this lack is remedied by the provision of a well-constituted and effective command structure by the nations cooperating in the provision of forces. Thus the United States has been correct not only in national-interest terms but also in moral terms to insist on retaining command of its forces when assisting in United Nations interventionary operations. Our national command authority is complete; that of the United Nations as currently constituted is not.

On the subject of right intention, I will simply observe that when the purpose of interventionary action is defined by humanitarian necessity, this goes a long way toward establishing right intent. Such intent is reinforced by a plan for ending the intervention at some future time or under some future conditions and, in the case of internationally sanctioned interventions, by rotation of national contingents over the period of the intervention.

Interventionary uses of military force should also be proportionate to the task at hand. There is a good deal of wrong thinking about this requirement in the moral debate, wrong usage that surfaces in arguments against such-and-such a use of military force as "disproportionate," that is, too large. This was a criticism directed against the US. use of force in the Gulf War, for example. It is a version of the *bellum contra bellum justum* identified earlier. But the just-war concept of proportionality does not equate to requiring that low levels of force should always be used. Rather, what proportionality requires is that the level and type of force be appropriate to accomplish the justified task and that the application of that force be such as to bring about more good than harm. This means that overwhelming force, sufficient to blanket hostile activities and snuff them out, may satisfy the criterion of proportionality better than a minimal commitment of force that soon finds itself confined to a fortified enclave and to patrolling and convoying, which may attract attacks and result in more harm than good. Understood this way, the criterion of proportionality reinforces the parallel requirement that uses of military force should be undertaken only when there is reasonable hope of success in achieving the justified mission of intervention.

Confusion also surrounds the way the criterion of last resort is used in recent debate. This criterion does not mean always postponing use of military force until every possible means short of force has been tried. If one comes into a situation late in the day, as is almost by definition the case when a conflict has created urgent humanitarian needs, working this gradualist way might simply postpone what is necessary until still later, perhaps making the situation worse and requiring a more robust, costly, and dangerous intervention when force is finally brought in. Rather, the just-war understanding of last resort is that in every case a determination should be made as to the kind of action that should be taken, with military intervention subordinated to other forms of action if they will work instead. This determination settles whether a situation of last resort exists. Thus it may exist at the initial point of national or international involvement in a crisis. This understanding of last resort also should be understood as serving the parallel requirements of proportionality, reasonable hope of success, and the aim of peace.

The criterion of reasonable hope of success implies, first, suiting the actions taken to the needs confronted, and in this sense it reinforces the conception of proportionality described above. But in the second place making a calculation of reasonable hope of success may serve as a brake on impulses toward a military intervention that is driven by the perception of urgent humanitarian need in the media. Requiring reasonable hope of success, along with last resort, serves as a reminder that military forces should not be seen as a cure-all for ills that other methods have not been able to remedy. The mere fact that nonmilitary forms of humanitarian intervention have been tried and failed in a given case does not mean that military forces should now be committed; in the case at hand they may not work either or may make for a worse situation. The truth is, moreover, that armies, navies, and air forces are not created for this as their primary purpose. The primary purpose of the U.S. military is our national defense, and the services are structured accordingly. These structures may not fit at all well the needs of a situation of humanitarian need, and there may be no reasonable hope of success in a military commitment.

Finally, the aim of peace is closely connected to the other just-war criteria already defined and can be said to be satisfied only when all the other criteria have themselves been met. Additionally, though, it should be noted that to satisfy this last criterion military intervention should be placed in the context of other means of addressing and solving the problem at hand. In some cases, nation-building may be a necessary adjunct to the provision of humanitarian relief or protection of relief efforts or the endangered population. In such cases, the idea of military intervention should include the possibility of not only fighters but engineers, communications teams, military police, and civil affairs units, or of civilian teams that would fulfill these functions and others necessary to the rebuilding of a stable civil order. Unfortunately, this implies a long-term involvement in the society into which intervention is made, and here moral re-sponsibility runs head-on into a lack of political will and, perhaps, resources. I am not sure what this means for given cases of possible military intervention: Are we not to intervene except in those cases where we are willing to make a long-term commitment? I would rather say that our commitment should extend to considering how to restore a peaceful and functioning civil society, and to encouraging and supporting domestic and international efforts in that direc-tion. Such consideration is an essential part of the moral debate about interven-tion, and it has been mostly lacking in recent American public discourse.

Explaining the aim of peace St. Augustine argued that no one in his right mind makes war in order to create more war; war is too terrible for that. Rather, one makes war in order to create the conditions for peace. We should judge not only war also but intervention by that standard and not lay our military forces on the line without a clear understanding of how their sacrifice will serve the cause of peace in the situation at hand.

Notes

1. Paul Ramsey, *The Just War: Force and Political Responsibility* (New York: Charles Scribner's Sons, 1968), 5.

2. See James F. Childress, "Just War Theories: The Bases, Interrelations, Priori-ties, and Functions of Their Criteria," *Theological Studies* 39 (September 1978): 427–45; Michael Walzer, *Just and Unjust Wars* (New York: Basic Books, Inc., 1977).

3. See National Conference of Catholic Bishops, *The Challenge of Peace: God's Promise and Our Response* (Washington, D.C.: United States Catholic Conference, 1983), paragraphs 10, 78–110, and passim; William V. O'Brien, *The Conduct of Just and Limited War* (New York: Praeger Publishers, 1981), 4, 5, 13, 15, 56, 67, and passim.

4. Paul Ramsey, "A Political Ethics Context for Strategic Thinking," in *Strategic Thinking and Its Moral Implications*, edited by Morton A. Kaplan, 101–47 (Chicago: University of Chicago Press, 1973), 124–25.

5. See Ramsey, *The Just War*, "Robert W. Tucker's *Bellum Contra Bellum Justum*," chap. 17 (pp. 391–424).

6. For the full statement of the "six conditions," see Caspar W. Weinberger, *Report of Secretary of Defense Caspar W. Weinberger to the Congress*, 5 February 1986 (Washington, D.C.: U.S. Government Printing Office, 1986), 78–79.

7. Cited from George P. Shultz, "The Ethics of Power," *Department of State Bulletin*, February 1984, 1–3. For a comparison of the positions taken by Secretaries Weinberger and Shultz in relation to the just-war criteria, see James Turner Johnson, "The Recourse to War: An Appraisal of the 'Weinberger Doctrine,'" *Small Wars & Insurgencies* 1, no. 2 (August 1999): 160–67.

8. H. Richard Niebuhr, *The Kingdom of God in America* (New York: Harper Torchbooks, 1959), 179.

9

Emergency Ethics

Michael Walzer

I

My subject in this essay is "supreme emergency." The phrase is Winston Churchill's, and it refers to the crisis of British survival during the darkest days of World War II.[1] Supreme emergency is a time for heroic decision, when nations and leaders are measured by the measures they take; but it is also a desperate time, when the measures taken are ones we would avoid if we possibly could. I wish no such time on my own country and my fellow citizens. Let this be a theoretical discussion and an educational exercise. We can test our everyday moral perceptions against an extreme case, and we can ask whether there are useful analogies between historical or hypothetical extremity and what passes today for normality. I suggest a certain wariness about the exercise. As hard cases make bad law, so supreme emergencies put morality itself at risk. We need to be careful.

More than a decade ago, in *Just and Unjust Wars*, I worked out an argument about supreme emergency that was driven by Churchill's account of the British crisis and by my own memory of and reflection on the struggle against Nazism.[2] I took the years 1940 and 1941, when a Nazi victory in Europe seemed frighteningly close, as my model. A supreme emergency exists when our deepest values and our collective survival are in imminent danger, and that was the situation in those years. Can moral constraints have any hold upon us at such a time?

What can and what should political leaders do when confronting danger on that scale? I gave a philosophically provocative and paradoxical answer to those questions. I argued, first, that the constraints did still have a hold on us; and second, that political leaders could do whatever was required to meet the danger. There are no moments in human history that are not governed by moral rules; the human world is a world of limitation, and moral limits are never suspended—the way we might, for example, suspend *habeas corpus* in a time of civil war. But there are moments when the rules can be and perhaps have to be overridden. They have to be overridden precisely because they have not been suspended. And overriding the rules leaves guilt behind, as a recognition of the enormity of what we have done and a commitment not to make our actions into an easy precedent for the future.

The example in my mind when I first made that argument was the British decision to bomb German cities—specifically the orders issued to bomber crews in the early 1940s to aim at the city center or at residential areas (that is, not at military bases, factories, shipyards, warehouses, and so on). The intention of the British leaders at that point in the war was to kill and terrorize the civilian population, to attack German morale rather than German military might. I won't rehearse here the technical arguments urged by Bomber Command, which had more to do with civilian housing than with civilian lives—as if the two were separable targets—but those arguments were not entirely straightforward.[3] In order to display the theoretical issue in all its difficulty, it is enough to say flatly that the intention was wrongful, the bombing criminal; its victims were innocent men, women, and children. If soldiers or "munitions workers" were also killed, it was only by accident, a morally defensible side effect of what remains an immoral policy. But if there was no other way of preventing a Nazi triumph, then the immorality—no less immoral, for what else can the deliberate killing of the innocent be?—was also, simultaneously, morally defensible. That is the provocation and the paradox. You can imagine the skepticism with which this account of emergency ethics was greeted, especially in philosophical circles, where even the appearance of internal contradiction is taken (as it should be taken) very seriously.[4] So let me try now to explain the argument.

The doctrine of supreme emergency is a way of maneuvering between two very different and characteristically opposed understandings of morality. The first reflects the absolutism of rights theory, according to which innocent human beings can never be intentionally attacked. Innocence is their shield, and though it is only a verbal shield, a paper shield, no defense at all against bombs and bullets, it is impenetrable to moral argument. The second understanding reflects the radical flexibility of utilitarianism, according to which innocence is only one value that must be weighed against other values in the pursuit of the greatest good of the greatest number.[5] I put the opposition crudely; both rights theory and utilitarianism can be developed in complex ways, so that the opposition I have just described is considerably attenuated. But it is never, I think, wholly abolished. Both these moral understandings have claims upon us, and yet they pull us in different directions. It is sometimes said with reference to domestic politics that we should let the courts worry about rights, while congressmen and presidents (and, I suppose, ordinary citizens when they are choosing congressmen and presidents) should think about the greatest good.[6] But this division of responsibility doesn't work. One has only to look closely at the processes of judicial deliberation and legislative debate to see that the two claims are repeatedly made and repeatedly acknowledged within each. In any case, judicial scrutiny in international politics and especially in wartime is notoriously light, and so the two claims necessarily fasten on the political and military leaders of the nation; otherwise they would have no fastening at all. What is the relative strength of the claims? Neither is strong enough to defeat the other; neither is so weak that we can disregard it. At the risk of philosophical muddle, we must negotiate the middle ground.

Why not opt for absolute rights? I have to begin with absolutism, since it represents a denial of the very existence of anything that might be called "middle ground." Morality is not negotiable. Innocence is inviolable. We may disagree, says the absolutist, over who the innocent people are and how they might be located sociologically, but once we have found them, we have also found the final limits of war-making. To protect the innocent or, at least, to exclude them from deliberate attack, is to act justly. And we must act justly whatever the consequences: *fiat justitia, ruat caelum* (do justice even if the heavens fall). The claim of the moral absolutist is that we acknowledge the true meaning of justice only when we ignore the consequences of acting justly—for justice is literally invaluable, beyond the possibility of estimate or measure. It can't be balanced against anything else; the bookkeeper doesn't exist who could strike such a moral balance. Religious absolutists may believe that God keeps his own accounts; they also believe, however, that human beings are bound by his unqualified prohibitions: "Thou shalt not."

This sense that there are things we must never do, forbidden things, taboos, proscriptions, is very old, perhaps older than anything else in our moral understanding. Rule utilitarianism, though it no doubt captures some of the reasons for moral taboos, fails utterly to explain their power. The prohibitions urged upon us by moral absolutists are in fact the common and inescapable rules of moral life. They are external constraints that have long ago been internalized, so that we know the crimes they name not as acts we want to commit but must not, but rather as acts we don't want to commit. Even more, we want not to commit them (not to be murderers, for example), and this desire commonly gets stronger, not weaker, when troubles begin and we find ourselves pressed to act badly. When we feel this pressure, we also feel, most of us, the need to resist. But can we sustain our resistance even when disaster looms, when the heavens are really about to fall? At that point absolutism represents, it seems to me, a refusal to think about what it means for the heavens to fall. And the history of the twentieth century makes that refusal very hard to justify. How can we, with our principles and prohibitions, stand by and watch the destruction of the moral world in which those principles and prohibitions have their hold? How can we, the opponents of murder, fail to resist the practice of mass murder—even if resistance requires us, as the phrase goes, to get our hands dirty (that is, to become murderers ourselves)?

These are rhetorical questions, but I acknowledge immediately that they don't always elicit the response they seem to ask for. Absolutism is by definition unresponsive, and even someone ready in principle to move away from an absolutist position might well respond skeptically. He or she will remind us of how quick some people are to say that the heavens are falling. At the first sign of trouble, they shout "supreme emergency!" and claim exemption from the moral rules. We should always be reluctant to grant such exemptions, for every exemption is also a concession to those who argue that justice has a price, which may sometimes be too high and which we need not always pay. And then the way is open for utilitarian calculation.

Well, what is wrong with utilitarianism? Jeremy Bentham designed his doctrine for political leaders, and the design seems to have been successful. Hasn't cost/benefit analysis become the standard form of moral reasoning in the arenas of public life? Isn't this the educational core of most university courses on decision theory and policy choice and, I would guess, on military strategy? We value and respect moral taboos but consign them largely to the private sphere. We expect our leaders to be goal-oriented, and we judge them more by the goals they attain than by the rules they uphold. "When the act accuses, the result excuses."[7] How can we avoid, why should we want to avoid, the kind of reckoning this maxim requires?

The problem is that it's too easy to juggle the figures. Utilitarianism, which was supposed to be the most precise and hardheaded of moral arguments, turns out to be the most speculative and arbitrary. For we have to assign values where there is no agreed valuation, no recognized hierarchy of value, no market mechanism for determining the positive or negative worth of different acts and outcomes. Suppose we agree that justice is not in fact beyond measure, invaluable. Then we have to find some way of measuring it, of fixing, for example, the moral cost of murder. How do we do that? Is the cost eight or twenty-three or seventy-seven? Eight or twenty-three or seventy-seven of what? We have no unit of measurement and we have no common or uniform scale. It's not the case, I suppose, that every valuation is idiosyncratic. We are able, for specific purposes (insurance is the common example), to set a dollar price on a human life—though not on the act of taking a human life; the hire of a hit man isn't a morally acceptable figure. In any case, market values for lives-at-risk rise and fall for morally irrelevant reasons. And in politics and war, cost/benefit analysis has always been highly particularistic and endlessly permissive for each particular. Commonly, what we are calculating is *our* benefit (which we exaggerate) and *their* cost (which we minimize or disregard entirely). Is it plausible to expect them to agree to our calculations?

Those first- and third-person plural pronouns ostensibly have no impact on utilitarian calculation; each and every person is valued in the same way; all utilities are measured as if there were a common scale. But this holds in practice only for men and women whose solidarity counterbalances all conflicts of interest among them. When solidarity collapses, in pure or almost pure adversarial situations—in war, for example—utilitarian calculation is zero-sum, and "we" commonly attach only negative value to "their" utilities. Negative valuation is clearest with regard to enemy soldiers when they are actually engaged in combat, but it is likely to extend (unless it is checked by absolutist prohibitions) across the entire population, first to soldiers who are not actually engaged, then to civilians at work in war-related industries, then to civilians who support the war effort indirectly, then to everyone who supports the supporters and the workers and the soldiers. Finally, no "enemy" life has any positive value; we can attack anyone; even infant deaths bring pain and sorrow to adults and so undermine the enemy's resolve. Of course, we can always juggle the figures and stop short of this horrific conclusion. But it is our sense of moral taboos that makes us want to stop short—and it is only by reflecting on the meaning of innocence and on the rights of the innocent that we can decide where in fact to stop.

So the weaknesses of utilitarianism lead us back to the theory of rights, and it is rights that fix the everyday constraints on war-making (and on all adversarial engagements). But these constraints seem to depend on some minimal fixed values, just as utilitarianism depends on some minimum solidarity of persons. When our deepest values are radically at risk, the constraints lose their grip, and a certain kind of utilitarianism reimposes itself. I call this the utilitarianism of extremity, and I set it against a rights normality. The two together, it seems to me, capture the force of the opposed moral understandings and assign to each its proper place. I can't reconcile the understandings; the opposition remains; it is a feature of our moral reality. There are limits on the conduct of war, and there are moments when we can and perhaps should break through the limits (the limits themselves never disappear). "Supreme emergency" describes those rare moments when the negative value that we assign— that we can't help assigning—to the disaster that looms before us devalues morality itself and leaves us free to do whatever is militarily necessary to avoid the disaster, so long as what we do doesn't produce an even worse disaster. No great precision is required in calculations of this sort. Just as a jury in a capital case doesn't look for a 51 percent probability of guilt but for overwhelming certainty, so we can only be overwhelmed by supreme emergency. And, of course, we must always be skeptical about political leaders who are, so to speak, too easily overwhelmed, just as jurors must always be skeptical about those of their fellows who are too quick to place themselves "beyond a reasonable doubt."

II

But how can we be properly skeptical unless we have some precise understanding of what a supreme emergency is and how it differs from the daily emergencies of military life? I want to approach this question indirectly, by asking another. If we are permitted to respond immorally when a disaster threatens us, why can't an individual soldier respond immorally when a disaster threatens him? From the standpoint of the combat soldier, war is a rapid succession of supreme emergencies: his life is constantly at risk. But we are very reluctant to allow soldiers to save themselves by killing innocent and helpless people. Consider the standard case of soldiers holding prisoners behind enemy lines. I can't repeat here all the arguments that have been made about this much discussed and not at all hypothetical example. There is a range of conclusions, and considerable disagreement among commentators, but almost no one would say that the soldiers can kill their prisoners simply in order to reduce the danger to themselves.[8] Perhaps they can kill them if that is or seems to be absolutely necessary for the success of their mission, but once the mission has succeeded, they are commonly expected to bear some risk, even considerable risk, for the sake of their prisoners. And yet, what is at risk is all they have, life itself. So far as individuals are concerned, supreme emergency doesn't make a radical exception to rights normality. In war, as in domestic society, there are limits on what we can do in self-defense, even in extreme situations. A moral person will accept risk, will even accept death, rather than kill the innocent. But a moral president or prime minister or military commander will not accept the risk or the fact of communal death. Why not?

The first answer to this question has to do with the theory of representation. I can, morally and psychologically, accept risks for myself, but I can't, either morally or psychologically, accept risks for other people. If I possess political authority, I can impose risks, but I have only a limited right to do that (both the rights and the limits are implicit in the governmental contract). Soldiers, for example, are conscripted and then trained for risk-taking by the government in the name of the political community. But no government can put the life of the community itself and of all its members at risk, so long as there are actions available to it, even immoral actions, that would avoid or reduce the risk. It is for the sake of risk avoidance or risk reduction that governments are chosen. That is what political leaders are for; that is their first task. This argument, however, faces a deep difficulty. If individuals have no right to save themselves by killing the innocent, how can they commission their government to do this on their behalf? They can't pass on rights they don't possess, hence their political leaders can do no more on their behalf than they might do themselves. Leaders can act to reduce or avoid risks only within the limits of rights normality.

The argument from representation doesn't work unless we add to it an argument about the value of the community.[9] It isn't only individuals who are represented, but also the collective entity—religious, political, or cultural— that the individuals compose and from which they derive some portion of their character, practices, and beliefs. I don't want to say that the whole is greater than the sum of its parts, for I don't know how to sum the parts or set a value on the whole. A certain number of individuals can always be found—so it seems—who value the whole more than their own part; they are ready to risk their lives for their country. But it doesn't follow from this that they (or their leaders, acting on their behalf) are entitled to risk the lives of other people who don't even live in their country. There can't be any such entitlement. The risks imposed on the others are criminally imposed. How can the community permit or require criminal actions?

Edmund Burke's description of the political community as a contract between "those who are living, those who are dead, and those who are yet to be born" helps us to see what is at stake here.[10] The metaphor, I suppose, is inappropriate, since it is impossible to imagine the occasion on which such a contract could have been agreed to. But there is an important truth here nonetheless: we do try to carry on, and also to improve upon, a way of life handed down by our ancestors, and we do hope for recognizable descendants, carrying on and improving upon our own way of life. This commitment to continuity across generations is a very powerful feature of human life, and it is embodied in the community. When our community is threatened, not just in its present territorial extension or governmental structure or prestige or honor, but in what we might think of as its *ongoingness*, then we face a loss that is greater than any we can imagine, except for the destruction of humanity itself. We face moral as well as physical extinction, the end of a way of life as well as of a set of particular lives, the disappearance of people like us. And it is then that we may be driven to break through the moral limits that people like us normally attend to and respect.

By contrast, when we tell an individual soldier that he can't make the same break, we are telling him that he must risk death and even die within the moral limits so that his children and children's children can hope to live within them. It may be small comfort to a soldier facing death to know that people like himself will survive and continue to uphold the principles and practices he values (including the normal defense of rights, for if he didn't value that, there would be no issue here). But that knowledge is comfort enough to rule out any claim he might make to exempt himself from the moral prohibitions. Take that knowledge away, and the claim begins to seem plausible; and only then do we enter the terrible world of supreme emergency.

If the political community were nothing more than a neutral framework within which individuals pursued their own versions of the good life, as some liberal political philosophers suggest, the doctrine of supreme emergency would have no purchase.[11] It would indeed be a bad thing for individuals to lose the protection of such a framework, and they might be persuaded to accept some risk to their own lives in order to guard against that loss—though it's a hard question, first posed by Thomas Hobbes, the first theorist of the neutral framework, why anyone should die for a "community" whose substantive meaning only he can provide, and only so long as he is alive.[12] In any case, this kind of a person, facing this kind of a loss, can hardly drag other men and women (and children) into the war zone, from which he is likely to make his own escape as soon as he can. The license of supreme emergency can only be claimed by political leaders whose people have already risked everything and who know how much they have at risk.

The fact that a "communitarian" political theory helps to explain the meaning of supreme emergency might well be taken as an argument against communitarianism. For if we didn't value the community (however we conceive community: people, nation, country, religion, common culture) in this intense way, we might fight fewer wars and face fewer emergencies. Fewer emergencies, and none of them supreme, for in an international society composed of countries that were nothing more than neutral frameworks, or in an international society that was itself one big neutral framework, individuals pursuing their private projects might find many occasions for quarrels and even for fights but few for wars—they would have every reason to stop short of the kinds of risk that war involves. But this is only to say that life would be safer without emotional entanglements. The statement is obviously true but not very helpful.

Supreme emergency is a communitarian doctrine. But to say that is not to diminish the moral significance of the individual. Communities need, and can't always find, morally strong citizens, soldiers, and political and military leaders. And *morally* strong is very strong indeed, for what the community requires of individual citizens and soldiers is that they risk their lives, first for their compatriots and then for the innocent members of other countries. And what it requires of its leaders is that they impose risks and sometimes, in rare and terrible moments, take on the guilt of killing the innocent. We may doubt that moral strength is really required in this last instance; after all, many, perhaps most, of the political leaders who figure in the history books or in our own memories of twentieth-century history seem to have had no difficulty killing innocent people. They had no sense of the guilt involved; they were simply criminals. A morally strong leader is someone who understands why it is wrong to kill the innocent and refuses to do so, refuses again and again, until the heavens are about to fall. And then he becomes a moral criminal (like Albert Camus's "just assassin")[13] who knows that he can't do what he has to do—and finally does.

III

Provocation and paradox again. And yet this is not an idiosyncratic argument; I didn't make it up. It conforms to the professional ethic of the soldier as this has developed over the course of time, and also to the professional ethic of the police, firefighters, and merchant sailors, all of whom are required to risk their lives to protect the innocent. And it also conforms to the doctrine of "dirty hands," according to which political and military leaders may sometimes find themselves in situations where they cannot avoid acting immorally, even when that means deliberately killing the innocent.[14] The effect of the supreme-emergency argument should be to reinforce professional ethics and to provide an account of when it is permissible (or necessary) to get our hands dirty. The argument is essentially negative in character, as arguments have to be, I think, when they are focused on extreme cases, for dirty hands aren't permissible (or necessary) when anything less than the ongoingness of the community is at stake, or when the danger that we face is anything less than communal death. In most wars, the issue never arises; there are no supreme emergencies; the normal defense of rights holds unquestioned sway, even at the moment of defeat. In a war over this or that piece of territory, for example, we are not called upon to calculate how many innocent lives the territory is worth. If we are considering a strategy that involves deliberate murder (I leave aside questions about the side effects of legitimate military actions), the territory has to be deemed worthless, and innocence, as the normal defense of rights holds, beyond price.

Even in wars where the stakes are very high, they may not be so high at every moment in the course of the war as to bring the supreme-emergency argument into play. Each moment is a moment-in-itself; we make judgments again and again, not once for each war. My claim that the British bombing of German cities might have been defensible in 1940 and '41 extends no further than those years. The bulk of the bombing that actually took place is certainly not defensible, for it took place after it had become clear that Germany could not win the war. The triumph of Nazism was no longer an imminent danger. Nor was the continued bombing designed (as it might have been) to deter or defeat the Nazi war against the Jews. The Holocaust might have constituted a new supreme emergency, but it did not figure in the minds of the men who decided on bombing policy; they did not conceive themselves to be acting on behalf of the community of European Jewry.

The evil of Nazism suggests the positive form of the supreme-emergency argument. It is that sort of evil, uncommon even in the long history of human violence, that pushes us beyond rights normality. The more ordinary sorts of military defeat, political subjugation, the establishment of puppet regimes and satellite states—none of this qualifies as a similar "push," for in these cases we commonly expect the physical and moral survival of the defeated nation; we even look forward to its renewed resistance. Conventional conquerors, such as Alexander or Napoleon, leave behind more or less intact political and religious communities. It was the Nazi intention, at least in central and eastern Europe, not to do that; and even in the west, a long-term Nazi triumph would have brought a loss of value greater than men and women are morally obliged to bear. Only a prospect like that invites—and then only insofar as it also requires—an immoral response: we do what we must (every legitimate alternative having been exhausted). And if we can see clearly, with the help of such an example, when the normal defense of rights can be overridden, we can also see clearly why it can't be overridden short of that. For the overriding is also a loss of value, an action of exactly the sort that we anticipate from the other side and hope to avoid. In supreme emergencies, we imitate our worst enemies (as the bombing of Germany imitated the bombing of Coventry and the London blitz), and that is not something to which we can ever be reconciled.

It follows from this argument that supreme emergency is a condition from which we must seek an escape. Mostly, we will want to escape, for we will dread the dangers we face and abhor the immoral acts to which we are driven. But just as a "state of emergency" may be politically convenient for leaders who prefer to rule outside the law, so a state of supreme emergency may be morally convenient for leaders who wish to dispense with prohibitions and taboos. It is not always the case, of course, that emergencies are temporary in character; great dangers can persist over time. But we are morally bound to work against the persistence, to look for a way out, lest we be thought to view our dirty hands with less than abhorrence. The obvious example here is the cold war "balance of terror" generated by the deterrent policies of the United States and the Soviet Union. I suggested in *Just and Unjust Wars* that nuclear deterrence was commonly defended, and rightly defended, in terms that follow closely the lines of the supreme-emergency argument. Were terror unbalanced—so both sides believed—country and culture, people and way of life, would alike be at risk. And so we permitted ourselves to threaten the same terrorism that we feared: the destruction of cities, the killing of vast numbers of innocent men, women, and children. The threat was immoral, for it is wrong to threaten to do what it would be wrong to do; and though the threat is obviously a lesser wrong than the act, it can hardly be taken lightly when it is accompanied by massive preparation for the act.

We accepted the risk of nuclear war in order to avoid the risk, not of ordinary, but of totalitarian, subjugation. If that second risk were to recede (as it has), we would be bound to seek alternatives to deterrence in its cold-war form. In any case, we are bound to look for ways of reducing the risk—by pursuing détente, for example, or by signing arms-control and arms-reduction agreements, or by undertaking unilateral initiatives that address the fears and suspicions of the other side. We must resist the routinization of emergency, reminding ourselves again and again that the threats we force others to live with, and live with ourselves, are immoral threats. Over the years we became habituated, callous, hardened against the crimes we were pledged to commit. But it isn't incompatible with the pledge to think concretely about those crimes and about our own unwilling criminality—for it won't be unwilling unless we think about it. This is the essential feature of emergency ethics: that we recognize at the same time the evil we oppose and the evil we do, and that we set ourselves, so far as possible, against both.

IV

I come back at the end to the communitarian foundation of emergency ethics. The strongest argument against supreme emergency is that it makes a fetish of the political community. Not, I want to stress, of the state: the state is nothing more than an instrument of the community, a particular structure for organizing collective action that can always be replaced by some other structure. The political community (the community of faith too) can't be similarly replaced. It consists of men, women, and children living in a certain way, and its replacement would require either the elimination of the people or the coercive transformation of their way of life. Neither of these actions is morally acceptable. But the reason for this unacceptability has nothing to do with fetishism. The political community is not magical, not mysterious, and not necessarily an "object of irrational reverence" (the dictionary definition of a fetish). It is a feature of our lived reality, a source of our identity and self-understanding. We can indeed make a fetish out of it, as countless nationalists and communalists have done; this is to engage in a collective version of self-worship, which is likely to have moral consequences of the same sort as the individual versions have. Egoists and communalists, who recognize no one's rights but their own, act badly on the smallest pretext, at the first hint of danger (perhaps also at the first hint of advantage) to themselves. A non-fetishized community, by contrast, sustains the discipline of its soldiers and the restraint of its leaders, who thus act badly only at the last minute and under absolute necessity.

Here is the final provocation and paradox: moral communities make great immoralities morally possible. But they do this only in the face of a far greater immorality, as in the example of a Nazi-like attack on the very existence of a particular community, and only at the moment when this attack is near success, and only insofar as the immoral response is the only way of holding off that success. We can recognize a moral community by its respect for that reiterated word "only." Supreme emergency is not in fact a permissive doctrine. It can be put to ideological and apologetic uses, but that is true of every moral argument, including the argument for individual rights. Properly understood, supreme emergency strengthens rights normality by guaranteeing its possession of the greater part, by far, of the moral world. That is its message to people like us: that it is (almost) the whole of our duty to uphold the rights of the innocent.

Notes

1. Winston Churchill, *The Gathering Storm* (New York: Bantam Books, 1961), 488.

2. Michael Walzer, *Just and Unjust Wars* (New York: Basic Books, 1977), chapter 16.

3. Churchill himself was entirely straightforward; see *The Hinge of Fate* (New York: Bantam Books, 1962), 770: the aim of the bombing was "to create conditions intolerable to the mass of the German population." This is from a memorandum written in July 1942.

4. For an effort to escape the contradictions (using examples from domestic society rather than from war), see Alan Donagan, *The Theory of Morality* (Chicago: University of Chicago Press, 1977), 184–89.

5. These two positions are put forward in near classic form in Thomas Nagel, "War and Massacre," and R. B. Brandt, "Utilitarianism and the Rules of War," which appeared together in *Philosophy and Public Affairs* 1, no. 2 (winter 1972): 123–65.

6. See, for example, Ronald Dworkin, *Taking Rights Seriously* (Cambridge, Mass.: Harvard University Press, 1977).

7. Niccolo Machiavelli, *The Prince and the Discourses*, intro. by Max Lerner (New York: The Modern Library, 1950), 139.

8. But see Telford Taylor, *Nuremberg and Vietnam: An American Tragedy* (Chicago: Quadrangle Books, 1970), 36.

9. In a critical review of *Just and Unjust Wars*, Kenneth Brown writes that "throughout his work, Walzer identifies the highest human aspirations with the supremacy of the nation-state" (Brown, "'Supreme Emergency': A Critique of Michael Walzer's Moral Justification for Allied Obliteration Bombing in World War II," *Journal of World Peace* 1, no. 1 [spring 1984]). No, I make no argument for the "supremacy" of the nation-state, only for its existence, and only insofar as its existence serves the communal purposes I describe in this essay.

10. Edmund Burke, *Reflections on the Revolution in France* (London: J. M. Dent, 1910), 93.

11. On the neutral state, see Ronald Dworkin, "Liberalism," in *Public and Private Morality*, ed. Stuart Hampshire (Cambridge: Cambridge University Press, 1978).

12. See Hobbes's discussion of military service in *Leviathan*, part 2, chapter 21, and my own commentary, "The Obligation to Die for the State," in *Obligations* (Cambridge, Mass.: Harvard University Press, 1970).

13. Camus, *The Just Assassins*, in *Caligula and Three Other Plays*, trans. Stuart Gilbert (New York: Vintage, 1958).

14. See my "Political Action: The Problem of Dirty Hands," *Philosophy and Public Affairs* 2, no. 2 (winter 1973): 160–80.

10

Terrorism and the Military Professional

MANUEL M. DAVENPORT

The Problem of Definition

In order to discuss terrorism without equivocation or begging the question, it is essential to begin with a clear and non-normative definition. Although most dictionary definitions of "terrorism" are normatively loaded, they do avoid ambiguity. The American Heritage Dictionary of the English Language describes "terrorism" as "violence toward private citizens, public property and political enemies promoted by a political group to achieve or maintain supremacy."[1] This definition captures three essential characteristics of terrorism: (1) it involves violence; (2) it is morally indiscriminate in its selection of targets; and (3) it is a political act.

The same dictionary, however, by defining "violence" as "the abusive or unjust exercise of power," assumes without argument that terrorism is immoral because it involves violence. If, however, we define "violence" as "power made operative against resistance," as this dictionary does elsewhere,[2] then the morality of violence remains an open question, as Richard Becka argues in "Violence and Its Justification," because the essential characteristic of violence is its use to "cause a person to change contrary to will."[3]

Whether terrorism is moral, then, depends on whether it is moral to change a person contrary to his or her will.[4] It is certainly plausible to contend that when dealing with children and other irrational beings, the use of violence may be morally justified when such beings, if not changed contrary to their will, may cause permanent harm to themselves and others. The morality of violence, then, should depend upon the circumstances of its use.

It is possible to argue, however, while conceding that violence may not always be immoral, that terrorism is nonetheless always immoral because, by definition, it targets the innocent. As Phillip Lawler argues, because the use of violence against the innocent is always unjust, "Terrorism is by its very nature morally indefensible."[5]

However, if, as Maurice Merleau-Ponty claims, no one is able to act in society at all without engaging in violence, then we do not have a choice between using or not using violence, but only "between different kinds of violence." Moreover, if, as indicated earlier, the essential characteristic of violence is that it is power used to cause a person to change contrary to will or, as Merleau-Ponty puts it, power that reduces "the others to objects," then violence, even directed toward the innocent, cannot be avoided and the real question becomes whether it can be used to make the world better than it is.[6]

For the sake of clarity and for those who might argue that terrorism is immoral merely because it is a political act, it may be useful to indicate the ways in which terrorism is political. As our dictionary says, it aims at achieving or maintaining supremacy, but, as stated in *The Public Report of the Vice President's Task Force on Combatting Terrorism*, it "has become another means of conducting foreign affairs"[7] in that it aims also at influencing government policy or changing the conduct of a government. Most commonly, terrorists try to provoke from the governments they attack reactions that in fact or appearance suppress the behavior and views of loyal citizens.

On April 26, 1984, for example, President Ronald Reagan submitted to Congress four bills to combat international terrorism that would allow the secretary of state, without court review or challenge, to decide which foreign governments or groups are terrorist and to subject any person "providing support services to organizations designated as 'terrorist'" a $100,000 fine or ten years in prison. Such laws would have led, for example, to the prosecution of Harvard professor Abraham Chayes for representing Nicaragua in the World Court.[8] If such laws, as a reaction to terrorism, arouse the opposition of loyal citizens to a government's attempts to control terrorism, then terrorism has succeeded as a political act.

Given these preliminary considerations, I shall define "terrorism" as "the use of violence against persons and their property without regard to the previous behavior of such persons for the purpose of maintaining political supremacy or causing the downfall of political enemies."

Types of Terrorism

In his classic work on terrorism, *The Rebel*, Albert Camus distinguished between individual and state terrorism. The individual terrorist, knowing that his death is highly probable and knowing that there is no continuing group to promote his dreams, engages in terrorism to protest the present for the sake of future unknown values.[9] State terrorism, usually called "international terrorism," is, as Stephen Rosenfeld indicated, "sponsored by governments as an instrument of foreign policy," and thus, as the Foreign Intelligence Surveillance Act of 1978 points out, involves "activities that . . . transcend national boundaries."[10] In what follows, our focus will be upon state, or international, terrorism, and I shall adopt the latter, more popular term in this discussion. Most terrorism today is international terrorism for a simple, practical reason: Without the support of a government terrorists could not obtain the necessary logistical and technological support to circumvent the counterterrorist measures of the governments they oppose.

A Case Study in International Terrorism

The particular example of international terrorism selected for closer examination is the bombing of Dresden by the British and Americans in February and March of 1945. I have chosen this example because detailed information recently available makes it clear, for reasons which will follow, that it is a case of international terrorism committed by "our side," and thus may allow us to be open to the possibility that not every act of terrorism is immoral by definition. In February 1945, the Russians were advancing westward toward Dresden and on February 8 crossed the Oder, driving before them into Dresden over 600,000 German refugees, who joined the 630,000 already residing there. The first wave of British bombers completed their attack on Dresden at 10:21 P.M., February 13. When the second wave arrived at 1:30 A.M. the next day, the city was on fire. American bombers made a third run at 12:12 P.M. and on February 15, at 12:30 P.M., dropped only 461 tons. Although Dresden was then a secondary target, the Americans hit it again on March 2.[11]

These bombing runs caused what has been called "the greatest firestorm of World War II," and by the most conservative estimate occasioned the deaths of 35,000 persons.[12] Dresden had strategic importance only as a regional railway center; and although the bombing did damage the railway yards, Dresden—which in February 1945 was "virtually an undefended city"[13] and would soon fall to the Russians—was not bombed to cripple German transportation or to kill retreating German soldiers. To understand why Dresden was bombed it is necessary to go back nearly four years to the early summer of 1941, when the British decided to switch from precision bombing, which was too costly in daytime and too inaccurate at night, to nighttime area bombing. According to Sir Arthur Harris, the RAF Commander, the aim of such bombing "was to break the enemy's morale." Given this new objective, the British switched from explosive to incendiary bombs so that "aiming points . . . would be easy to see" and adopted a "principle of concentration in time and space," to start "so many fires that no fire fighting services could get them under control. . . . It was also decided in 1941 that aircraft should not bring their bombs back from Germany."[14]

Contrary to what many thought, then and later, Harris was personally opposed to such area bombing for pragmatic reasons. Area bombing, unless directed at German industry, he argued, would not slow German war production, would cost too much in terms of men and materiel, and, most critical, would not bring about the intended goal of breaking civilian morale.[15] Nonetheless, due to the success of a 1,000-bomber night raid on Cologne on May 30, 1942, in which only 39 bombers were lost, Churchill became convinced that area bombing of civilians was "an immensely powerful weapon" that could allow the Allies to take the offensive. Harris believed, however, that he had won a victory in principle when the Casablanca Directive of January 1943 declared that the primary aim of air war was "[t]he destruction and dislocation of the German military, industrial and economic system," and made "the undermining of the morale of the German people" a secondary objective.[16]

American Air Force officials, especially Major General Laurence S. Kuter, General "Hap" Arnold's staff assistant for Plans and Combat Operations, preferred daylight precision bombing for both tactical and moral reasons. When the Combined Chiefs of Staff issued a revision of the Casablanca Directive at Malta on January 31, 1945, in which the new objectives were stated as bombing eastern Germany's transportation facilities to confuse civilian evacuation and prevent Germans in the west from moving east, Kuter asked General Carl Spaatz, commander of the American Air Force, if this meant that U.S. bombers would be used in area bombing. Spaatz replied in the negative and assured Kuter that Americans would attack eastern transportation facilities only at Russian requests and would follow Directive 3, of January 12, 1945, which limited bombing to industrial and military targets and specified that only the RAF would engage in "blind attacks."[17] Kuter raised this question because he knew that in 1944 the British Joint Intelligence Commission was looking for a way to prevent the Russians at the Yalta Conference, scheduled for February 4–11, 1945, from claiming all of eastern Europe. This commission and other British officials proposed Operation Thunderclap,[18] an all-out daylight area bombing raid of some large German city to impress the Russians with Allied power and thereby deter them from moving into eastern Europe. The Russians and the rest of the world would be told that this operation was aimed at assisting the Russian advance.

Operation Thunderclap can be traced back to a memo of August 1, 1944, which Sir Charles Portal, the British chief of Air Staff, addressed to the Combined Chiefs of Staff through Secretary of State for Air Sir Archibald Sinclair. In this memo, Portal argued that the aim of air offense must be to force Germany to surrender without having to use Allied offensive or occupational ground forces. To realize this aim, Portal suggested,

> Immense devastation could be produced if the entire attack was concentrated on a single big town other than Berlin and the effect would be especially great if the town was one hitherto relatively undamaged.[19]

Harris, however, continued to follow his own plan, which was to destroy the sixty leading industrial centers of Germany, and despite the objections of Portal, Harris continued bombing them, one by one. By November 12, 1944, when Portal ordered him to stop, Harris had destroyed forty-five of them.[20]

Behind the scenes on the American side, General Kuter was raising objections to the bombing strategies of both Portal and Harris. During the war itself Kuter's reasons for opposing nighttime area bombing, whether of civilian or industrial targets, were overridden by the dictates of military command and courtesy, but in 1980 his wife, Ethel, made available to the Academy Library of the US. Air Force his collected papers, numbering some 50,000 items. These papers, together with an Office of Air Force History interview of Kuter conducted in 1974, lend strong support for the thesis that it was Kuter, and perhaps Kuter alone, who developed and advocated an "American concept of air power," which led him and eventually his superiors to oppose the British policy of "terror bombing."

In a field service regulation of July 2, 1943, Kuter distinguished between the strategic air force, which uses bombs to destroy an enemy nation's "lines of communication" and "economic system," and the tactical air force, which uses fighters, attack bombers, and reconnaissance aircraft. The tactical air force aims, first, "to obtain and maintain air superiority in the theater" by destroying the enemy air force. Its second priority is "isolation of the battlefield," and its third priority is to support ground forces.[21]

In a speech entitled "American War Doctrine," delivered on November 9, 1954, at the Air Command and Staff College, Kuter stated his opposition to the use of "aviation in support of ground forces" and concluded, "I cannot emphasize too strongly that the first objective of air forces must be to achieve control of the air."[22] It is possible that, like Eisenhower, he did not believe in but only tolerated the concept of a strategic air force.[23] In a memo of April 22, 1943, Kuter listed as "Profitable Targets" for bombers: "troops, artillery, tanks, fuel dumps, ammo dumps, aircraft, bridges, pill boxes, repair installations, railways and highways." "The most important target at a particular time," the memo concluded, "will be that which constitutes the *most serious threat* to the operation of supported ground forces."[24] Given his later opposition to using air power for strategic purposes, this suggests that Kuter believed that if one must have a strategic air force, then its use should be restricted to the destruction of military targets that immediately threaten one's own ground forces.

What is beyond question is that Kuter opposed area bombing of cities, which he consistently called "terror bombing." In the 1974 interview he said:

> From the very beginning, I believed it would be ineffective, and I was pretty much alone on that. Tooey was pretty well persuaded for a while that that would win the war. . . . Tooey was living with Bomber Harris.[25]

"Tooey" was General Carl Spaatz, who, with Arnold, persuaded the Combined Chiefs of Staff to approve on May 19, 1943, a plan to select seventy-six military targets, including oil-producing sites, to be bombed in precision daylight raids. This plan, called "Operation Pointblank," was strongly opposed by both Harris and Portal but was consistent with, if not the product of, Kuter's concept of air power. In the year that followed, even some British officials, primarily Sir Arthur Tedder and Sir Trafford Leigh-Mallory, agreed with the concept but wanted to bomb railways in France rather than oil fields in eastern Europe. After nearly a year's delay, Eisenhower ordered the bombing of both types of targets.[26]

In the months that followed, May 1944 through January 1945, Portal and Sinclair persuaded Churchill to approve "Operation Thunderclap," a devastation bombing of a large, undamaged German city. The contrast of the names "Thunderclap" and "Pointblank" sums up the contrast between the strategic views of Portal and Kuter. The public justification for "Operation Thunderclap" was to be the delaying of the German retreat from the east and, thereby, the hastening of the Russian advance. However, as noted earlier, Kuter knew that the real purpose was to provide the Russians with a demonstration of Allied air power so terrible that it might prevent them from occupying eastern Europe. General Spaatz, forewarned by Kuter, denounced "Operation Thunderclap" as a plan to engage in terror bombing and gained assurance from Eisenhower that American bombers would take part only if no targets within the selected city except military ones were to be designated. Harris, too, opposed the operation—because it would not impair the German war effort— and delayed it by claiming that he could not find sufficient fighter escort.[27] In January 1945, however, Churchill was urging most strongly that "a dramatic strike" be scheduled for the close of the Yalta Conference and proposed as targets "Berlin, and . . . other large cities in East Germany."[28]

General Spaatz, knowing that his superiors had approved Operation Thunderclap, agreed to a joint attack on Berlin, but with the comment: "The Americans would not permit their bombers to be sent for any purely terror-raids directed solely against the German populace"; Americans, he added, would only bomb during the day to light fires to guide the British at night. It was decided at Yalta that the dramatic strike to impress the Russians and thereby limit their absorption of eastern Europe would be the bombing of Dresden. Air Marshall Sir Norman Bottomley was the first to mention Dresden as a possible target, but since the city was to be large and relatively undamaged and must be in the path of retreating Germans and advancing Russians, the eventual selection of Dresden was almost inevitable. General Kuter, who was at Yalta, protested but was overruled.[29]

On March 28, 1945, after being subjected to strongly negative reactions to the bombing of Dresden from all parts of the world, Churchill addressed a memo to his Chiefs of Staff which read in part: "The question of bombing of German cities simply for the sake of increasing the terror . . . should be reviewed." In a rare gesture of defiance, his Chiefs of Staff refused to accept the memo, and it was withdrawn and revised to request only a review of "the so-called 'area bombing.'"[30] Air Marshal Harris would later write: "Here I will only say that the attack on Dresden was considered a military necessity by much more important people than myself."[31]

Terrorism and Ethics

Most military historians agree with my claim that American Air Force leaders in World War II opposed bombing enemy civilians to destroy their morale as ineffective and immoral. This claim, however, has been challenged recently as "substantially fictitious and misleading" by Ronald Schaffer, a professor of military history. Schaffer admits that Generals Arnold and Ira C. Eaker consistently rejected proposals to bomb civilians for the purpose of destroying morale, but argues that they did this "for reasons of conscience. Rather it was because they considered selective bombing more efficient militarily, better suited to the image they wished to project, [and] more likely to verify their theory of strategic air power." He quotes from a letter in which Eaker overruled a proposal to bomb small towns and villages in Germany: "we should never allow the history of the war to convict us of throwing the strategic bomber at the man in the street," but Schaffer claims that this is a pragmatic rather than a moral position. He acknowledges that General Spaatz's policy was to oppose area bombing but concludes that because it was Spaatz's practice "to permit indiscriminate bombing of German civilians when his superiors required him to," it follows that his policy was not really a moral policy. It is Schaffer's avowed aim to make it more difficult "to distinguish the ethical conduct of the United States in World War II from its conduct in Vietnam . . . and from the morality of other nations."[32] Although it is not my aim to show that our conduct in World War II was ethically superior to that of other nations or to our own in later wars, I do want to argue that it was ethical, and thus I must address Schaffer's contentions.

Schaffer labors under two critical misapprehensions. First, he assumes that choosing an action because it is more effective than another cannot be an ethical choice; and second, he assumes that the disagreement between the Americans and British concerning area bombing was based solely upon differences in air power theory or concern for public image.

It is certainly true that both Harris, on the British side, and Kuter, on the American side, condemned the proposed bombing of Dresden on the grounds that it would serve no desired military objective. It is equally certain that neither Harris nor Kuter believed that such an act could be justified regardless of the nature of the means to be used. Each was concerned, in his own way, with the moral nature of the means used and not merely with the result.

Extreme act-utilitarianism, which Schaffer mistakenly characterizes as "pragmatism," is an ethical theory that would be indifferent to how many children or cathedrals or how few troop trains or combatants are destroyed as long as the result is "good." Schaffer to the contrary, it is an ethical theory. It is, however, a poor ethical theory, and if this is what Schaffer means, I would agree, but then hasten to repeat that neither the British nor the Americans followed it.

Harris, as noted earlier, condemned the area bombing of civilians because it did not kill sufficient numbers of combatants, did not slow war production, and didn't even succeed in breaking civilian morale. He did not condemn all forms of area bombing but insisted that considerations concerning "the ethics of bombing" must involve comparative judgments. If we do not bomb the enemy, what mode of attack do we employ and will it be more or less ethical than bombing?[33] By making such judgments, Harris avoided extreme act-utilitarianism by insisting that the means used in war should be intended to reduce the future need for violence, and in this respect his moral position closely resembled that of Merleau-Ponty.[34]

Harris did not doubt that those who ordered the bombing of Dresden intended to reduce future violence in the world, but for him the ethical question was: What is the relation between this intended result and the means selected? Was there, in other words, any good reason to believe that the Russians would indeed change their policies upon witnessing the destructive power of British and American bombers? Although the bombing of Dresden was announced as tactical support for the Russian advance, at Yalta and even earlier the British and Americans had condemned the Russian occupation of Bulgaria and Rumania.[35] Assuming, then, that the Russians knew the bombing of Dresden was a warning, would it have persuaded them to change their plans for the permanent domination of eastern Europe and, thereby, bring about a net reduction of future violence in the world?

This ethical approach, which allowed Harris to determine that the proposed means would not bring about the intended results, is flawed, however, in that it rests upon the false assumption that acts of terrorism, in themselves, can reduce the total amount of violence in the world. All that acts of terrorism can do, at best, is bring about a situation in which it might be possible, *given additional nonviolent actions*, to reduce violence. If, for example, Harris's plan to destroy all German industrial centers had been completed and somehow had prevented the Russian takeover of eastern Europe, it still would have been necessary, in order to create more humane and less violent social relations, to have also done something less violent than bomb cities. And there is no logical or ethical reason for believing that any act of international terrorism, including the bombing of Dresden, will lead to the necessary positive actions. Berlin today is more peaceful and prosperous than it was at the end of World War II, but it was not brought to its present condition by being bombed. It was made more peaceful and prosperous by airlifts, financial aid, and hard work, none of which were the direct and necessary results of its being bombed.

Harris's and Merleau-Ponty's ethical justification for international terrorism is plausible if, and only if, we can reasonably predict first, that it will bring about a situation in which a net reduction of violence is possible; and second, that it will be followed by positive, nonterroristic actions that will lead to a net reduction in violence. It is correct that there are situations in which the only way to create conditions in which violence may be reduced is to use violence now, but it is wrong to believe this is so in all situations, and it is wrong to believe that the use of violence in itself will lead a reduction in violence.

As indicated earlier, Kuter, as well as Harris, condemned the bombing of Dresden on the grounds that it would not lead to the desired result and, like Harris, did not follow extreme act-utilitarianism. Kuter's position concerning area bombing, however, can be distinguished from that of Harris in that Kuter believed that terrorism, including area bombing, was always wrong. Kuter, in other words, modified Harris's "dirty hands" utilitarianism[36] by blending it with a distinctively Kantian rule-guided ethical theory.

Kant, in contrast to Merleau-Ponty, did not focus on the intended result or its relation to the selected means but contended that actions are right if they conform to rules that tell us what we ought to value. These rules, Kant argued, should preserve, at the very least, the "oughtness" of values. Thus, we should not value any action that we could not will to be what ought to be valued. It is a fact that different persons do value different actions because of differences in inclination and culture, but what ought to be valued ought to be valued by all persons regardless of inclination and culture. Thus, what I ought to value is what I could will that all persons ought to value regardless of inclination and culture.[37]

Could I will, then, that tens of thousands of Germans be killed to save millions from communism, assuming that the bombing of Dresden would have done so? Could I will, in other words, that all persons ought to value the killing of some human beings in order to save many others from political oppression?

Following Kant, I could do this only if the Germans had in some way forfeited their human rights. Otherwise I could not will any act of killing some people to save any number of others from any evil. According to Kant, there are things that ought to be valued for their own sake and things that ought to be valued only as means to other values. The only thing that is valuable for its own sake is a human being acting as a moral agent, because only such a moral agent can determine what ought to be valued. If anything else—for example, food—were to be viewed as valuable for its own sake, then one could justify eliminating the human race to preserve food, which would be absurd, because in the absence of humans' making value judgments food would have no value. Thus, to treat human beings who are moral agents as a means by which to realize other values would be an absurd confusion of what is valued with what makes it valuable.[38] Moral agents, however, who deprive other moral agents of the right to make moral choices by killing or enslaving them forfeit their own right to act as moral agents and may be killed, punished, or in other ways used as a means to realize other values.

In Harris's mind, as in Churchill's, all Germans had lost the right to be treated as moral agents, and thus neither he nor Churchill would have claimed that terrorism directed against the Germans was always wrong.[39] But for Kuter, as well as Kant, to assign collective guilt to the Germans would be wrong because human rights can be forfeited only by and for individual moral agents. Because at least 6,500 of those killed in Dresden were children,[40] it seems unlikely that each and every one killed there had forfeited their humanity. From a strict Kantian point of view, however, such arguments are really beside the point because, given the meanings of "terrorism" and "violence," there can be no ethical justification at all for international terrorism. "Terrorism" involves "the use of violence against persons without regard to their previous behavior," and "violence" is "power used to change a person contrary to will." And if the victims of international terrorism are victims "without regard to their previous behavior," they have not necessarily forfeited their moral agency, as Kant would insist upon.

Terrorism and Military Ethics

As noted above, despite the fact that Harris was not opposed to terror bombing in principle, his actions in opposing the bombing of Dresden were clearly more overt and persistent than those of Kuter. Kuter, on the other hand, never violated military protocol but was more successful in modifying the behavior of his superiors. Thus, it might seem that Harris had greater moral integrity, while Kuter was the better tactician, but in making such a comparison we are overlooking a fundamental point: both men were military professionals and therefore faced a special and unique set of obligations. Thus, before we make comparisons in terms of moral character or tactical skill, we should consider what each was required to do by military law, which means we need to consider the difference between British and US. military law in regard to superior orders. British military law in 1944 stated that members of the military forces "are bound to obey lawful orders only," but US. military law at the same time stated that if alleged war crimes "were done pursuant to order of a superior or government sanction," then "this may be taken into consideration in determining culpability, either by way of defense or in mitigation of punishment."[41] British military law, then, would have encouraged Harris in taking a strong and overt stand against superiors who ordered the bombing of Dresden. US. military law, in contrast, would have encouraged Kuter to constrain and keep private his opposition to his superiors. The moral question, then, becomes: Given the military codes they were bound to honor, should Harris and Kuter have done more than they did to oppose the orders of their superiors regarding the bombing of Dresden?

At one point, Harris did threaten to resign, but at Portal's request he stayed on and followed the orders of his superiors. He was opposed to the bombing of Dresden, it must be remembered, not because he was opposed to area bombing in principle but because he believed it would accomplish in this particular instance no military purpose. This disagreement with his superiors, then, was not based on a moral difference but on a difference as to a question of fact. Therefore, although he may have resigned or made public protests because his cognitive judgment was challenged, he was not obligated to do so for moral reasons.

Given Kuter's opposition to area bombing in principle, his disagreement with his superiors concerned not only a question of fact but also a question of morality. Thus, it might seem that despite his particular military code he did have at the very least a moral obligation to resign and go public in order to prevent the bombing of Dresden. What seems evident is that he thought he had gained as much moral ground as he could hold, that to push further might jeopardize his future moral credibility. Kuter, in other words, was not an absolutist. Had he been an absolutist Kantian—one who could accept no deviation from principle regardless of circumstances—it could be claimed that this failure to go further was immoral. But, as noted, Kuter was a "rule-utilitarian," one who believed that the rules of war, once justified because they maximize long-range utility, are absolute only in the sense that they cannot be broken for the sake of expediency alone. A rule-utilitarian, as Richard Brandt writes, would endorse in regard to area bombing the rule that "substantial destruction of lives and property of enemy civilians is permissible only when there is good evidence that it will significantly enhance the prospect of victory."[42]

Thus, the moral question for Kuter becomes:

Suppose . . . that a superior officer commands one to do something that is permitted by the actual rules of war (that is, not explicitly forbidden) but clearly would be forbidden by the morally justifiable rules of war. The question is whether a moral person would refuse to do what would be permitted only by an unjust institution but would be forbidden by a just one.[43]

To answer this question we would have to consider, as Kuter did, which course of action would contribute most significantly to winning the war and saving the peace: obedience after making one's moral objections known or a refusal on moral grounds to continue to participate in the war. General Kuter clearly believed that he could contribute more to both the moral awareness of his superiors and eventual victory by retaining his military office than by resigning it and becoming a public critic of those who had been his superiors. Only an absolutist Kantian can condemn him with absolute certainty, and only an extreme act-utilitarian can be certain that he was right. Being neither, he leaves us, as he left himself, constrained to preserve his integrity and serve his nation in the face of moral uncertainty.

To acknowledge one's finitude and fallibility and yet take a stand according to one's best insights takes a high degree of moral courage. It is much easier to act as a moral coward and refuse to take a moral position out of fear of being mistaken or unpopular, and it is easier still to act on the arrogant and foolhardy assumption that one knows what is best for all humans in all times. The morally brave person fears the harms that come from failing to act and fears the harms that come from blind adherence to absolutes. General Kuter was a morally brave person; let us remember him as a true moral hero and a true military professional.

Notes

1. *The American Heritage Dictionary of the English Language* (Boston: Houghton Mifflin Co., 1979), s.v. "terrorism."

2. Ibid., s.v. "violence."

3. Richard Becka, "Violence and Its Justification," unpublished manuscript, 5.

4. Ibid., 16–19.

5. Phillip Lawler, "Just War Theory and Our Military Strategy," *The Intercollegiate Review* 19, no. 1 (1983): 13.

6. Maurice Merleau-Ponty, "Humanism and Terror," in *Existentialism*, ed. Robert C. Solomon (New York: The Modern Library, 1974), 227, 273, 270.

7. Quoted in "All Political Violence Is Terrorism," in *Terrorism: Opposing Viewpoints*, ed. Bonnie Szumski (St. Paul: Greenhaven Press, 1986), 16.

8. Ira Glasser and Moel Salinger, "Reagan's Rule," *Civil Liberties* 350 (Summer 1984): 2.

9. Albert Camus, *The Rebel* (New York: Vintage Books, 1958), 153.

10. Stephen S. Rosenfeld, "Terrorism Oversimplified," *The Washington Post*, June 29, 1984, p. A19.

11. David J. C. Irving, *The Destruction of Dresden* (New York: Holt, Rinehart and Winston, 1964), 100–102, 132-52, 217-23.

12. More probably the dead numbered about 55,000, the same as the number of members of British bomber crews killed during the war. See *Encyclopedia Britannica* 9 (1965): 308.

13. Irving, *The Destruction of Dresden*, 76.

14. Arthur T. Harris, *Bomber Offensive* (London: Collins, 1947), 78-83.

15. Hans Kumpf, *The Bombing of Germany* (New York: Holt, Rinehart and Winston, 1963), 166-67, 206-7, 235-36.

16. Harris, *Bomber Offensive*, 112-13; see also Kumpf, *The Bombing of Germany*, 229.

17. *Europe: Argument to V-E Day, January 1944 to May 1945*, vol. 3 of *The Army Air Force in World War II*, ed. Wesley F. Craven and James L. Cate (Chicago: University of Chicago Press, 1951), 721-26.

18. Irving, *The Destruction of Dresden*, 92-95.

19. Barrie Daskins and Michael Dockrill, *The Ethics of War* (Minneapolis: University of Minnesota Press, 1979), p. 36.

20. Ibid., p. 39.

21. This regulation was published by the Department of War on July 21, 1943, as *Command and Employment of War Power*. Kuter Papers, Series One: B.9.5. (US. Air Force Academy: Academy Library, Special Collections, 1980), pp. 9–13.

22. Ibid., B.30.5., pp. 24-25, 33.

23. Hugh N. Ahmann and Tom Sturm, "Interview of General Laurence S. Kuter," *US. Air Force Oral History Review* (Washington: Office of Air Force History, 1974), 290.

24. Training memo no. 33, "Air Support," *Kuter Papers*, B.2.2., pp. 11-12.

25. Ahmann and Sturm, "Interview of General Laurence S. Kuter," 375.

26. Daskins and Dockrill, *The Ethics of War*, 21-22, 34-35.

27. *The Army Air Force in World War II*, 284-85.

28. Irving, *The Destruction of Dresden*, 90-93.

29. Ibid., 92–95, 39–41, 101–2.

30. Ibid., 229–31.

31. Harris, *Bomber Offensive*, 242.

32. Ronald Schaffer, "American Military Ethics in World War II: The Bombing of Enemy Civilians," *The Journal of American History* 67, no. 2 (1980): 319, 333, 328, 332, 334.

33. Harris, *Bomber Offensive*, 176–77.

34. Merleau-Ponty, "Humanism and Terror," 270.

35. *Encyclopedia Britannica*, 23:872–73.

36. Utilitarianism, if not blended with some absolute rules, cannot justify any result regardless of the means selected in the way that extreme act-utilitarianism can, but it can justify the use of means that are *prima facie* wrong if their use makes no difference to the total amount of social good: thus, it can be insensitive to the demands of personal integrity.

37. Paul W. Taylor, *Principles of Ethics: An Introduction* (Belmont, Calif.: Wadsworth Publishing Co., 1975), 105–8.

38. Ibid.

39. Irving, *The Destruction of Dresden*, 90.

40. Kumpf, *The Bombing of Germany*, 161.

41. Telford Taylor, "Superior Orders and Reprisals," in *War, Morality, and the Military Profession*, ed. Malham M. Wakin (Boulder: Westview Press, 1968), 384.

42. Richard B. Brandt, *Morality, Utilitarianism, and Rights* (New York: Cambridge University Press, 1992), 338, 345.

43. Ibid., 352.

11

Unchosen Evil and the Responsibility
of War Criminals

PETER A. FRENCH

During the ethnic conflicts in the Balkans, the news releases were regularly filled with reports of rape, torture, mutilation, and murder carried out by combatants in the name of "ethnic cleansing." War crimes charges have been filed in the appropriate world court. I am not concerned with the possible war criminality of the political leaders of the various factions. Instead I am interested in trying to understand what sort of evil can be legitimately ascribed to typical perpetrators of war crimes such as those described in the reports of ethnic cleansing in Bosnia and Kosovo. These are people who, when not engaged in ethnic cleansing, were the ordinary tradespersons and farmers of the region. And I am concerned with what our reaction to those who committed these atrocities should be, that is, whether we should hold them morally responsible for what they did and what that requires of us.

Aristotle distinguishes three types of character that are to be avoided, that may be called evil: moral weakness, wickedness, and brutishness.[1] People are morally weak when they have good moral principles but fail to act on them. They are wicked when they just act on bad moral principles. Morally weak persons believe that what they do is wrong. Wicked persons believe incorrectly that what they do is right, or they know it is not right and don't care.

It is difficult to imagine that the war criminals of the Balkan conflicts were (or are) morally weak. They didn't commit atrocities against those from other ethnic backgrounds believing that what they were doing was wrong and wanting to alter their behavior, but being so weak of will that they could not do so. Admittedly, in the frenzy of killing, raping, and torturing that occurs in massacres during wartime, perpetrators can be so swept up in the carnage and the sheer exercise of violence against a hated enemy that it is difficult to identify their belief states or to make sense of the idea that their wills are too weak to resist what they believe to be wrong—if, in fact, they believe it is wrong. Nonetheless, brutishness and wickedness appear to be stronger candidates than weakness of will to account for their vicious actions. Let's first consider brutishness.

Aristotle distinguishes between two types of brutishness. He tells us that brutishness is typically found in barbarians, where he attributes it to nature. Then he allows that civilized folk may be afflicted with brutishness as a result of habit. His example is startlingly modern: "when someone has been sexually abused from childhood."[2] The idea seems to be that if one is abused as a child, one may develop a brutish disposition that makes such behavior habitual. Aristotle is clear that those who are brutish by nature or by habit should not be categorized as morally weak.[3]

It seems reasonable to assume that those who are naturally brutish do not believe that what they are doing when behaving brutishly is wrong or bad. Perhaps they never think of what they are doing in moral terms. After all, they're brutes. The habitually brutish apparently do not care that what they are doing is not the morally right thing to do. Due to the experiences that ingrained the brutish habit, they are indifferent to the demands of morality, at least over some range of their behavior. It is not as if they are indulging themselves in some desired behavior over which they know or believe they should exercise control to prevent themselves from doing it. Brutes, whether natural or habitual, just do what they do.

The Balkan war criminals, I feel safe in saying, are not brutish by nature. To my knowledge, there is no credible evidence that those who inhabit the former Yugoslavia possess some natural attribute of beastliness that most of the rest of the human race, thankfully, lacks. Those who committed the atrocities in Bosnia and Kosovo were not members of a pack of werewolves, driven by natural forces to rape, torture, mutilate, and murder.

Some might argue that the Balkan war criminals are brutish by habit, owing to a long history of past experiences in which they were brutalized. They have become indifferent to the constraints of morality when they confront those they regard as their former oppressors. I do not want to give short shrift to the hypothesis that those who have been abused and oppressed may become habitually brutish and respond in kind when encountering their oppressors and abusers or act in similar ways toward others when they are in dominant positions. The problem with classifying the Balkan war criminals in this way, however, is that, by and large, they do not come from the ethnic groups that were the most oppressed in Yugoslavia, and the Bosnian Muslims and ethnic Albanians in Kosovo, who have suffered the most at the hands of the Serbian war criminals, were not oppressors.

Let's look at wickedness. A person of wicked character is someone who acts on morally bad principles and believes either that what he or she is doing is the right thing to do or that it is the wrong thing to do but prefers doing it anyway. In the first case, the person is perversely wicked; in the second, preferentially wicked. Perverse wickedness is the only sort the Greeks thought was possible.

Preferential wickedness, on the other hand, can be identified with the Christian conception of evil. For the Christian, "wickedness consists in knowingly doing what is morally wrong without any compunction or scruple."[4] Doing what one believes will realize a desired end is preferred to avoiding doing what one knows or should know is wicked.

Most media accounts of the Balkan war criminals suggest a perverse rather than a preferential reading of wickedness. The reports make it appear that the perpetrators did what they did believing (albeit perversely) that it was the right thing to do. They imply that the war criminals were steadfastly convinced that mutilating, raping, torturing, and murdering those of other ethnic groups is morally demanded of them. Not infrequently, they are described as brimming with righteousness while carrying out the atrocities of ethnic cleansing. If the news stories are correct, the Balkan war criminals were notably different from the American soldiers of Charlie Company of the Americal Division in the village of My Lai 4 in March 1968. There is undoubtedly a wide range of accounts with respect to the actions and belief states of those American soldiers on that day, but very few, it appears, actually believed that what they were doing was morally right.[5]

Perverse wickedness can be understood in two rather distinct ways: (1) we might decide that a person who commits "a perversely wicked act does something that is morally wrong because he or she is ignorant that acts of this sort are morally wrong and falsely believes that such acts are right."[6] Or (2) we could say that someone is perversely wicked because he or she does "what is morally wrong because of one's acceptance of a *bad* moral principle."[7] The first description is a cognitivist's account, and the second one is a noncognitivist's version.

Think of an average Balkan war criminal, a Serb, who, in a small mountain village, has raped Bosnian Muslim women, tortured and mutilated them, and then murdered them. Did that Serb act out of ignorance? If he is ignorant, of what is he ignorant? Surely not of what Aristotle would have called the particulars of the case,[8] such as exactly what one is doing, on what or whom one is actually acting, with what specific instruments one is acting, and the intensity of one's emotions. Aristotle maintains that ignorance of the particulars (or at least the most important factors) may be involuntary and therefore pardonable. But he also adds the condition that "an action upon this kind of ignorance is called involuntary, provided that it brings also sorrow and regret in its train,"[9] which is apparently not something that our Serbian war criminal evidences. Aristotle's point is that only factual ignorance whose cause is external to the evildoer is excusable. In the case of the Balkan war criminals it is hard to imagine of which particular circumstances they may have been ignorant due to external forces. They surely knew who the persons are on whom they were acting, and they knew the results their actions would produce. If they were ignorant of anything, it must have been moral principles. And that, Aristotle insists, is not pardonable. Such perverse wickedness reflects a bad moral character.

Suppose that the Balkan war criminals do have bad moral characters. Why should that render them ignorant of moral principles? What blocks someone with a bad character from granting the truth of propositions to the effect that what he or she is doing is morally wrong? Maybe perversely wicked people are so morally sick that their intellectual capacities are impaired. They are afflicted with a cognitive blindness or, at least, cognitive myopia. There is something quite appealing in that imagery, but it really provides no insight into how perverse wickedness or bad character produces ignorance of moral principles. If that cannot be explained, then it is conceivable that someone could have a preference for doing something while believing that it is the morally wrong thing for one to do in the circumstances or under any circumstances. Some people, I am convinced, just do what they prefer doing regardless of the fact that they believe it to be morally wrong or improper to do it, and not because they are weak of will. They reveal what they care most about: not doing what is morally right in those circumstances.[10]

If we are to believe that the Balkan war criminals are perversely wicked, we would have to also assign to them beliefs to the effect that it is morally right to rape, torture, mutilate, and murder other human beings. The Balkan war criminals must believe that committing such atrocities on women of another ethnic group is not morally wrong, but that it is morally permissible or even morally required. How else could they do it? How indeed![11] We may be told that they believe that it is morally wrong to rape, torture, mutilate, and murder. It is just that they also believe that what they are doing to women of another ethnic group is not really rape, torture, mutilation, and murder. It is ethnic cleansing. Nonsense!

To make accounts of this sort plausible, one must maintain that it is possible to believe that there are no kinds of acts such that, if one knows what it is for an act to be morally wrong, one *must* believe that acts of that kind are morally wrong. For any act, it is possible to believe that it is either morally right or morally wrong.

Surely the Balkan war criminals knew that they were committing forced sexual intercourse on, torturing, mutilating, and killing their victims. If one knows what it is for an act to be morally wrong, you would think, one should know that acts of that sort are prima facie morally wrong. The further fact that these acts are being performed on defenseless noncombatants also cannot be ignored by anyone who understands what "morally wrong" means. By and large, the Balkan war criminals are not morons or brutes. They have, we may suppose, perfectly adequate moral vocabularies. So I think it more closely mirrors the facts to say either that they do not care that they are acting in violation of moral principles, or that they care more about performing acts of ethnic cleansing on the women of the Bosnian Muslim villages than they do about acting in accord with moral principles that would forbid them the very things they do to ethnically cleanse the villages. Their evil isn't perverse; it is what they prefer.

Aristotle departs from his defense of perverse wickedness because he cannot adopt the position that there are no kinds of acts such that, if one knows what it is for an act to be morally wrong, one *must* believe that those acts are morally wrong. He tells us that, for example, there are some types of actions

> whose very names connote baseness, e.g., . . . adultery, theft, and murder. These and similar . . . actions imply by their very names that they are bad. . . . It is, therefore, impossible ever to do right in performing them: to perform them is always to do wrong. In cases of this sort, let us say adultery, rightness and wrongness do not depend on committing it with the right woman at the right time and in the right manner, but the mere fact of committing such action at all is to do wrong.[12]

If Aristotle is correct, and I think he is, then one cannot both know what it means to believe that some action is morally wrong and also believe that raping, torturing, mutilating, and murdering defenseless women is not morally wrong. So where murder, adultery, and theft are concerned, one cannot be perversely wicked. If you know (or believe) you are committing adultery, for example, you must know (or believe) it is wrong or bad to do it. Only those adulterers who do not know what adultery is, and so do not know that what they are doing is adultery, can be perversely wicked. If you know it is adultery, you know it is wrong to do it. Then if you do it, you are preferentially, not perversely, wicked.

Further, if you do not know what it means to believe that some action is morally wrong, you cannot have beliefs about the rightness or wrongness of what you are doing in the first place, so you cannot properly be described as perversely wicked. The most we could say about you is that you (sometimes) just prefer to do things that you *should* know are morally wrong or bad, but for some reason do not. But that would also make you preferentially wicked.

So perverse wickedness, despite its original attraction to explain the behavior of the Balkan war criminals, loses its persuasive power. If they are wicked, they are preferentially wicked, which seems to make them more reprehensible than if they were perversely wicked.

Suppose we adopt the second way of understanding perverse wickedness and simply describe the Balkan war criminals as accepting bad moral principles or, perhaps closer to the case, as accepting and acting on morally bad principles. In either case they are acting on their preferences, attempting to realize their desired ends regardless of the moral status of their actions. But if they act on their preferences, they don't necessarily have to believe that they are doing what is morally right. They might prefer to promote their own ends, such as ethnic cleansing, by doing something they even believe to be morally wrong, though not caring that it is. If one's preference is to ethnically cleanse one's neighborhood by raping, torturing, mutilating, and murdering women of different ethnic origins, it would seem fair to say that one has extraordinarily perverse preferences. In the end, both accounts of perverse wickedness collapse into preferential wickedness.

A pathetic naïveté seems to afflict those who believe that if only the Balkan war criminals could have been convinced that what they were doing was raping, torturing, mutilating, and murdering other human beings, they would have been caught up by the scruff of their necks by some moral invisible hand and just stopped what they were doing. Nothing, I fear, is farther from the truth. I am convinced that they knew full well that they were raping, torturing, mutilating, and murdering. That is what they understand ethnic cleansing to be, and that is what they preferred doing in the circumstances. They are not that morally ignorant. They are the living moral monsters, the possibility of whose existence has been denied by a legion of moral philosophers from ancient times to the present. Yet our history books and newspapers and newscasts are replete with accounts of them and their kind.

The preferentially wicked cannot claim the morally redeeming feature of being conscientious, as the perversely wicked may. They cannot claim that if they had known or believed that what they were doing was wrong, they would have refrained from doing it. They knew it was wrong, and they preferred it anyway. Normally they would be treated as fully morally responsible for the evil they do. But should they be held morally responsible if their preferences for doing the evil things they do are the result of a cultural inculcation over which they had no choice?

I think it is probably fair to say that the Balkan war criminals did not choose to be racial and ethnic bigots. They were raised in a centuries-old culture of hatred, distrust, and conflict. In such a culture the preferences that form their characters were cemented. Although acting on those preferences and performing acts of ethnic cleansing, instead of following moral principles, is wicked, their wickedness, at an important level for moral evaluative purposes, was not chosen by them, even though it was preferential. Their preferential wickedness is what we may call "unchosen evil."[13] They "do not decide to cause evil, yet they do so as a regular by-product of their characters and actions."[14] Preferences need not be chosen. They can be, and typically are, habituated unconsciously.

Those who flogged slaves, burned witches, treated their enemies as vermin, tortured criminals before execution, or gassed Jews[15] did not act on mistaken moral principles while applying correct or good moral principles in their dealings with people of their own ethnic background. They believed, I think it fair to surmise, that moral principles did not take priority in their dealings with certain human beings or groups of human beings. Other things were more important, such as ethnically cleansing the area, exterminating threats to their superiority, and punishing those on whom they have heaped the cause of their own misfortunes. Still, in most cases, those doing the evil deeds *did not choose* the root cause of their actions: those inbred, ingrained preferences. They did not (do not) have perverse moralities. They had (have) immoral preferences on which they felt (feel) compelled to act.

Suppose we grant, as I am prepared to do, that the vile actions of ethnic cleansing, by and large, are the products of vices or faults in character that were not chosen by the Balkan war criminals in Bosnia and Kosovo. From the dominant point of view in moral philosophy, persons are not held fully morally responsible for such actions because they cannot do other than they do, because they cannot have preferences other than the ones they have. If the Balkan war criminals do not have the capacity to act in ways other than they did when confronted with the opportunity to ethnically cleanse their region, their behavior does not fit the typical criteria for chosen action, and they should not be held responsible for it. This is the tack taken by what we may call "the choice version" of moral responsibility.

I am convinced that the Balkan war criminals are dominated by their ingrained, unchosen ethnic bigotry. They are, if you will, possessed by it. It controls them, disposes them to act as they do in certain situations. It is who they are, their form of life, and they do not have the ability to dispossess themselves of it. That is the way they were raised. Had they been more independent in their thinking, had they questioned their upbringing, had they critically appraised their cultural traditions and heritage, they might have determined that their preferences were morally improper. But that is not the way they are. They are immersed in their culture of ethnic hatred, baptized in it from birth. It is an unquestioned, unexamined part of their lives. They know that what they are doing to those of other ethnic groups inflicts pain and harm on them, but they are convinced that doing so is preferable to acting in any other way toward those of the hated ethnic groups.

How can people become this way? That is a no-brainer. There are centuries of cases to examine, and they all seem to share the characteristic that the members of prejudiced and bigoted communities, whether ethnic or racial or sexual, regularly reinforce those kinds of views in each other and over many generations. When the vast majority of the members of the community expresses a singular set of pernicious, perverse views and when those views are incessantly echoed and enlarged upon by those in positions of authority, the questioning of the veracity and the morality of the dominant view diminishes to a virtually invisible point. The perverse preferences of that culture are among its essential features, and they dominate the characters of those who share it. They are the inescapable mark of belonging to those raised in that community, and the individual members of the community have no effective control over their own adoption of those preferences. The preferences of that culture are learned by its members, but the process is predominantly one of "unconscious habituation,"[16] rather than rational reflective acquisition. It is unlikely that the members ever had an opportunity to alter the course of their character development, "since doing so would have required of them a sus-

tained effort to act contrary to the social context that favored their development in a particular direction."[17] The very virtues that might have stood them
in good moral stead and withstood the pressures of their culture are exactly the
ones that they lack because they were never encouraged or trained in them.
None of this, however, makes their raping, torturing, mutilating, and murdering those of other ethnic origins one iota less wicked, preferentially wicked.

The Serbian war criminals do not sincerely believe that what they did to
women in the Bosnian Muslim villages was "deserved punishment, a necessary
corrective, justified self-defense, or only a way of instilling discipline."[18] They
do not subscribe to a mistaken set of moral principles. When they are with
their own kind, they honor all of the standard moral principles. They just prefer what raping, torturing, mutilating, and killing Bosnian Muslim women
means to them: ethnic cleansing. A morally timid view of them is insupport-
able. The morally robust view is that they are preferentially wicked people
whose bad characters were, unhappily, molded by unchosen habituation in an
ethnically bigoted culture. I think that only the morally robust view is truly
consistent with the facts.

So what should we do to these Balkan war criminals, if and when we catch
them? Two sorts of responses will typically be registered. One will censure the
raping, torturing, mutilating, and murdering they perpetrated, but it will excuse them on the grounds that their evil was unchosen by them. That is the
"soft reaction,"[19] or the "choice-based response." It is the morally timid response. It condemns the actions, but not the people who performed them.

The second type of response—call it the "hard reaction,"[20] or the morally
robust one—holds the Serbian war criminals morally responsible for the evil,
regardless of whether or not it was chosen by them. As I feel strongly that the
Balkan war criminals are condemnably evil, I reject choice-basing as the sole
justification of ascriptions of moral responsibility. In fact, I believe that choice
(the possibility of doing otherwise) should not be even the primary basis of
justifiable ascriptions of moral responsibility.

Suppose we ask, "What is the point of ascribing moral responsibility to an
agent?" In *Responsibility Matters*, I maintained that there are at least three social
practices that utilize and are codependent with responsibility ascription.[21] One
sets the targets for burden shifting, the second concerns the determination of
who merits punishment, while the third identifies appropriate subjects of blame
or praise. The second and third practices are fundamental to moral responsibility. Why punish? Because if we do not, morality has no causal power in our
lives. Why identify proper subjects for blame (or praise)? Because morality is

essentially the attempt to prevent evil, to bring about a better community. One way, perhaps the dominant way, we do that within the moral sphere is to evaluate characters, ours and those of others, to ask ourselves what sort of people we ought to be and with whom we ought to associate. We must hold responsible those who are not the sort of people that they ought to be if our community, our world, is ever to become, or even approach, a truly moral, good place to live. Moral judgments have no causal power unless we empower them.

Without compunction, we should regularly express disapproval of a person's character, regardless of how that person came to have such a character. What that means is that unchosen evil, at least when it arises from or reflects the character of the offender, warrants taking action against him or her, blaming and punishing him or her. What is important is not whether the offender chose to do what he or she did, but that what was done was evil. If morality is basically about preventing evil, then it must apprehend evil where it finds it.

The *New York Times* reported that Dr. Charles Epstein, one of the victims of the Unabomber, Theodore Kaczynski, said: "I looked at him in court and I came to the decision, this is a profoundly evil person. He is really the essence of evil."[22] When Epstein was asked if Kaczynski's mental illness affected his judgment of the man, he replied: "that doesn't take away for me from the fact that he is evil."[23] In my view, Epstein has captured the essence of morality. Calling someone evil is to use our most severe term of moral censure. Importantly, it is not a choice-based term. Even, to paraphrase Epstein, if Kaczynski's mental illness, which Epstein characterized as paranoid schizophrenia, determines the very preferences he has, determines that he has no effective scope of choice when he is in its throes, he is no less evil, "the essence of evil."

There is another side to moral responsibility that is worth noting: the members of the moral community are expected to make identifications of evil persons and to censure and punish them on pain of losing their own moral standing. The condoning of evil is itself evil. The average Balkan war criminal is a horrible human specimen, an example of what we must all try to avoid if we are to strive to make this a better place to live. People who do evil deserve to be treated as evil, and to have evil visited on them.

Does the fact that the evil was unchosen, the outcome of culturally habituated preferences, alter the moral responsibility we should ascribe to these war criminals? I think not. In fact, it is one of the best reasons for holding them morally responsible. They are dominated by evil in that they are culturally habituated to do evil. If we are feeling merciful, the fact that they do not really choose to do evil may count with us as mitigatory when we address questions of punishment. Epstein is reported in the *Times* as saying that he "would not have been unhappy if Kaczynski had been executed. But other than the need to keep Kaczynski away from society for the rest of his life, he had not concerned himself greatly with the question of what penalty was appropriate."[24]

Holding people morally responsible and punishing them are not separable practices. Ascriptions of moral responsibility have no effect in this world unless we empower them through our actions. For it to matter that what someone did was evil, even if it was unchosen evil, we—as individuals or as a community or as a community of civilized nations—must cause the moral evaluation to have a significant impact on the offender's life. It should come as no surprise that I believe that the Balkan war criminals ought not to escape severe, indeed capital, punishment for the atrocities they committed. Our very conception of moral responsibility requires nothing less.

Notes

1. Aristotle, *Nicomachean Ethics*, trans. Martin Ostwald (Indianapolis: Bobbs-Merrill, 1962) 1145a (hereafter cited as NE).

2. NE 1148b.

3. NE 1149a.

4. Ronald Milo, "Wickedness," *American Philosophical Quarterly* 20, no. 1 (January 1983): 69.

5. See the BBC production *My Lai Remembered* for accounts by those who participated in the massacre.

6. Milo, 70.

7. Ibid.

8. NE 1111a.

9. Ibid.

10. See Peter French, *Cowboy Metaphysics: Ethics and Death in Westerns* (Lanham, Md.: Rowman & Littlefield, 1997), chapter 1, for a discussion of cares.

11. For a related account of the weakness of moral imperatives, see Philippa Foot, *Virtues and Vices, and Other Essays in Moral Philosophy* (Oxford: B. Blackwell, 1978), chapter 11.

12. NE 1107a.

13. The term is taken from John Kekes. See his *Facing Evil* (Princeton: Princeton University Press, 1990), chapter 4.

14. Ibid., 70.

15. Kekes's examples.

16. The term is borrowed from Kekes.

17. Kekes, 75.

18. Ibid., 71.

19. Ibid., 85.

20. Ibid., 86.

21. Peter French, *Responsibility Matters* (Lawrence: University Press of Kansas, 1992), chapter 2.

22. *New York Times* wire story carried in *St. Petersburg Times*, January 24, 1998, 1A, 8A.

23. Ibid.

24. Ibid.

12

The Core Values in Combat

GENERAL RONALD R. FOGLEMAN

When it comes to discussing accountability and core values for the United States Air Force, I have a special motivation and interest. I emphasized these topics during my time as Chief of Staff. But my focus on core values is part of a larger commitment. That larger commitment flows from a continuing interest in military issues and in issues of national security.

My intent here is to put into perspective Air Force core values, not only as we learn them in an academic sense, not only as we practice them in peacetime, but also as they apply and have applied in combat. We're talking, of course, about three core values: integrity first, service before self, and excellence in all that we do.

In my view, you cannot sensibly talk about core values without also putting them into a larger context that includes accountability. Clearly, recent events involving our military (to include the Navy's Tailhook incident, the rape of a schoolgirl in Okinawa by some Marines, the Air Force's Kelly Flinn case, and the Army's problems with Aberdeen and Command Sergeant Major of the Army McKinney) have generated questions within the public and among our own people about accountability, core values, and the need for our military to live by standards that are higher than those of the society that it serves. It is this larger context of accountability and one's success or failure as a member of the profession of arms, particularly in the crucible of combat, that I would like to address.

Due to its importance, I would propose to start this discussion with an examination of the concept of accountability. As I understand it, and for our present purposes, accountability involves a moment or a day of reckoning when one is judged on his or her adherence to the standards and values of an institution or profession. Such a day of reckoning has two possible outcomes (and professional practitioners have a right to expect the outcome to be fair and specific): that is, when you are called to task, you will face either a positive or negative outcome. Notice that I do not restrict accountability to the negative, and that I did not say a day of reckoning only for failing to meet standards and values. That would assume we are only judged on our failures. But I think we should judge both on successes and failures, and I would hope that a proper understanding of accountability would always have it be so.

Reflecting on this premise, I think it points to some more fundamental principles. I believe the key element in this understanding of accountability is adherence to standards and values. Professional standards may or may not be codified or written down, but for accountability to be workable and fair, standards and values must be universally known and uniformly applied. This seems obvious, but some recent cases would indicate that there may not be a universal knowledge of what constitute our standards and our values. Or, as I think Voltaire said, common sense is not so common.

Maybe this seeming lack of knowledge is a good reason for codifying our standards. General Bill Creech, when he was the commander of Tactical Air Command and I was one of his wing commanders, said it like this: You should remember when dealing with the Forces that the spoken word is philosophy, and the written word is guidance. While over the years I have come to recognize the importance of standards and values being codified, the fact remains that workable standards also come to us in other forms.

One of the oldest and clearest forms of standards for military professionals is the oath that is taken by the practitioners of the profession of arms. The oath we take is well known. We swear to support and defend the Constitution of the United States against all enemies, foreign and domestic, and to bear true faith and allegiance to the same. We take the oath freely, without any reservation or purpose of evasion, and swear to discharge faithfully the duties of the office we enter. Our enlisted troops in addition swear they will faithfully obey the orders of the president and the officers appointed over them, according to regulations and the Uniform Code of Military Justice.

Indeed, one of the most vivid recollections I have of my four years at the Air Force Academy happened during my basic cadet summer. I remember the day that we were advised by our Air Officers Commanding and our upperclassmen that this was the day of reckoning, and that if we were going to turn back, we should do it then, because we were about to take the oath. In those days, the oath was administered en masse to the class. The class formed up on the upper terrazzo in front of Harmon Hall, looked toward the superintendent's office, and the superintendent stepped out on the balcony and administered the oath. It was from that moment on that something changed in my life. I had never been asked to take an oath or to think through what this meant in a higher sense, and in all candor, I had no real understanding of what it meant for the future. But something fundamental had changed beginning with that oath. I had publicly acknowledged and embraced an important set of professional standards.

Another standard for the military is the current version of our Code of Conduct. It came to us as a result of U.S. military experiences in the Korean War, in which our soldiers, our sailors, our airmen, and our Marines in many cases did not hold up very well in North Korean captivity. And so it was that the Congress of the United States, after investigating this situation, decided to promulgate a Code of Conduct. Like so many of our standards, not everyone was able to meet the standards set out in the code. But we had to have a set of standards that were universally known and could be uniformly applied, and the Code of Conduct serves that function for us.

Yet another set of professional standards is found codified in our laws. In the case of the military, it's the Uniform Code of Military Justice (UCMJ). During some recent congressional testimony, I was chagrined to discover that there were members of the Congress who did not know that the UCMJ is the law of the land. It is not something that was invented by the Department of Defense, but rather was enacted by Congress. Even so, I was asked about certain articles of the UCMJ and whether they were outdated or no longer applicable. When these members of Congress questioned the UCMJ, my response was simple: Take out whatever you do not like. If you do not like Article 134, which applies to adultery (or, as a close reading will show you, adultery when adultery affects good order and discipline), remove it. If you do not like the article that applies to treason, remove it. If you do not like the article that applies to murder, it can go too.

Of course, Congress will not remove any of these articles. The UCMJ has been well crafted to regulate our military, which is a large organization with special needs. Out in the field, the leadership does not look at the UCMJ as something that always leads to one of those outcomes that is negative. It is instead something that provides a framework in which our officers, our airmen, and our senior leaders can function. There is great value in having set down what our expectations are, and what our standards are and will be as we go forward. These expectations, these codified standards, are not to be feared, but to be valued.

In addition to written codes, standards can also come from what I could best refer to as the professional culture or ethos. This is really where our Air Force core values come to the fore. Integrity first. Service before self. Excellence in all that we do. Capturing this cultural aspect of our standards is something that we worked long and hard on when we put together the Little Blue Book on core values. As we said in that book, the core values exist for all members of the Air Force family. They exist for officers, enlisted, civilian, active, reserve, retired, senior, junior, middle management, civil servants, uniformed personnel, and contractors. The core values are much more than minimum standards. They are intended to remind us what it takes to get the mission done. They inspire us to do our very best at all times. They are the common bond among comrades in arms, and they are the glue that unifies the Forces and ties us to the great warriors and public servants of the past. The culture and the ethos of our profession is what we were trying to capture.

I sincerely believe that effective professional standards and values, in whatever form we find them, must have some things in common. I think first and foremost they must serve a purpose for the profession and the larger public served by that profession. In our military institutions, an important purpose that they serve is to promote good order and discipline within the force, which in turn provides the public an effective fighting force. Second, I think that standards and values generally evolve slowly over time, as a result of practicing the profession (even though on occasion we may find them suddenly thrust upon us because of some perceived shortcoming). Last, I would suggest that professional standards and values generally involve some interplay between individuals and institutions. And I am sure I take nothing away from anybody in terms of human dignity or individual worth when I say that in most cases, and certainly in the case of the military, satisfying the needs of the institution is more important than individual pride, prestige, and appetites. The professional institution and its mission are paramount, as those institutions will rise and fall on the sum total of the efforts of the individuals who constitute them.

Standards and values serve the guiding purposes for an entire organization. They must certainly be known, practiced and supported by the leaders of that organization. I believe that the central leadership challenge for military officers begins with the public understanding of why the military exists. It is a profession that is dedicated to defend the nation, to ensure life and liberty and the pursuit of happiness of this nation's citizens—as the oath says, to support and defend the Constitution of the United States against all enemies, foreign and domestic.

With this task of defending the nation comes the reality that our core expertise, the thing that allows us to be called professionals, is fighting and winning wars. We are not part of a social engineering experiment. We are not an employment agency. We are a *military* organization. So when it comes to standards and values and leadership, the greatest challenge for any individual or for any military leader will be battle and battle leadership. The tools of our trade are lethal. We engage in operations that involve risk to human life and untold national treasure. And we should never forget the fact that the most precious treasure of all is the young men and women who serve.

Associated with some of these responsibilities comes a recognition of something else, something that ought to be understood fairly easily by the military professional, less so by the public we serve. When we take that oath, we also agree to live by something that was best described in the early 1960s by a noted British soldier-scholar, General Sir John Winthrop Hackett, in a series of lectures at King's College in which he talked about the profession of arms. He talked about the thing that sets us apart from other professions in our culture and our society—he said we agree to live by an "unlimited liability clause." Nowhere do you see it written, and rarely will it be discussed, but basically implied in that oath, and part and parcel of that unlimited liability clause, is the idea that if called upon to do so for your nation, your family, your friends, your fellow warriors, and your freedoms, you are expected to lay down your life in this profession.

I have a friend who recently retired from the Air Force Reserve, a major general by the name of Bill Cohen (no relation to the former secretary of defense). He has spent his life studying the art of leadership. He is a West Point graduate, and in 1990 he published a book called *The Art of the Leader*, which I believe you will find on the Chief of Staff's reading list. Bill Cohen is in the process of publishing another book, in which he specifically talks about the challenges of combat leadership. He says that

> . . . in combat, conditions are severe. There are terrible hazards and poor working conditions. There's probably greater uncertainty than in any other activity. Workers may need to perform their duties with little food and irregular sleep. All must take great risk. Most followers and leaders alike would prefer to be somewhere else and doing something else. And while there are true military geniuses in battle, the vast majority, as in

most organizations, are ordinary men and women. In most battles many are not professionals, and not all are suited for their jobs. But professional or amateur, all are stressed far more than in any civilian situation or occupation for, moreover, leaders must not only carry out the mission, but they must do their best to protect the lives of those they lead at the same time. And so it is no wonder that traditional motivators such as high pay or good benefits and job security aren't much good. There is no "business as usual" on the battlefield. (Cohen, *The Stuff of Heroes*, ii–iii)

It is this essence which Cohen is describing that separates what we do from what most people do. We must look upon our work as a calling. If one comes to the Air Force for training or a good education, that is fine. One will get a good education. But we must think beyond that, in terms of how we will pay back this nation for that education and what that will entail. And for the military professional, that time will come, as it has in the past. Eventually, we will be challenged again and will have to answer the call to arms for this country. I would like to think that this is not true, that we can change the nature of humanity, but I must tell you that it will happen . . . it will happen. And that treasure, the young men and women of this country, deserves the very best in leadership, those who understand our standards and our values and who have developed within themselves a moral compass that will allow them to lead.

People who have been in combat agree with me. From my own experience, I remember in particular one individual. I attended the Army War College during 1975 and 1976, and in my class was a chaplain whose story is told by Bill Cohen in his book. This chaplain stood out because he wore a tremendous number of medals for a chaplain, many of which were for gallantry. I had to find out more about this man. I discovered that Kermit Johnson had been an infantry platoon leader in Korea, then resigned his commission, went to Princeton, and earned a degree in divinity. He reentered the Army as a chaplain and eventually retired as the Chief of Chaplains of the United States Army. But when we were at the Army War College, immediately after the Vietnam War era, there was a lot of cynicism and sarcasm among the class. One of our classmates made the statement to Kermit that "ethics never won a battle." And it was interesting to see what happened in that seminar as the rest of the people took the speaker apart piece by piece. Every one of the people in that room had been in battle, and they knew better. They knew that moral standards and values are an essential component for success in leading in battle.

Cohen also surveyed combat leaders as part of his investigation. His study of combat and combat leaders moves through an elaborate process and arrives at eight laws that determine success for leaders in most situations, especially in the military. But digesting Cohen's eight rules for leadership in combat led me to the conclusion that they are reducible to our three Air Force core values: integrity first, service before self, and excellence in all that we do.

It is difficult to be more specific about how the core values function in the context of combat, but I would relate to you two stories that I hope will be instructive. I cannot pick out a specific incident that illustrates each value, but I think it will be easy to see how all of them together operate in both of these stories. The first one happened to me. It has to do with cohesion of the armed forces, and the idea that from core values comes a firm belief that no matter how dark it may look, you can depend upon your fellow warrior.

On September 12, 1968, I was on a combat mission in the F-100. I was shot down in an area of IV Corps called the Uh Minh Forest. It was very hostile territory. There were no friendlies in the area. After taking quite a bit of fire in the parachute coming down, I managed to get on the ground, get out of my chute, get up on a canal bank, and run several hundred yards without being severely wounded or killed. While running down the trail on the canal bank I came around a turn, and there, sticking out of what we called a spider hole, an underground bunker, was a small child. I remember drawing my weapon. The child disappeared very quickly. I was prepared to kill that child, but his presence shocked me into reviewing my situation and actions.

Something then came home to me that said, "This is really stupid. Here you are with combat boots running down a muddy trail next to a canal." I turned around and could see the cleat marks from my boots. I am not a good swimmer, and I hated being in murky water. But nonetheless I knew I needed to get off that canal bank, and so I turned and jumped into the canal. After I was in the water, I concealed myself under a bank.

I did all those things that you think only occur in John Wayne movies. I smeared mud on my face and neck. I thought for a minute that I was well hidden, then looked down and saw two yellow pencils in my flight suit, shining like beacons. I took those yellow pencils and quickly threw them away, but a few minutes later those two pencils floated by in the water, brighter than ever. I thought that maybe I ought to stick them in the mud, where they would stay submerged. I waited for help to arrive in the form of a forward air controller (FAC) and rescue helicopters.

After some time, an FAC arrived on the scene and started a search-and-rescue effort. Things looked bleak. There was a Viet Cong (VC) force only a couple of hundred yards away, and they were starting a sweep across the rice paddy toward my position. At one point when I was in the water, underneath this bank, there was a soldier standing above me, shooting at the forward air controller, the empty shells from his AK-47 falling into the water in front of me. I guess you could say we were in close proximity. Eventually, when the FAC got established in the area, the VC backed away, and I started talking on my radio. The FAC told me that he had a flight inbound that was going to provide cover for me until I could be rescued, and he gave me the call sign of that flight.

It was Ramrod Zero One. Ramrod Zero One was the call sign of the squadron commander of a sister squadron, the 531 TFS. The man flying that airplane was a guy by the name of Bob Bazely, Lieutenant Colonel Bob Bazely. He had gone to Vietnam from the Air Force Academy, where he had been on the commandant's staff. He was an experienced, superb F-100 pilot. His silver-gray hair earned him the nickname of "The Silver Fox." When I heard that Bob Bazely was in that airplane, suddenly all hope returned, because somehow I knew he would do whatever was required to get me out of there. He was known for excellence in all that he did. He was known for service above self. His integrity was above reproach.

And so time passed, and eventually the VC decided they were going to come across this rice paddy again. On my radio I asked for close air support, but the FAC did not want to employ the fighters because he was afraid that the air strikes would kill me too. They were afraid I was disoriented and did not know where I was, because I was giving them instructions to make their strike relative to my chute. Finally I convinced them with a hard-to-argue-with logic that said, "Look, it doesn't matter whether you kill me, they're going to get me if you don't do this." And so Bazely came in and he eliminated the threat.

After that, we were still faced with the situation of how to get me out of this position. As it turned out, there were no Air Force rescue choppers that could reach me. But there happened to be an Army helicopter unit in the vicinity, some fifty miles away. It was a gunship unit that was stationed in the Delta to support special forces. The FAC called me and said, "Look, we have some Army gunships that will come in, and they will rescue you. However, they don't have any room inside the helicopter, so you're going to have to hang on to the outside of the helicopter to be flown to safety."

Now, the only Army gunship I had ever seen was a Huey, and there is plenty of room to get inside one of those. Just to show you how service rivalry comes through even in your darkest moments, and forgive me the profanity, this was the thought going through my mind: "Just like the god-damned Army.

They're not going to let me inside the helicopter." I figured that I would be able to get inside anyway.

I was in for a big surprise when they arrived on the scene. That was the first time I ever saw a Cobra helicopter. To my surprise and chagrin, it was truly a gunship, with no room inside. Interestingly enough, when these choppers came in, with one holding high to provide suppressive fire, the VC respected them and did not interfere. The other one came in and landed. I got out of the mud and ran to the helicopter. I sat down on the skid, grabbed hold of it, and was ready to get out of there. The gunner in the front opened his canopy and pointed to a couple of latches, which I then disengaged. The gun-bay door fell open. It was about fifteen by thirty inches, and it had a couple of cables attached. I put a leg through one, an arm through the other, and away we went, twenty miles to a special forces camp. They had to replace that door, I think, because it became warped in the ride back (maybe from my grip on it). It was an interesting rescue.

Waiting for me at the special forces camp was an Air Force medical evacuation helicopter, which took me to a field hospital. In order to meet me, Bob Bazely had landed on a short, 5,000-foot strip where the field hospital was located. I'll never forget what Bazely did. The medics took me off the helicopter to work on me, but Bazely said, "Not so fast. This boy drinks bourbon; nobody touches him until you get him some bourbon." Now, they had all kinds of stuff at this hospital, but they didn't have any bourbon. This kind of threw them into a flip, but eventually one of the NCOs got some bourbon, came back, and we were okay.

Later, when I got back to my home base, my wing commander contacted the Army two-star in charge of all rotary wing aircraft in Vietnam. He wanted to thank this crew for rescuing me. And the word went out: "Anybody who rescued an Air Force pilot at such and such a place on such and such a date take one step forward." Nobody stepped forward. The reason was that the Cobras were so new in theater they were prohibited from landing anywhere except at home base, and these guys were not about to admit they landed in a rice paddy to pick me up. Eventually, the general had to go out with another message that said, "Look, this is a no-kidding, all-is-forgiven come forward." And I was pleased that they did, because here were some folks who risked violating a standing order to take care of a fellow warrior who was in need. They needed to be recognized and held accountable in a positive way.

There is a mixed but interesting ending to this story. The front seater, the gunner in that helicopter, turned out to be from a small town about twelve miles from where I grew up. Unfortunately, he was killed before he made it home. He ultimately gave up his life for his country and his comrades. So again, we see that service before self, excellence in all that we do, and integrity are vitally important in combat, both personally and professionally. Lt. Colonel Bob Bazely, the Silver Fox, went on to wear four stars and command the United States Air Force in the Pacific during the late 1980s.

I promised two war stories. The second one is also in Bill Cohen's upcoming book and begins with General Jay Kelly's predecessor at Maxwell Air Force Base, General Chuck Boyd. When Chuck Boyd was at Maxwell, which is where we now have all of our professional military education, the citizens of Montgomery came to the base and said, "We want to help you build an air park. We will buy a historic aircraft and put it out there so you can complete your collection." And Chuck Boyd said, "Well, I appreciate that, but why don't we do a statue of an Air Force leader who has had a major impact on our Air Force?" And the town fathers, led by their great mayor, Emory Folmer, said, "We will back whatever you want, Chuck, and we will agree to have a statue of whatever leader you choose."

And so General Boyd was faced with a great decision. Would the statue be of Billy Mitchell, who had fought so hard for the independence of the Air Force? Would it be of Claire Chennault, who had taught at the Air Corps Tactical School while stationed at Maxwell? Would it be of General Hap Arnold, the first Chief of Staff of the Air Force? Or maybe somebody like Curtis Lemay, who had built the Strategic Air Command? General Lemay served longer as a four-star in the Air Force than any other general officer. But in the end, General Boyd chose none of these distinguished leaders. Instead, he chose a lieutenant by the name of Carl Richter.

Carl Richter lost his life during the Vietnam War. Potential critics said, "But so many people gave the full measure. Why Carl Richter, and how could a young lieutenant be considered to have such a large impact on the Air Force?" And so Chuck Boyd told them about Carl Richter. Graduated from the academy in 1964, he went directly to pilot training. From pilot training he went immediately into training for the F-105, the legendary THUD. The THUD was a fighter bomber, and wasn't really designed for what we were using it for in Vietnam. But it was a much sought-after fighter assignment, and First Lieutenant Carl Richter gave up his predeployment leave, went to Southeast Asia, and began his combat tour as quickly as he could. He arrived for duty with the 338th Wing in April 1966, a time when the 388th was carrying a lot of the weight of the air war. They were taking the fight to downtown Hanoi, which at that time had the world's heaviest concentration of air defenses. Five months after arriving, Carl became one of the first F-105 pilots—and the youngest—to shoot down a MIG 17. This was done in spite of the fact that the F-105 was really not an air-to-air machine.

These were tough days for the Air Force. Historians aren't generally aware that the United States Air Force suffered a 16-to-1 loss ratio. For a time in 1966 and 1967, we lost sixteen aircraft for every aircraft that we shot down. But the rule was that pilots must fly one hundred missions over the North. When you completed one hundred missions, you went home. But 43 percent of the people flying these missions were either killed or captured before they went home. So to reach one hundred missions was quite an accomplishment.

Richter completed his hundred missions successfully, and he promptly volunteered to fly another hundred. He believed that he had learned so much about his business as a combat fighter leader that he could save lives of less experienced fellow aviators. The senior leadership agreed to let him fly another hundred missions. Here we see, without any question, service before self and excellence in all that we do. He personally led many raids as a junior officer. He taught many more senior officers, including some of his commanders, how to survive and employ the F-105 in this intensely hostile environment. And along the way Richter won numerous decorations for his heroism and his leadership. On one occasion he was awarded the Air Force Cross, the second-highest award this nation bestows upon its warriors.

Richter completed his second hundred missions, and he immediately volunteered for a third tour of duty. But this time it would not be up North—the leadership would not allow it. This time it was to fly F-100s in the South, supporting the ground war. But just before his transfer, he was once again out in front. He was checking out a newly assigned pilot. The target was a very heavily defended bridge. Richter told the new guy to hold high and dry, and that he would make the first attack. His luck ran out that day. His aircraft was hit, and he punched out. There was a locator beacon, so rescue forces came in, found Richter, and picked him up. But he had been so severely injured, probably as a result of being dragged through rock formations with his parachute, that he died in the helicopter.

The statue of Lieutenant Carl Richter bears an inscription from the Bible, and it quotes the prophet Isaiah: "Whom shall I send, and who will go for us? Here am I; send me." Now, Richter wasn't a squadron commander or a wing commander, but he was a leader. He understood his profession and its values, and he wasn't that long out of this institution when he was called upon to do those things. In my view he continues, and he should continue, to lead and inspire other Air Force leaders and young officers in the future.

So, to conclude, our standards and core values are vitally important to what we do. Recently I brought thirty-four years of active duty, thirty-eight years of total service, to a close. And some people have asked me, "Well, how do you feel now that you are retired? What is it that you reflect upon?" I will tell you. When I was assigned to the Air Force Academy between my tours of duty in Southeast Asia, I served on the faculty in the history department. One of my additional duties during that tour was to serve as the executive director of a military history symposium. We brought General Sir John Winthrop Hackett here to give a lecture on the profession of arms. He gave a presentation titled "The Military in the Service of the State." I remember very clearly one paragraph from that lecture, because it has certainly proven true in my personal and professional experience, and I believe that it continues to be applicable to those who would lead the Air Force:

> For the military life—whether for sailor or soldier or airman—is a good life. The human qualities it demands include fortitude, integrity, self-restraint, proven loyalty to other persons, and the surrender of the advantage of the individual to a common good. None of us can claim total command of all of these qualities. The military man sees round about him others of his own kind also seeking to develop them, and perhaps doing it more successfully than he has done himself. This is good company. Anyone can spend his life in it with satisfaction.

So it was, and so it is.

THE JUST WAR TRADITION AND
MORAL PROBLEMS OUTSIDE WARFARE

13

The War Metaphor in Public Policy

Some Moral Reflections

JAMES F. CHILDRESS

I n this essay I want to offer some moral reflections on both war as reality and
war as metaphor. I will begin with some reflections on the morality of real
war, but I will concentrate on the morality of using war as a metaphor. Military
professionals are often told that they should learn about the limits of war from
nonprofessionals—that is, the public—but my theme here is different. My
claim is that military professionals have a tremendous responsibility to help society think about both the moral use of war and the moral use of war as a metaphor. I will examine the relation between our moral discourse about real war
and our moral discourse about social policies and practices, which we often
discuss in the language of war.

Throughout I will stress the following point: In debating social policy
through the language of war, we often forget the moral reality of war. Among
other lapses, we forget important moral limits in real war—both limited objectives and limited means. In short, we forget the just-war tradition, with its moral
conditions for resorting to and waging war. We are tempted by seedy realism,
with its doctrine that might makes right, or we are tempted by an equally dangerous mentality of crusade or holy war, with its doctrine that right makes might
of any kind acceptable. In either case, we neglect such constraints as right intention, discrimination, and proportionality, which protect the humanity of all
parties in war.

Let me briefly offer my perspective on the moral reality of war. I come from a Quaker background, i.e., the Society of Friends, which is one of the historic peace churches but also tolerates a wide range of views about war among its members. In college and divinity school, I read several works by Reinhold Niebuhr, a Christian realist, and I became convinced that war can sometimes be justified, but that it always requires justification. Then through reading various theological and philosophical writers, including Paul Ramsey and Michael Walzer, I came to appreciate more fully the moral limits on the conduct of war, which are recognized by the broad just-war tradition but largely ignored by Niebuhr.

I also came to the conclusion that pacifists and just warriors share an important starting point: a moral presumption against war because of the important individual and social duty not to kill others. Pacifists deny that this duty can ever be morally overridden; just warriors hold that it can be morally overridden, because, as fundamental as that duty is, it is only prima facie or presumptively binding and must sometimes yield to competing moral principles or values.[1]

I draw on the "historical deposit" of just-war criteria in the West to interpret the right to wage war (*jus ad bellum*) and rights or right conduct within war (*jus in bello*). As an ethicist it is not my task merely to repeat what has been held traditionally but also to think critically about moral traditions regarding war, thus respecting them as living, vibrant traditions that must be thought through again and again, especially in new contexts. And I have tried to reconstruct the traditional just-war criteria in what follows.

The prima facie duty not to kill binds societies as well as individuals, but not absolutely so. Killing always requires moral justification, and its justification must meet a heavy burden of proof. When killing is justified, the prima facie duty not to kill doesn't just evaporate—it continues to exert moral pressure on our conduct and on our attitudes, leading to what St. Augustine called "a just and mournful war."

When other important moral duties come into conflict with the duty not to kill—say, the duty to protect the innocent—then we do (and should) engage in a process of reasoning that includes traditional just-war criteria. These criteria were explicitly used in the public and military debates about the Gulf War. The criteria of the *jus ad bellum* (the right to go to war) include: legitimate authority to undertake the war; just cause, i.e., a serious and weighty competing prima facie duty; last resort or necessity, i.e., the exhaustion of reasonable alternatives to waging war; explanation and justification of one's course of action to the enemy and to other parties (often expressed in a somewhat legalistic way as a declaration of war); a reasonable hope of success; proportionality, i.e., determining that the probable good effects outweigh the probable bad effects for all the parties affected; and right or just intention, which includes pursuit of a just cause, peace as the end of war, motives of nonhatred and regret. The criteria of the *jus in bello* include discrimination between legitimate and illegitimate targets, particularly between combatants and noncombatants, with direct attacks permitted on combatants but not on noncombatants; and, again, proportionality, i.e., balancing probable good against probable harm in particular actions in the war.

In Michael Walzer's language, I thus view war as a rule-governed activity rather than as murder or a hell where anything goes.[2] When war is viewed as hell—as pacifists and realists are inclined to do—the only moral question is whether to enter this criminal or hellish state that lacks all moral limits. The pacifist says "Don't enter"; the realist says "Enter and get out as quickly as possible"; the just warrior says "Enter reluctantly, fight fairly, and restore the peace as soon as possible." For the just warrior, it makes a moral difference how the war is fought.

Now, there is an important and irreducible difference between peace and war—so that crossing from peace to war requires discharging a heavy burden of justification—but the difference is not between day and night, not between morality on the one hand and immorality or amorality on the other hand. And criteria similar to those of the just-war tradition appear in our reflection about other conflicts of duties in peace: for example, whether to lie or whether to force someone to do something, as in involuntary hospitalization. Thus, there is an important continuity or overlap between the justification of war, which infringes on the prima facie duty not to kill, and the justification of other acts that also infringe on prima facie duties, such as the duty not to lie. This point will be important when I turn to war as metaphor.

I apologize for this quick—and perhaps cryptic—statement of my interpretation of the moral reality of war, but since my position is not totally novel, even if it is distinctive, perhaps its main lines are clear enough. After all, one shouldn't expect great originality in this area, for as one philosopher put it, "originality in social and political thought is almost always a sign of error." Or as another wag put it, originality is forgetting where you got it. My theory of just war builds on our common morality of war as expressed in the tradition of just war in dialogue with other moral traditions about war, including pacifists, realists, and crusaders.

Let's now turn our attention to some moral issues in the use of war as a metaphor in social and political discourse. Following an introduction to general moral issues in the use of war as a metaphor, I'll take some examples from my other areas of work in ethics, particularly biomedical and religious and social ethics: the construal of medicine as warfare; society's war against AIDS, particularly in relation to screening and testing for antibodies to the human immunodeficiency virus (HIV); and our recent and continuing culture wars.

Moral Issues in the Use of War as a Metaphor

George Lakoff and Mark Johnson have written an important book, *Metaphors We Live By*, which argues that our metaphors (often subconsciously) shape how we think, what we experience, and what we do.[3] Our metaphors use us as often as we use them. In each use of metaphor, we see something as something else; we experience or understand one thing through another. For example, we see X as Y, human beings as wolves, love as a journey, and argument as warfare.

Take an example that Lakoff and Johnson use—argument as warfare. We develop *strategies* of argument, *contend* with one another, *attack* positions as *indefensible*, *win* arguments, and so on. With this metaphor of argument as warfare, we interact with one another in certain ways. Imagine how different our interactions would be if we had a different metaphor for argument—for instance, if we viewed argument not as combat but rather as a collaborative search for the truth (along the lines, say, of Gandhi's thought) or as a collaborative work of art. Such approaches to argument sound odd and even bizarre, and we might not even recognize what the agents are engaged in as an argument. This example clearly indicates Lakoff and Johnson's point about how metaphors both highlight and hide features of their subject. The metaphor of warfare highlights the conflict involved in argument, but it hides the cooperation and collaboration, involving shared rules, that are also indispensable to argument.

The war metaphor was rampant in several headlines on the first page of the *New York Times* on April 23, 1990:

MILLIONS JOIN BATTLE FOR A BELOVED PLANET: A Global Call to Arms Is Seen in Festivities Marking Earth Day

AIDS WAS SHUNNED BY MANY DOCTORS: Patients Are Said to Miss Out on Life-Prolonging Drugs. [The follow-up inside headline is: In the AIDS War, Many Doctors Are Happy to Stay in the Reserves]

A COVERT AND MAJOR VICTORY IS REPORTED
IN THE DRUG WAR.

It is easy to view such headlines as merely dramatic and even exaggerated ways to make a point. To be sure, we do sometimes use metaphors as merely decorative or dramatic ways to call attention to some point we want to make. But often our very interpretations of what is going on, and our actions in response, are structured by metaphors that use us. Frequently we are not even aware that we are thinking metaphorically—as is probably true in the cases of argument as warfare and, as I will argue later, medicine as warfare. Only when we or others probe our language can we grasp how much our conceptual framework is shot through with particular metaphors. Metaphors are ways of orienting ourselves in the world, and they orient us by highlighting and hiding features of the principal subject, such as argument or medicine, by the commonplaces associated with war.

We cannot avoid metaphors, but we can become conscious of our metaphors—individual, professional, or social-cultural—and critically assess them. We can even try to change the ones that distort more than they illuminate, to modify them or even, if necessary, to replace them. All of these responses are important for the metaphor of war in some contexts. Our approach to any particular metaphor should depend on its value, its illuminative power, that is, how well it helps us see and understand what is going on, and how well it helps us see what we ought to do. The first test involves looking at reality from all angles; the second test involves examining the moral principles and values highlighted and hidden by the metaphor.

Medicine as Warfare

The metaphor of warfare is prominent in health care, where it shapes much of our conception of what is and should be done. Consider the way this metaphor emerges in the day-to-day language of medicine, which I have drawn from conversations and from medical literature: The physician as the captain leads the battle against disease, orders a battery of tests, develops a plan of attack, calls on the armamentarium or arsenal of medicine, directs allied health personnel, treats aggressively, and expects compliance. Good patients are those who fight vigorously and refuse to give up. Victory is sought and defeat is feared. Sometimes there is even hope for a "magic bullet" or a "silver bullet." Only professionals who

stand on the firing line or in the trenches can really appreciate the moral problems of medicine. And they frequently have "war stories" to relate. As medicine
wages war against germs that invade the body and threaten its defenses, so a society itself may also declare war on cancer or on AIDS, under the leadership of
its chief medical officer—the surgeon general. Articles and books may even herald the "Medical-Industrial Complex: Our National Defense." As one writer
notes, "where once it was the physician who waged bellum contra morbum, the
war against disease, now it's the whole society."[4] Medical organization, particularly in the hospital, resembles military hierarchy, and medical training is probably closer to military training than any other professional education in our
society.

The military metaphor first became prominent in the 1880s, when bacte-
ria were identified as agents of disease that threaten the body and its defenses.
It now clearly structures much, though by no means all, of our conception of
health care. And it both illuminates and distorts health care. Its positive implications are widely recognized—for instance, in galvanizing support to fight
against disease. It can also, among other things, engender a positive attitude
and hope.

Perhaps surprisingly, the metaphor also has its problems. Susan Sontag, a
distinguished intellectual, was diagnosed with cancer in the late 1970s, and her
suffering, she reports, was intensified by the metaphor of warfare against cancer,
which was so dominant in medicine and in society. She wrote her superb little
book, *Illness as Metaphor*, in order to calm the imagination and direct people
with cancer to appropriate practical actions. The controlling metaphors in the
descriptions of cancer are drawn from the language of warfare: Cancer cells
don't just multiply; they are "invasive." They "colonize." The body's "defenses"
are rarely strong enough. But since the body is under attack ("invasion"), by
"alien" invaders, counterattack is justified. Treatments are also often described
in military language:

> Radiotherapy uses the metaphors of aerial warfare; patients are "bom-
> barded" with toxic rays. And chemotherapy is chemical warfare, using poi-
> sons. Treatment aims to "kill" cancer cells (without, it is hoped, killing the
> patient). Unpleasant side effects of treatment are advertised, indeed over-
> advertised. ("The agony of chemotherapy" is a standard phrase.) It is im-
> possible to avoid damaging or destroying healthy cells (indeed, some
> methods used to treat cancer can cause cancer), but it is thought that
> nearly any damage to the body is justified if it saves the patient's life. Of-

ten, of course, it doesn't work. (As in: "We had to destroy Ben Suc in order to save it.") There is everything but the body count.

Furthermore, Sontag continues, "Military metaphors contribute to the stigmatizing of certain illnesses and, by extension, of those who are ill."[5]

Certainly one contemporary implication of the metaphor of warfare in health care is overtreatment, particularly of terminally ill patients, because if disease is the immediate foe, death is the ultimate enemy. It is difficult for physicians and families under the spell of this metaphor to let a patient die. "Heroic" actions, with the best available weapons, befit the military effort that must always be undertaken against the ultimate enemy. Death signals defeat and forgoing treatment signals surrender. Some physicians even feel more comfortable withholding (that is, not starting) a treatment, say, for cancer, than they do withdrawing (that is, stopping) the same treatment, in part because withdrawing treatment smacks of retreat.

What has happened in this use of the war metaphor is the loss of the sense of limits. Let's just keep in mind the limits of discrimination—distinguishing combatant from noncombatant—and the limits of proportionality. The opposing combatant is the disease or death, not the patient, and the patient's suffering must be balanced against the probable benefits. There should be a reasonable prospect of success and also proportionality, that is, a balance of good over bad effects in light of the patient's own values.

Some other ambiguous implications of the war metaphor can be seen in the allocation of resources for and within health care. First, it is no accident that two major terms for the allocation and distribution of health care under conditions of scarcity emerged from, or have been decisively shaped by, military experiences: triage and rationing. As Richard Rettig and Kathleen Lohr note:

> Earlier, policymakers spoke of the general problem of allocating scarce medical resources, a formulation that implied hard but generally manageable choices of a largely pragmatic nature. Now the discussion increasingly is of rationing scarce medical resources, a harsher term that connotes emergency—even war-time circumstances requiring some societal triage mechanism.[6]

Triage involves sorting out casualties according to the degree of severity of their illness: those who can survive without treatment; those who can be salvaged only with treatment; and those for whom treatment would be futile. This approach involves judgments of medical utility—urgency of medical need and probability of successful treatment. But sometimes triage includes judgments of social utility and social worth.

A widely discussed example was reported in World War II. In North Africa, the Allies had a limited supply of penicillin and could not treat everyone in need. They chose to treat the men "wounded" in the brothels rather than those wounded on the battlefield, because those suffering from venereal disease could be restored to fighting capacity sooner and contribute directly to the war effort. This was a social utilitarian calculation, based on the needs of a focused community at war.[7] But however much such an approach can be generalized to some civilian emergencies (say, following a disaster such as an earthquake), it does not translate well into the routine allocation decisions in health care, where a commitment to equality and medical utility trumps or should trump social utility.

Second, within the health care budget, the military metaphor tends to assign priority to critical care over preventive and chronic care. It tends to view health in negative rather than positive terms, as the absence of disease rather than a positive state, and then concentrates on critical interventions to cure disease. It tends to neglect care when cure is impossible. Lawrence Pray noted that he originally tried as a teenager to conquer his diabetes, but his struggles and battles were futile and even counterproductive. Then over time he came to view his diabetes not as an "enemy" to be "conquered" but as a "teacher." Only then did he find a satisfactory way of living.[8]

A third point is closely connected: In setting priorities for research and treatment, the military metaphor tends to assign priority to killer diseases over disabling and crippling diseases. But that is not how we as individuals order our lives. As Franz Ingelfinger once noted, if we concentrated research and treatment more on disabling diseases, such as arthritis, rather than on killer diseases, then national health expenditures would reflect the same values that we affirm as individuals: "It is more important to live a certain way than to die a certain way."[9]

This leads to our fourth ambiguous implication of the military metaphor. Medicine as war concentrates on technological interventions, such as intensive care units, over other technologies, such as prostheses. It downplays less technological modes of care.

Fifth, society's health care budget tends to be converted into a defense budget to prepare for and conduct war against disease, trauma, and death. As a consequence, society may put more resources into health care than it can justify, especially under a different metaphor, in relation to other social goods. Indeed, society may overutilize health care, especially since technological care may not contribute so much to the national defense of health itself, the reduction of morbidity and premature mortality, as many other factors, including poverty.

In short, the military metaphor has some negative or at least ambiguous implications for a moral approach to health care decisions. It tends to assign priority to health care (especially medical care) over other goods and, within health care, to critical care over preventive and chronic care, killer over disabling diseases, technological interventions over less technical interventions, and heroic treatment of dying patients rather than allowing them to die in peace.

I do not propose that we abandon the military metaphor—it illuminates and directs much of health care in morally significant ways. I have concentrated on its negative or at least ambiguous implications for health care because I believe its positive implications are clear enough. We can avoid some of the negative implications of the war metaphor for health care if we retrieve and respect the just- or limited-war tradition. "Modern medicine," William May writes, "has tended to interpret itself not only through the prism of war but through the medium of its modern practice, that is, unlimited, unconditional war," in contrast to the earlier, just-war tradition. Modern war has often become "total, unconditional war with the commitment of all means, extraordinary as well as ordinary, to the victory. Just so, hospitals and the physician-fighter wage unconditional battle against death."[10] No wonder the Dr. Kevorkians of the world have found a receptive audience for those wanting to escape from the terrorist bombardment of this warfare. Hence, rather than giving the war metaphor a dishonorable discharge, we should instead make it accountable to the moral tradition of just war.

But we also need to supplement the war metaphor with other metaphors. It is not the only one in health care, and it is not even the dominant one now, given the pervasiveness of the language of economics and business. In the new way of talking about health care, there is a health care industry, with providers who deliver care to consumers. Productivity is sought, and cost-effectiveness or cost-benefit analysis offers the key to decision making. This metaphor also highlights and hides features of health care, including the relevant values. One major concern is what this economic metaphor implies for the relationship between health care professionals and patients, particularly when the language of efficiency or the bottom line replaces the language of care and compassion for the sick. Nevertheless, this metaphor is becoming more and more pervasive as concerns about costs dominate the discussion. And now patients are beginning to fear undertreatment as hospitals and professionals seek to reduce costs, in contrast to their fear of overtreatment under the war metaphor as remarkable technologies emerged for prolonging life (or the dying process).

We probably need both military and economic metaphors to understand contemporary health care. But they may not be adequate, even together, to guide and direct health care. Whether any metaphor is adequate or not will depend in part on the principles and values it highlights and hides. The military metaphor tends to emphasize the goal of conquering disease, and this goal, with the necessary discipline and sacrifice, may triumph over the patient's autonomy and value preferences. It may also triumph over a society's other values in the allocation of resources. By contrast the economic metaphor tends to emphasize efficiency, even when equity and care have to be sacrificed.

One promising supplementary metaphor is nursing, with its attention to caring more than curing, to hands-on rather than technological care. This metaphor is not adequate by itself, just as the military metaphor (or any other metaphor, such as business) is not adequate by itself, but it could direct society to alternative priorities in the allocation of resources for and within health care, particularly for chronic care.

Society's War against AIDS: Fighting and Caring

For several years, a professor of medicine and I cotaught a seminar entitled Confronting Plagues, which considers historical and contemporary societal responses to epidemics. From our review it appears that societies often react (and, at least in retrospect, overreact) with coercive measures to epidemics of communicable diseases, and they frequently do so in the name of war against those diseases. In a sensitive discussion of major vocabularies of concern about AIDS, Monroe Price notes that "the question is whether the AIDS epidemic will become such a serious threat that, in the public's mind, it takes on the stature of war."[11] In fact, the metaphor of "the war against AIDS" has been very prominent in debates about social policies, particularly in efforts to justify coercive interventions, for example, through mandatory screening and testing for antibodies to the human immunodeficiency virus (HIV).

In our society it is natural to use the metaphor of war when a serious threat to a large number of human lives requires the mobilization of vast societal resources, especially when that threat comes from biological organisms, such as viruses, that attack the human body. And AIDS activists have appealed to the military metaphor in an effort to galvanize society and to marshal its resources for an effective counterattack against the AIDS virus.[12] However, the military metaphor has other entailments that must not be overlooked.

From the beginning of the war against AIDS, identification of the enemy has been a major goal. Once the virus was identified as the primary enemy, it became possible to develop technologies to identify human beings who carry or harbor the virus. This led to what Ronald Bayer calls the "politics of identification."[13] How are HIV-positive individuals to be viewed? As carriers of HIV, are they enemies to be fought? Should society try to identify them? And how should society act on the information that a particular individual carries or harbors the virus? What may and should be done?

Surgeon General Everett Koop insisted that this war is against the virus, not against people, but that distinction is too subtle for many. The distinction between the virus and the carrier becomes very tenuous, and the carrier tends to become an enemy as much as the virus he or she carries. Furthermore, many actions that lead to exposure to HIV are not considered "innocent," and the associated lifestyles are sometimes viewed as a threat to dominant social values. Thus, it is not surprising that this metaphor of war often coexists with metaphors of AIDS as punishment and as otherness.[14]

Here again, the metaphor of war against AIDS could be appropriate and less risky if our society regularly recalled the moral constraints on resorting to and conducting warfare represented in the just-war tradition. Just as the "moral logic of war" entails justification for overriding the prima facie obligation not to kill, so the "moral logic of war" against AIDS through mandatory identification of carriers requires overriding some of our society's important principles—respect for individual autonomy, liberty, and privacy. Of course, those are not absolute values—just as the prohibition of killing is not absolute—but they are important values and cannot be lightly dismissed. Mandatory screening and testing can be justified under some circumstances, but most proposals simply fail to meet the conditions for overriding those values, conditions that are analogous to those for a just war: Is there a weighty competing goal (usually there is—public health)? Is mandatory screening/testing necessary, or are there other morally acceptable ways to realize the same goal? Would mandatory screening/testing probably be effective? Would its benefits outweigh its costs, including its economic costs? And is the screening/testing employed the least intrusive and invasive available?

By the criteria implied in these questions, it is clearly possible to justify mandatory testing of donated blood, organs, sperm, and ova, and also mandatory screening in settings where there are no effective ways to avoid spread of the virus. But HIV is transmitted only through a few routes. And in most settings mandatory screening is not necessary, would not be effective, and would be very costly. For instance, it seems intuitively plausible to consider state-mandated HIV-antibody tests of all couples who apply for a marriage license. However, the one state that implemented this policy dropped it after a brief period because the policy failed these tests. In the war against AIDS, as in real wars, it is important to proceed with limited means as well as limited objectives. Here again, the justificatory conditions are analogous to those that govern just wars.

In addition to retrieving the just-war tradition in the use of the war metaphor, we need to consider other metaphors in response to the AIDS epidemic. Metaphors of community and solidarity, metaphors that express caring, are promising. Whereas the military metaphor tends to conflate the virus and the carriers of the virus, metaphors of community and solidarity tend to express concern for the individuals who carry the virus and for others at risk of infection. The metaphor of war against AIDS tends to divide the community insofar as HIV-infected individuals are viewed as enemies, and in the process it undermines some of the conditions that could make voluntary testing effective without resort to mandatory policies. People who are aware that they may be HIV-infected often do not seek testing because of the psychological risks of a positive test result—such as stigma, discrimination in insurance, housing, and employment, and breach of confidentiality. Some of those risks can be reduced by a caring community. And reducing those risks would encourage more people to seek voluntary testing and, if they are not infected, to protect themselves or, if they are infected, to protect others.

When we combine the war metaphor with efforts at identifying carriers, it is not surprising that marginalized groups often respond with suspicion. And those groups most affected by AIDS—gay men and intravenous drug users—belong to marginalized subcommunities. The war metaphor tends to exclude HIV-infected individuals as enemies from the larger community, while the metaphor of community and solidarity tends to include them in an orbit of care.

Many (but not all) coercive policies in response to the AIDS epidemic would also set a precedent of overriding individual rights in a crisis—in a war against disease—even when it produces limited or no benefits, or the burdens outweigh the benefits, or there are alternative ways to protect the public health. We need other metaphors in addition to the war one, but if we use the metaphor of war against AIDS, we need to keep in mind the moral commitments of our society and the justificatory conditions for overriding prima facie principles—parallel to the ones that operate in the just-war tradition. How we respond will shape and express our "identity and community in a democracy under siege."[15]

Culture Wars

The war metaphor also emerges in our contemporary debate about American culture. James Hunter, a colleague at the University of Virginia, has written a book entitled *Culture Wars: The Struggle to Define America*, which attempts to make "sense of the battles over the family, art, education, law, and politics."[16] According to Hunter, "America is in the midst of a culture war" over "our most fundamental and cherished assumptions about how to order our lives" and about "who we are as Americans." The conflict between the "orthodox" and "progressivists" within various faiths is about "the power to define reality," that is, to interpret society's collective myths and symbols of national identity. As Hunter wrote recently in the *Washington Post*, "the culture war is about who we are as a nation and who we will choose to become. Rather than blame it for demeaning democratic discourse, the 'war' should be acknowledged as the proper subject of democratic debate."[17] He accuses cultural warriors, such as Pat Buchanan, of trivializing the culture war by reducing it to particular struggles rather than seeing that it is in fact "a fundamental struggle over the 'first principles' of how we will order our life together. Through these seemingly disparate issues we find ourselves, in other words, in a struggle to define ourselves as Americans and what kind of society we want to build and sustain."

Reflecting on Hunter's and others' interpretations of the culture war (he prefers "war" to "wars"), Peter Steinfels notes that Americans tend to toss the word "war" around carelessly, and that the term "cultural war" was appropriated by neoconservative intellectuals from the German term "Kulturkampf," which referred to Bismarck's campaign against the Roman Catholic Church in Germany in the 1870s and which suggests a Prussian harshness.[18] Other parts of the social and political spectrum in the United States also use the term, at least in self-defense. Participants in this societal debate view themselves as combatants in a war.

Here, yet again, we see little evidence of the just-war tradition of restraint, for what we have, to some extent on both (or all) sides, is much more a holy war and even a crusade. Even though he is somewhat sympathetic to themes in the conservative camp, Hunter calls for a deflation of the rhetoric and for leadership with "great courage" and "wisdom"—wisdom to recognize "that however well the term 'culture war' may describe the battles being waged in America today, the term cannot be embraced as a call to arms. It is, then, time to stop the drum-beating. What we require is serious and substantive argument inspired by a leadership that is both bold and rhetorically circumspect. For in a democracy, how we contend in public life is as important as *what* we contend for." In short, Hunter uses the war metaphor descriptively while questioning its normative use, that is, its use as a guide to action in the current setting, other than to downplay the war and to concentrate on how the conflict is waged.

However, as Steinfels notes, Hunter's description makes it difficult not to take sides. For if the metaphor of war expresses what is "the inevitably dominant reality" and "if the stakes are so high, the competing moral visions so nonnegotiable and rational moral discussion so unlikely, then isn't the responsible thing to choose sides and plunge in?" Hunter has been criticized by conservatives for remaining neutral, and he makes it clear that he is deeply dissatisfied with the dualism of the culture war. Steinfels continues: "By describing the reality, he wants to correct it, not perpetuate it. But can he do this without questioning the adequacy of the military metaphor itself? When culture becomes the continuation of war by other means (to paraphrase Clausewitz), something is seriously wrong." I'm not even sure how well the metaphor of warfare helps us understand what is going on in our cultural conflicts, but I am quite certain that it does little to guide our actions properly in relation to this conflict. Not all efforts to define society are conflicts, and not all conflicts are best understood as warfare; but when they are properly understood as warfare, it is important to ask whether the moral constraints from the just-war tradition are being respected, or whether instead the crusade or holy war has taken over, with a real threat to our society's fundamental commitments to ordered liberty.

Conclusion

Do these various uses of the war metaphor, through highlighting and hiding features of certain issues, generate insights about what is and about what ought to be? Donald Schoen gives a fine, simple example of a generative metaphor, that is, one that generates insights.[19] Researchers were trying to improve the performance of a new paintbrush with synthetic bristles; the new brush applied the paint to the surface in a "gloppy way." Nothing the researchers tried made the artificial bristles work as well as the natural bristles. But then one day someone observed "You know, a paintbrush is a kind of pump!" That was a generative metaphor: Pressing a paintbrush against a surface forces paint through the spaces or "channels" between the bristles, and painters sometimes even vibrate brushes to increase the flow. Once the researchers began to view the paintbrush as a kind of pump, they were able to improve the brush with synthetic bristles.

We have to ask of each use of war as a metaphor: Does it generate insights or does it obscure what is going on and what should be done? In each use of the war metaphor we have considered, distortion occurs in part because of the failure to hold the war metaphor accountable to the just-war tradition, with its limiting conditions for waging and conducting war. Analogous conditions apply elsewhere in conflicts, particularly when a prima facie duty is overridden. And at each point we need both limited objectives and limited means, again in line with the just-war tradition. We need to maintain the just-war tradition not only in order to be able to wage real wars justly—the most important reason—but also to instruct our society about ways to approach its own internal conflicts.

In view of the limited illuminative power of any particular metaphor, we also need to supplement the war metaphor, if we use it, with other metaphors. I do not propose a war of metaphors as much as a creative juxtaposition of metaphors that can illuminate complex matters. In some conflicts, perhaps in the so-called culture war, we may need to replace it altogether because of its distortions and risks. It is a sad commentary on our society if we cannot say that something important is at stake in a societal debate without resorting to the inflated rhetoric of warfare.

Finally, we also need to be cautious about the loose use of the metaphor of war. Otherwise we will trivialize real wars and exaggerate other conflicts and problems our society faces. War, real war, remains one of the most significant human activities, but it is an exceptional activity that can be justified only under exceptional circumstances and, even then, should be fought within appropriate moral limits.

In short, we need imagination. David Eerdman says that imagination is reasoning in metaphors.[20] But we also need imagination in our selection of metaphors, noting what each highlights and hides. The war metaphor is important and often indispensable, but it must be used thoughtfully and with appropriate restraint.

Notes

1. For a fuller statement of my views on war, see my *Moral Responsibility in Conflicts: Essays on Nonviolence, War and Conscience* (Baton Rouge, LA: Louisiana State University Press, 1982), especially chapter 3, "Just War Criteria."

2. Michael Walzer, *Just and Unjust Wars* (New York: Basic Books, 1977).

3. George Lakoff and Mark Johnson, *Metaphors We Live By* (Chicago, IL: University of Chicago Press, 1980).

4. Susan Sontag, *Illness as Metaphor and AIDS and Its Metaphors* (New York: Doubleday Anchor Books, 1990), p. 98. The essay "Illness as Metaphor" was published separately, first in the *New York Review of Books* in 1978 and later that year by Farrar, Straus and Giroux, which also published the essay "AIDS and Its Metaphors" separately in 1989 before the combined edition appeared.

5. Ibid.

6. Richard Rettig and Kathleen Lohr, "Ethical Dimensions of Allocating Scare Resources in Medicine: A Cross-National Case Study of End-Stage Renal Disease," unpublished manuscript (1981).

7. Paul Ramsey, *The Patient as Person* (New Haven, CT: Yale University Press, 1970), chap. 7.

Historian David J. Rothmann dismisses this story as a "widely repeated but apocryphal tale." See his *Strangers at the Bedside* (New York: Basic Books, 1991), p. 40. No available evidence indicates that this was ever a formal policy. However, British government policy in allocating penicillin in 1944 was apparently social utilitarian in restricting its use to pilots and bomber crews on military grounds, but at least one case was reported of a breach of these established rules of allocation to save another enlisted person. See Stuart W. Hinds, "On the Relations of Medical Triage to World Famine: An Historical Survey," in *Lifeboat Ethics: The Moral Dilemmas of World Hunger*, ed. George R. Lucas, Jr., and Thomas Ogletree (New York: Harper and Row, 1976), p. 37.

8. Lawrence Pray, *Journey of a Diabetic* (New York: Simon and Schuster, 1983), and "How Diabetes Became My Teacher," *Washington Post*, July 31, 1983.

9. Franz Ingelfinger, "Haves and Have-Nots in the World of Disease," *New England Journal of Medicine* 287 (December 7, 1972):1198–99.

10. William May, *The Physician's Covenant* (Philadelphia, PA: The Westminster Press, 1983), p. 66.

11. Monroe E. Price, *Shattered Mirrors: Our Search for Identity and Community in the AIDS Era* (Cambridge, MA: Harvard University Press, 1989), p. 84. For a fuller statement of my position on mandatory screening and testing for HIV antibodies, see "Mandatory HIV Screening and Testing," in *AIDS and Ethics*, ed. Frederic Reamer (New York: Columbia University Press, 1991), 50–76. See also my *Practical Reasoning in Bioethics* (Bloomington: Indiana University Press, 1997), chap. 6.

12. Larry Kramer, "A 'Manhattan Project' for AIDS," *New York Times*, Monday, July 16, 1990.

13. Ronald Bayer, *Private Acts, Social Consequences: AIDS and the Politics of Public Health* (New York: Free Press, 1989).

14. See Judith Ross, "Ethics and the Language of AIDS," in *The Meaning of AIDS: Implications for Medical Science, Clinical Practice, and Public Health Policy,* ed. Eric Juengst and Barbara A. Koenig (New York: Praeger, 1989), 30–41, and Ross, "The Militarization of Disease: Do We Really Want a War on AIDS?" *Soundings* 72 (1989): 39–50.

15. Price, *Shattered Mirrors*, p. 189.

16. James Davison Hunter, *Culture Wars: The Struggle to Define America* (New York: Basic Books, 1991).

17. Hunter, "America at War with Itself: Those Debates over Sitcoms and Motherhood Aren't Froth—This Is a Cultural Showdown," *Washington Post*, September 11, 1992, C 1 & C 4.

18. Peter Steinfels, "Beliefs: Metaphors are Flying . . .," *New York Times*, December 12, 1991, p. 10.

19. Donald Schoen, "Generative Metaphor: A Perspective on Problem-Setting in Social Policy," in *Metaphor and Thought*, ed. Andrew Ortony (Cambridge, England: Cambridge University Press, 1979), pp. 254–84.

20. David Eerdman, "Coleridge as Editorial Writer," in *Power and Consciousness*, ed. Conor Cruise O'Brien and William Dean Vanech (New York: New York University Press, 1969), p. 197.

14

The Control of Violence, Foreign and Domestic

Ethical Lessons from Law Enforcement

REVEREND EDWARD A. MALLOY, C.S.C.

What will we face in the future? We live in a time of rapid and sometimes unpredicted social and political change. What social scientist can claim to have known what was going to happen in Russia, in Eastern Europe, in Chile, in Afghanistan, in Namibia, or in any of the other places in the world that have recently experienced radical change? Who has an overview that sufficiently incorporates the tremendous variety of social, political, and economic circumstances that exist in our world today upon which to base accurate predictions? Much is unknown, but I feel there are certain claims that we can safely make.

It is probable that smaller-scale conflicts will persist: Think of what has been happening in Ethiopia, Cambodia, Lebanon, Angola, El Salvador, and many other places like them. We have also seen the introduction of terrorism and the capacity of a few to seize the high technology that previously was restricted to a limited number of experts. This no doubt will continue to be a serious problem. We face—and will most probably continue to face—narcotics traffickers who in a sense take over legitimate governments, corrupt them from within, and have the economic power of multinational corporations. As a response, both the military and law-enforcement agencies will be asked to undertake roles that often are uncomfortable. In the midst of all of this we see our federal government struggling with the national debt in debates over defense budgets for the years ahead. These situations will have an impact on all of us as citizens of this country. The role that the military will play is only roughly determinable. We need to think through not only the changes that will be predictable but also the unforeseen circumstances that will challenge us all.

I come out of a religious tradition—Roman Catholic—that is committed to a broader frame of reference relative to war and peace. Called the just-war tradition, it is a way of analyzing the context of the use of violence by the military. It dates to the Greco-Roman period and was adapted and modified through the ages by various representatives of the Christian tradition particularly, though not exclusively so. There are many ways of describing the criteria that emerged from this process, but certain well-established criteria are generally accepted.

The criterion of legitimate authority states that war cannot be declared arbitrarily or by the whim or fancy of a few but rather must be prepared for and promulgated by a legitimately established government. It must be for a just cause, often described in terms of national defense. It must take place as a last resort, that is, only after every effort has been expended to keep it from happening, in recognition of the terrible human tragedy that accompanies the making of war. It must be motivated by right intention: Each person who prepares for or participates in the conflict must have prepared him or herself in terms of the moral scheme of things, thinking through what is acceptable and appropriate and what is not, being prepared to say no even when that is an unpopular decision. And we know that the momentum of events and the difficulty of ascertaining facts in the midst of conflict make all of this difficult.

Much of just-war theory in the twentieth century has been devoted to reflection about the fifth criterion, moral means. Because of the scale and destructive capability of our weaponry, because of the integrated nature of modern life, where military forces are very seldom isolated from the civilian populations, we have had to undertake an analysis of forms of fighting, the very legitimacy of which is in question. In discussing the question of moral means, three governing principles have been developed. The principle of discrimination, or noncombatant immunity, traces its origins to the beginning of the Greco-Roman period and has been a constant feature of the analysis that has taken place over the last two thousand years. This considers the necessary distinction between those who can be legitimately described as the enemy—those who bear arms against our side—and the civilian population. But we know, looking back on the First and Second World Wars, on Korea, on Vietnam, and on many smaller-scale conflicts, that maintaining this distinction is extremely difficult. We have creeping into our language the notion of collateral damage, whereby some percentage of civilians are put at risk because there is no other way of winning in a particular kind of engagement.

The second principle we have placed under the rubric of moral means is the principle of proportionality. Common sense dictates that we should not enter a war that we cannot win. In addition to that, as human beings who can exercise our intelligence and weigh and evaluate things, we should seek to participate only in such conflicts from which, all things being equal and acceptable, a greater good will result than the evil that will be suffered. But how difficult this is to evaluate, not simply in the short term—in terms of body count—but also in the long term, with the destruction of infrastructure and the continued or renewed hostility and hatred in the next generation!

The final principle derived from moral means is that of humane treatment—to respect the dignity of the enemy, as difficult as that may be. Examples of this principle can be found in the treatment of prisoners, the immunity of those who are serving as medics, ambassadors, or negotiators with the other side, and in trying to preserve certain other civilized practices in war that developed in the Middle Ages and that have been incorporated into the statutes of international law. These three items grouped under the general criterion of moral means are flexible in their applications and, like the other general criteria of the just-war theory, are designed as ways to help us think through creatively the questions of morality in war.

I would like to suggest that the large issue of controlling violence and maintaining justice can be viewed at the macro level in terms of military conflict; at the micro level under the rubric of law enforcement; and at a mixed level when considering agencies like the CIA, the FBI, the National Security Council, and various other groups with a mandate that exceeds the normal restrictions of law-enforcement agencies but is not quite tantamount to the mission of the military. Let me further suggest that thinking morally about the use of violence is a *professional* responsibility at each of these levels.

To make my case, I must say something about what it means to be a professional. The historical learned professions of law, religion, and medicine have evolved over time. Now a number of areas of human work also claim to be "professions." But becoming a professional requires, first of all, specialized training. One must acquire a broad general background, develop a technical expertise appropriate to the discipline, and master a certain set of principles before one is able to competently practice a profession. Second, there is invariably some sort of certification. At the end of the training program, the professional body or those otherwise involved in the profession must in a sense confirm that one has accomplished all that is required; only then is one inducted into the profession. Third, in the training and early periods of practice, the inculcation of a code or set of values or way of thinking about moral responsibility as a professional person is an essential part of any profession. Finally, a profession usually conveys status and/or a higher than usual level of financial reward. The desirability of these attributes is reflected in the results of popular opinion surveys. What would young children like to be? There's a kind of ranking that normally finds the professions clumped near the top, but that can change. After certain kinds of scandals are given public exposure in a given profession, its status commonly suffers, which suggests that being a professional carries with it high levels of expectation placed upon one by the public one is sworn or somehow committed to serve.

It is the third characteristic I find most interesting for this discussion: the unique moral responsibilities we claim to carry as professionals. We are all familiar with the Hippocratic oath. Whether it is directly attributable to the Greek philosopher Hippocrates or not, it has a long-standing significance in the way members of the medical profession think about themselves, the quintessentially professional convictions they have about themselves and that are shared by patients entrusted to their care. The oath codifies an attitude of service and the receipt of a solemn trust. For example, it expresses concern about confidentiality, about protecting information that one gains in a privileged context so as not to abuse what has been entrusted. For a profession to be a profession in the sense of which we are speaking (as opposed to merely taking money for one's services), this element of trust and service to the client or society is indispensable. The codes that we find in the various professions simply make this attitude explicit.

Perhaps the most difficult task for a professional person and for the profession as a whole is enforcing the code. In the end, nobody is comfortable turning someone else in. People may espouse the value, they may even live by it themselves, but it is quite another matter, a much more difficult task, to hold a peer accountable. Nobody likes a whistle blower; nobody likes somebody who seems self-righteous or cannot respect the limitations of human nature and human weakness. Yet for a profession to be held in consistently high regard, the willingness to hold others accountable must be present.

The problem is not peculiar to any particular profession and might be found in medicine, law, the military, law enforcement, and teaching. I have observed it in the many facets of my professional life. Unfortunately, most of us have had some occasion to see teachers who are ill-prepared, professors who are incompetent for one reason or another. No one wants to hold them account-able, lest the profession as a whole be tainted; yet the result of such inaction and rationalization is that over time the profession itself is tainted and the level of trust broken down. It is estimated that 20 percent of the physicians in this country have a problem with some type of substance abuse. At the very least, this would lead one to be more wary about medical care when its practi-tioners have such easy access to drugs. Clearly, one ought to recognize that when a few are incompetent, the whole profession suffers.

In light of these comments on the moral responsibilities of the professions in general, I would like to focus on some ethical responsibilities of the law-enforcement professional. Perhaps the most difficult moral issue for the law-enforcement professional is how to control violence. I've suggested that law en-forcement deals, at the micro level, with the same kinds of problems that the military must face at the macro level. With this in mind, I want to test out the applicability of just-war theory for those in law enforcement. Indeed, I think it will work very well, because in some ways law enforcement is a more controlled setting than is a military operation in wartime. We can look at what the difficulties are and why the profession is more or less successful in facing cer-tain dilemmas.

Prior to 1829, there really weren't any police forces as we know them today. There were constables, sheriffs, and watchmen. They were generally unedu-cated and ill-prepared for the role assigned to them. One of the first police forces was established, at least indirectly, because gin was introduced into England. Gin, which was originally distilled as a way of reducing the corn surplus, created a terrible problem with alcohol abuse in London and other English cities. Re-sponding to the resulting violence and other crime, Sir Robert Peale took the initiative in establishing a group that could ensure safety in English cities. In fact, the word "bobbies" comes from his first name. From the days of Peale until the present we have seen in most countries of Europe and North America a mul-tiplicity of police agencies, some 40,000 in this country alone.

Law-enforcement agencies have had a difficult time dealing with profes-sionalization. In fact, right up to the present, the very desirability of profession-alizing the police has been debated in various public-policy journals. In order to attract the very best people to this crucial work, agencies have paid great atten-tion to the recruitment and selection process, to police training, and to better pay scales.

However, there still remains the question as to whether police officers should be college-educated or not, and this question must be settled before law enforcement at all levels can be compared to the professional model we outlined earlier. Certification to practice is also an unsettled issue. Should there be lateral entry? Should one be able to move from a police force in Chicago to another in Denver? Today, this is not generally done, excepting transfers at the very top level. More typically, police officers live a relatively isolated existence, spending their entire careers in one place. This is very different from other professions, where, for example, lawyers or doctors can take certification examinations in a state other than where they received their professional training. There's a kind of transferability. And surely the military profession provides a clear example of how effective certification permits mobility of the widest scope. I would argue that because of the complexity and the central significance of the law-enforcement function, its practice should be more thoroughly professionalized, with a great deal more attention paid to recruitment, selection, training, certification, and—perhaps most important—the inculcation and enforcement of a code.

One of the most significant aspects of law enforcement that demands professionalization and, by the way, distinguishes it from military service is police discretion. By discretion I mean the breadth of choice, the leeway in decision making, given to the individual officer. In fact, the lowest-ranking officers, the beat officers walking the streets or driving a patrol car in a certain area on a regular basis, and those working undercover have the most discretion, while those at the top of the "pecking order" have the least. It's a very interesting deviation from the kind of military organization that is evident simply from walking around the campus of a military academy, where one sees the deference to ranking officers, the recognition of the chain of command, the leadership role that calls upon officers to make the basic decisions and for enlisted personnel to carry them out. When you turn to the police force, it's just the reverse, and that creates some very interesting questions about accountability as well as professional preparation. In any case, we can see that police discretion calls for a greater degree of professionalization at the lowest levels, since the officer on the beat is making most of the basic decisions as to what constitutes crime, when to enforce a particular law, what to charge a suspect with, and what procedures to follow in arrests and evidence gathering—procedures that could gain or lose a conviction.

It is also interesting to note that police discretion is a necessary and an unavoidable feature of a feasible law-enforcement system, because it's impossible for the police to enforce all the laws all the time. As it stands now, this discretion is exercised unevenly across law-enforcement agencies, and for various reasons. Some agencies tend to overlook laws that are on the books at some other level of government, as when municipal police overlook certain laws or state police overlook certain statutes. Other agencies tend to be very selective, depending upon the signals they receive from their constituencies. For instance, laws against gambling or prostitution might be ignored in response to veiled communications from the political leadership, as might highway speed limits.

Decisions like these are made all the time, and the use of discretion varies not only from one law-enforcement agency to another but also within the larger departments and from one precinct or area to another. Surely potential for abuse lies here. One example is prejudicial enforcement—more severe enforcement against inner-city blacks than suburban whites, more severe enforcement against young males in general than against older people, less enforcement of white-collar crime than of crimes committed by the less fortunate, and so on. Besides being manifestly unfair, prejudicial law enforcement has the pernicious effect of breeding disrespect for the law.

There are other types of selective enforcement, such as the various categories of immunity. A system in which information is obtained from informants can also mean that a full-time burglar might never go to jail if he provides evidence in narcotics or rape cases. The fairness of this system is, of course, a separate issue, with its own set of accompanying problems; still, we are all at least casually acquainted with the system and are for the most part used to the arrangement. Another form of selective enforcement involves the revival of antiquated laws. An individual officer knowledgeable about such laws might enforce, say, a "quiet law" that hasn't been in use for more than fifty years as a way to block downtown streets from so-called "undesirables" who otherwise were doing nothing against the law.

The last abuse of discretion I want to mention here is selective action taken against societal corruption, either that perpetrated by distinct individuals or as part of entrenched patterns of behavior. We have already considered the difficulty of holding individuals accountable within a profession, and that difficulty makes abuse of this type that much more pervasive.

The necessities and difficulties associated with discretion in law enforcement give us something to think about in terms of the way the military functions, particularly with regard to the use of violence. Notwithstanding the difference in who exercises discretionary authority in law enforcement and in the military, comparing the two provides a rich topic for discussion. Is discretion distributed optimally in the military structure? Could military command structures be modified to gain some of the advantages inherent in the way the police use discretion? Are the holders of discretion in the military, wherever that authority might ultimately lie, subject to the same sorts of temptation to abuse this power or exercise it incompetently? If little or no discretion is available to the individual in the military, who should be called to account when mistakes are made by higher-ups? All of these questions related to discretion should be addressed when discussing the nature of the military or, indeed, of any profession. In this country, police are armed and trained in the use of force. They have discretion in both the use of force and the kind of force used—such as handcuffs, tear gas, pistols, shotguns, and automatic weapons. We all have seen the comparisons of our police with those in England, where the officer on the beat is generally not armed. Are our police officers armed because of our fascination with firearms, our "Wild West" syndrome? Or does it have to do with the idea that if firearms are available to criminals, law-enforcement agents must have them to enforce the law? Whatever the historical origins or justifications, I think it foolish to entertain the idea of adopting a police system like that in England. We live in circumstances where normally our police officers will be armed. Given an armed police force, then, a force exercising a high degree of discretionary authority, the criteria of just-war theory are applicable to law enforcement.

First, with regard to legitimate authority, the police officer can only validly use coercive force when he or she in fact represents the body politic. In some parts of the world, police death squads, or so-called right-wing death squads, exercise deadly force outside the legitimate political machinery. That is simply unacceptable within our constitutional tradition and our standards of right and wrong, as are any personal vendettas by the police in the use of force. So legitimate authority suggests a control over the exercise of violence by law-enforcement agents.

Second, with regards to just cause, the police should have written guidelines for the use of guns, mace, choke holds, and all the other means of constraining or harming another person. The discretion of the individual officer must be exercised only within the constraints of this established code, which is only to say that law enforcement needs a code, just as the military needs a code, as clerics need a code, as teachers need a code.

The criterion of last resort in the context of law enforcement means that the police should exhaust all possible methods for controlling a situation before resorting to the more severe levels of force. One of the most difficult circumstances that law-enforcement agents can face is domestic violence. Entering a household, police find a husband and wife, sometimes parents and children, fighting; sometimes there are weapons. Often, as soon as an intervention takes place, family members turn against the officer. The question of the appropriate use of force or style of interaction requires a high level of training; more and more, there are—and need to be—specialists for this kind of situation, as for potential suicides and other specific circumstances.

If they are acting from right intention, police will use the full force available to them only when they are convinced that the common good is being served, not for personal safety alone or because of some emotional response. In certain military engagements verbal provocation or the witnessing of horrendous acts can precipitate a breakdown of restraint, and the same is true in law enforcement when, perhaps in the course of an arrest, suspects resort to verbal or physical provocation. Restraint in such situations—acting from an intention to enforce the law, not to respond to insults—requires a level of training and self-control that exemplifies why both the military and law enforcement ideally should be professions.

Under the criterion of moral means, we can find examples of all three subordinate principles: discrimination, proportionality, and humane treatment. Police use of force must never be indiscriminate, that is, directed at groups of people in general. We demand this of the police, even when it is difficult, as in mass demonstrations, yet we all can recall in our own lifetimes vivid examples, such as the march on Selma, Alabama, where official mass hostility by the police was the direct cause of violence and injury. The principle of discrimination also calls for considering seriously the impact that specific force will have on innocent participants in an event. When, for example, can tear gas be used, and what about hot pursuit? There is nothing more frustrating for a law-enforcement agent chasing a felon in a car than to abandon the chase because of the risk to pedestrians and other motorists, but when the risk to innocents is real, the principle of discrimination requires that restraint be exercised. The same is true with kidnapping, skyjackings, and other crimes involving innocent bystanders. To exercise restraint because too many lives are at stake is to recognize that people of good will, those who try to do the right thing, will sometimes have to refrain from doing what would otherwise be right because of the collateral impact on others.

The principle of proportionality calls for weighing the good and evil results of an action or policy in both the short and the long term. Applying it to a hypothetical firearms policy, how much discretionary authority should an officer have in the discharging of his or her weapon? What sort of weapons ought he or she to have? Most police agencies today prohibit the use of warning shots simply to capture a suspect because of the risk inherent in firing a weapon; the risk involved is disproportionate to the task at hand. Still, it is very difficult to maintain this principle when officers' lives are at stake. Similarly, when a police officer does use a gun, the prime intention should be to incapacitate rather than to kill the suspect; that is, there is no general warrant for deadly force in every case where it may be legitimate to use a weapon. Once again, there are difficulties maintaining this principle—especially in some drug cases, because of the firepower available to the dealers, because of the brazenness with which certain dealers operate, and because of the desperation that law-enforcement agents often feel in fighting what they perceive as a losing battle.

For all these reasons, in every instance where a police officer fires a gun in the line of duty, there should be full investigation by responsible representatives of the people, some kind of civilian review board. Of course, few police officers would like that; they would take it as an affront to their trustworthiness and their internal departmental procedures. But in the first three months of 1990 there were approximately eighteen incidents in which civilians have either been killed or seriously wounded by police just in the city of New York. Perhaps every one of those instances was a legitimate exercise of force in a violent society, but perhaps not. The city's new police commissioner might have been too inexperienced to properly review or respond to these incidents, and the inclination to tolerate them, which we discussed previously, is invariably present. Credibility is indispensable for a profession and for its members. A civilian review board is a way to gain that credibility, particularly if those who make it up have the confidence of the public.

Again applying the principle of proportionality, it seems obvious that the type of weapon and ammunition police officers are allowed to carry while on duty should be, and in most agencies is, clearly specified in department regulations. The power of the revolver or automatic weapon, the kind of ammunition, the use of concealed weapons, and other such considerations must be tailored to the situation at hand. Proportionality dictates that different responses are appropriate in different situations. Certainly undercover officers are routinely called upon to use different levels and types of force. One example is those assigned to riot control. Police must be trained to recognize the difference between normal patrol duty, where a high level of discretion is called for, and group confrontations, where strict obedience to the chain of command is most effective. In riots police should probably become more like the military in terms of individual discretion; conversely, when the National Guard or other military units are called to riot control duty, they must act like police agencies rather than as troops engaging in warfare.

Riot control illustrates another aspect of proportionality: Decisions on the form and levels of force employed in group confrontations should always be based on the priority of persons over property. That's particularly problematic when such things as looting or arson are taking place. I've experienced a riot myself. After Martin Luther King, Jr., was killed, I was in Washington, trapped on 14th Street N.W. in the midst of a riot. People were throwing rocks through my windshield, and the car stalled out. I finally got it started and, filled with fear, beat a hasty retreat, driving down a city street at what seemed to be eighty miles per hour. I had this sense of chaos and that everything was out of control. It was easy to understand why under those circumstances it is so difficult to always place the lives and welfare of people first, and how easy it would be to respond disproportionately.

It also is essential that we view proportionality in terms of human dignity, which should include respect for privacy. Electronic surveillance should be prohibited; that is, private detectives, business competitors, and others should never have the authority to conduct that kind of surveillance. Only those properly certified by the government should have such license. Electronic surveillance by the police and other law-enforcement agencies should only be done with explicit court approval; that is, there should be no blanket permissions. Privacy rights must be prominent in these sorts of circumstances, although certain kinds of criminal activity may be controllable only by surveillance techniques. A balance must be struck between the evil produced by the means employed (that is, violations of legitimate privacy rights) and the good resulting from these enforcement techniques.

Finally, there is the principle of humane treatment. How does this apply to law enforcement? Certainly it is applicable to interrogation methods. The use of torture as a means of interrogation, for example, is never justified. Yet I've had debates in my classes with students who don't accept that principle. They offer up all sorts of hypothetical situations in attempts to support their positions, but I see this issue as one of the great test cases of our attitude about the dignity of the human person. Torture that we deem unacceptable is administered all over the world by regimes of the left, the right, and sometimes the center. We have no difficulty in condemning them, yet we entertain all too easily scenarios that might legitimize our own use of torture. In law enforcement, a confession is often seen as crucial in making a case, yet there's very little evidence of that in court records; in fact, a confession often gets in the way of a conviction because of the way it was obtained or because of the legal controversies that surround it. For both moral and purely instrumental considerations, procedures of interrogation should place maximum emphasis on the rights of the accused.

Conclusion

To conclude, I have five summary comments. First, professional life for all of us presupposes training, certification, a professional code involving moral and professional standards and the courage to enforce them, and the trust and respect of the clients or society we serve. The hardest part of a code, that hardest part of being a member of a profession, is enforcing the code—enforcing it in our own lives and, with even more difficulty, applying it to our fellow professionals.

Second, just-war theory is an attempt to approach morally the great human problem of violence and its control. We all wish that violence would go away, we all wish that we lived in a more peaceful and just world, but it's not that way. We struggle as moral beings relative to our religious and cultural heritages to find a set of guidelines to help us think through the challenges that we face. Just-war theory is a powerful and flexible framework for that purpose and will serve us well if we will but use it.

Third, just-war theory is more readily applicable to law-enforcement practices than to modern military engagements. Nonetheless, it is very difficult to effect good law enforcement, and it is vitally important to have thought through in advance the kinds of decisions the professional will be called on to make.

Fourth, we should realize that personal integrity is a quest rather than an achievement. A person of character will seek to do the right thing for the right reason and will also admit mistakes or errors of judgment when they occur. It isn't simply what we profess, it isn't simply trying with all our might to achieve a life of integrity; it's also being willing to admit our mistakes, publicly when that is called for, but more importantly, privately, in the innermost recesses of our hearts.

Finally, the proper exercise of leadership within a profession calls forth all that is best and most risky in the human condition. I applaud the efforts of all who take this challenge seriously, who think through what it means to be a person of integrity, a practitioner in an honored profession, and a leader in a very complex world.

THINKING ABOUT HARD CASES

15

When Integrity Is Not Enough

*Guidelines for Responding to
Unethical Adversaries*

RICHARD T. DE GEORGE

The Gulf War added new urgency, poignancy, and relevance to discussions of just-war theory and issues in military ethics. Although some claim that morality has no place in war, President Bush's use of just-war theory, the comments of those who agreed with and those who opposed his analysis, and the concern of the American people for the lives of civilians and our own forces engaged in combat argue otherwise. The reaction of Americans to the savings and loan and to the Boesky-Levine insider trading scandals indicates that the American public believes that ethics has a place in business as well. The cynic may claim that "it's only immoral if you get caught," but the media coverage of the war and the media investigations of business activities show there are few places to hide.

I shall draw lessons from the Gulf War and from business. But my purpose goes beyond both that war and business to the broader theme of integrity and ethical responses to unethical adversaries. I shall start with integrity, and then move on to areas in which integrity is not enough.

I

Joining business ethics and military ethics may seem odd to some. But morality is a seamless fabric that binds all human beings. We cannot have one morality for our private lives, another when we enter the offices of corporate America, and still another when we put on a military uniform. If we did, we would be moral schizophrenics, and moral integrity would be an impossible ideal. Even though we speak of business ethics and military ethics, there is no special morality for business or for the military. We are not allowed to do in business or in the military what we are prohibited from doing in other areas of life.

Because moral norms are the same no matter what the field of activity, we can apply general moral principles across the board. We can thus learn from ethical analyses of similar actions in different areas. The analysis in business ethics of when whistle-blowing is morally permissible, for instance, initially relied heavily on earlier analyses of the justification of civil disobedience. The doctrine of just-war theory is an extension of the theory of justifiable self-defense, which pertains to individual morality. Just-war theory in turn provides a paradigm for considering how businesses should react when facing at least some unethical competitors and provides guidelines for determining which reactions would be allowable and which reactions would not be, and why. What we do in each case is think and argue by analogy.

In all cases integrity is at the core of what it means to be a moral being. Acting with integrity means both acting in accord with one's highest self-accepted norms and imposing on oneself the norms demanded by ethics and morality. Although integrity requires that norms be self-imposed and self-accepted, they cannot be arbitrary. The norms must be justifiable, proper, and integral to the self-imposed process of forming a whole with a set of positive values. It is a misuse of the term to talk about the integrity of a Hitler who acted on his beliefs in order to achieve racial purity through genocide, or of a Mafia hit man who lives up to the code of his profession.

Yet integrity does not imply reluctance to compete or to fight. It is compatible with being a wily, fierce competitor, opponent, or enemy, even while exercising the restraint that precludes certain actions in which the unscrupulous might engage. Competing with integrity is not synonymous with competing successfully, but it is by no means antithetical to it. IBM is an example of a successful, fierce competitor that is widely acknowledged as acting with integrity.

A reputation as a reliable, ethical company commands a premium from those who use its products or services. The story of how Johnson & Johnson's credo and culture emboldened the leaders of its Tylenol division to order an immediate recall after seven deaths were linked to the product in Chicago in 1982 has almost passed into legend. Employees take pride in working for a well-reputed company, trust their futures to it, and assume that they will be treated fairly. Their loyalty to the company reflects the company's loyalty to them. Subcontractors and other firms prefer to do business with a firm known for its integrity, and feel secure in doing so. Customers similarly prefer to deal with a firm they feel they can trust.

The same is true of the military. Troops are more likely to demonstrate courage and loyalty when they believe in the integrity of their leaders and the justness of the cause for which they are asked to fight. Reactions of the military personnel on both sides of the Gulf War provide ample testimony to this claim.

Why, then, is integrity not enough? When is it not enough? And in such cases, what is enough?

Integrity is not enough in one sense because moral demands are not the only kind of pressures, even though in cases of conflicting demands they override all others. In business and in the military, leaders have the obligation to perform their assigned tasks and they aim for success, whether this means making a profit or winning a war. Good intentions, and therefore personal integrity, are not enough to get one's job done. One needs skill, knowledge, and usually hard work as well. But, assuming competence, integrity is not enough when an individual response will be inadequate to the task one confronts. I shall exemplify those situations by dealing with the question of how to respond ethically to an unethical opponent. Because our general ethical intuitions develop in a context where corruption tends to be the exception rather than the rule, there is no obvious, easy, or intuitive solution to the problem of responding to corruption. Yet, generalizing from a variety of cases, I shall develop ten rules of thumb that can guide us in developing appropriate responses to unethical actions by a competitor, opponent, or enemy. What are these?

II

1. *In responding to unethical activity, do not violate the very norms and values that you seek to preserve and in terms of which you judge the adversary's actions to be unethical.*

One is never ethically permitted to do what is unethical. In confronting immoral opponents the temptation is to retaliate in kind, or even to go them one better—to "kill them, smash them, nuke them." The temptation is a natural one and is a manifestation of righteous anger. But to give in to the temptation is to stoop to the adversary's level, to give up one's own integrity, and to give up morality in the process.

A company must counter a competitor's lies with the truth, not with lies of its own. An army must not respond to torture by the enemy of captured military personnel with torture of the prisoners it captures. The answer to those who kill innocent people cannot be to kill other innocent people in return. Retaliation in kind is permitted in some instances. One can sometimes respond to an enemy that breaks the convention of war concerning the use of chemical weapons against troops by reacting similarly, if that is necessary to restore the status quo ante. Yet one cannot respond to an enemy that gases innocent civilians by gassing the enemy's civilians in turn.

The moral cynic will reply that following this rule puts a person of integrity at a disadvantage vis-à-vis an unethical adversary. The unethical adversary is not inhibited by moral rules and so has the competitive edge, while the person of integrity is constrained by morality. Those not worried about the morality of their actions are free to do whatever they want and whatever they need to do to win. If winning is one's goal, then being hamstrung by rules and moral qualms simply gets in the way of achieving one's end. There is some truth to what the cynic claims. But success or victory won at the cost of one's own principles will be hollow. Principles cannot be turned on and off at will. If they do not guide one's response to immoral activity, there is no assurance they will guide one's response at all. Morality may demand the difficult. It cannot allow the contradictory without our having to give it up as an intelligible, much less defensible, enterprise.

Some firms that operate in corrupt environments claim implicitly or explicitly that it is ethically justifiable for them to do whatever they must to stay in business. Their frequent assumption is that a corporation has not only the right but for some reason the obligation to continue to exist. Their frequent justification is that unless the corporation does so, it cannot do all the good it might be capable of doing. From an ethical perspective, such a claim is much too broad to be defensible. If valid, it would justify anything, including engaging in immoral acts, which would be self-contradictory from an ethical point of view.

Yet ethics does not require that a business or an army capitulate to corruption. Although turning the other cheek and martyrdom may be personal ideals, they are not usually corporate or military ideals or ethical requirements. When economic survival and self-defense are morally justifiable aims, they must be pursued ethically.

2. *Since there are no specific rules for responding to an unethical opponent, in responding ethically, use your moral imagination.*

An ethical response to unethical activity must be at least as imaginative as the unethical activity. Gandhi's technique of passive resistance is an example of using one's moral imagination. Gandhi countered British armed force with a technique that captured the imagination of masses of people, and it achieved his goal more effectively than force could have. This response is not always appropriate, yet imagination is always preferable to brute force.

The injunction to think and act imaginatively is designed both to offset the tendency to consider morality only in terms of rules and to encourage us to reconceive the situation in which we find ourselves. Often there are many more alternatives open to us other than simply suffering at the hands of an unscrupulous opponent or fighting him on his terms. Either/or situations are in reality much more rare than we tend to think. Moral imagination pushes us to seek advantages we may have that we do not ordinarily consider, to look for the chinks in the armor of our adversary, and to search for analogies in the responses of others whom we admire. Literature, stories, the lives of saints and heroes, are here more helpful sources for coming up with ethical responses than any set of rules.

3. *When the response to immorality involves justifiable retaliation or force, apply the principle of restraint.*

That principle states that whenever force is used, it must be used only in reaction to unethical acts or practices, it must be justified as the ultimate solution, and it must be the minimal force necessary. The reason is obvious, since force always involves harm and the basic moral minimum is the injunction not to do avoidable intentional harm.

The Vietnam War led many Americans to think that war was unwinnable and therefore to be avoided at all costs. Ironically, the Gulf War has made war seem not only winnable but easy. The Air Force did such an effective job that the war seemed to many to be a series of surgical strikes—clean, ethical, controlled. The massive destruction seemed almost sanitary. War, we had been told, is hell. But war from the sky, with precision weapons, seemed not to be hell at all. And in a month the Air Force had done so thorough a job that the land war lasted only one hundred hours and turned out to be scarcely more than a mopping-up operation. If it is not hell for us, the temptation is to see war not as a last resort, to be avoided at almost any cost, but as a means to achieve our ends.

That is a temptation that the principle of restraint demands we resist. The principle of restraint requires that the powerful, regardless of the immorality of the enemy's actions, use no more force and cause no more harm than necessary to accomplish one's justifiable aims. The more powerful one is, the greater is the restraint required. In dealing with children, adults need to apply more restraint than in dealing with other adults, because of the difference in power. Police are given civil force but are expected to be restrained in their use of it, even against suspected criminals. Armies are given a monopoly of the major implements of force and are accordingly expected to be restrained in its use.

More is required of the strong than of the weak, and appropriately so. Large, powerful countries must be slower to react, because they can withstand damage better than smaller, weaker ones, and they must react with more restraint, because they can inflict so much damage. If we hold that human life is sacred, such that we must do all we can to protect the lives of our people, we cannot look with indifference on the killing of others, even if they wear the uniform of an opposing nation.

The need for restraint in turn leads to the next principle, with which it is closely linked.

4. *In measuring your response to an unethical opponent, apply the principle of proportionality.*

This principle requires that any force used must be proportional to the offense and harm suffered and to the good to be achieved, and that those who use the force must have some hope of being effective in achieving the end for which they use it. The principle of proportionality is widely used in military ethics and surprisingly rarely invoked in business ethics, where it is also applicable—for instance, in discussions of the legitimacy of whistle-blowing. The principle applies to economic and political force as well as ultimately to military force. Proportionality, so central in discussions of the morality of the war *(jus ad bellum)*, is equally central in discussions of morality in war *(jus in bello)* and tends to blur the distinction between them.

Had Saddam Hussein simply occupied the disputed oil fields on Kuwait's northern border, the principle of proportionality would not have justified the massive destruction the coalition visited upon Iraq. However, given Iraq's actual invasion, the American entry into the Gulf War passed the proportionality test according to most commentators. Whether it passed the proportionality test in the destruction done to the Iraqi infrastructure—on which civilians as well as military depend—is a matter of current debate. Communication networks, roads, bridges, electricity, and supplies of many kinds serve civilians as well as the military. To interdict their use to the one automatically interdicts their use to the other. To destroy them is to harm the civilian population as well. The greater ability to pinpoint targets without killing civilians paradoxically leads to bombing more targets in cities and more quasi-military rather than directly military targets. Imposing hardship on civilians is not immoral, if justified by proportionality. But cutting off water to the military that also cuts it off to civilians and so condemns both to death would be immoral. The Gulf War case raises the issue of how much destruction of the infrastructure of a country proportionality allows, granted that smart weapons can hit their targets with minimal collateral damage to civilians.

In the Gulf War, Allied lives were saved by killing masses of Iraqi military personnel. Had the Allies killed another 100,000 through another several weeks of bombing, it is unlikely they could have saved any more Allied lives. Hence such overkill would not have been justified by the principle of proportionality. Could the Allies have achieved the same ends that they did by killing half as many Iraqis? If so, then the principles of proportionality and of restraint were both violated. The difficulty is that calculations made in ignorance before the fact may look different from calculations made with knowledge after the fact. Yet the technological superiority the Allies enjoyed vis-à-vis Iraq placed moral burdens on them, including the burdens of restraint and proportionality, and changed the kind of thinking in which those in such a position must engage.

Clearly the actual Scud missile attack on Israel by Iraq was not sufficient in its damage or in its threat to the survival of the nation to justify Israeli retaliation by the use of a nuclear bomb on Baghdad. This does not mean that no retaliation was appropriate or justifiable, but that any such retaliation had to be proportional to the harm and to the threat. The principle of proportionality played an important role in evaluating Israel's response.

5. In responding to an unethical foe, apply the technique of ethical displacement.

Ethical displacement involves rising to a higher level in order to solve the dilemmas that an individual faces. Moral dilemmas are situations in which neither of one's choices is morally acceptable. If they are true dilemmas, their solution cannot be found on the level at which they appear. Thus a dilemma for an individual on a personal level may only find a solution on the corporate level, in the sense that solutions to personal dilemmas may require changes in corporate structures. Corporate dilemmas, in turn, may require changes in industry structures to guarantee fair conditions of competition. Industry dilemmas may require changes in national policies or legislation. And national business dilemmas, such as pollution problems, may require changes in structures or agreements on an international level.

The technique of displacement analysis is initially a descriptive technique and then a diagnostic technique. Any solution that results from it will not be intuitive and will not be easy. The idea that ethical issues are easy and are easily resolved intuitively by ethical people is precisely what has to be overcome, both at the personal and at the organizational level.

Business supplies an example. Bribery is unethical because it subverts the competitive system and gives unfair advantage to those who engage in the practice. It is unfair because someone other than the one receiving the benefit pays—either consumers, shareholders, or taxpayers. In a situation in which bribery is the going game, a company that acts with integrity seems to have no option but to opt out of it, and therefore lose business. This is blatantly unfair, yet a company with integrity cannot either demand or accede to bribery. At the level of the individual company, injustice seems to triumph. It is only by rising to a higher level that the disadvantage can be overcome. Legally outlawing bribery is a way to make the field of competition fair on the national level.

The same is true on the international level. After the Lockheed Tri-Star scandal with Japan, the United States passed the Foreign Corrupt Practices Act, which precluded American firms from soliciting or paying bribes. This equalized the playing field for all American companies. By making the unethical act illegal, the law made it possible for individuals and firms of integrity not to have to shoulder the complete burden of their integrity. Some argued that it then placed the American firms at a competitive disadvantage with respect to firms of other countries. Those firms, not restricted by American law, sometimes engaged in bribery to the disadvantage of the American firms. The solution to that situation required other countries to pass legislation similar to that passed by the United States, and in fact the United States pressured the European Community to adopt similar rules for European firms. American-European groups have next to apply pressure to get Asian nations to similarly outlaw the practice. The full solution is a slow process. But in the long run this is the only adequate response. Simply saying that all individuals and all firms throughout the world should act with integrity and not solicit or pay bribes is not enough.

Nor should one draw the conclusion that law is the only solution. Americans and American companies operating in South Africa were faced with demands that they practice discrimination, as specified in the South African apartheid laws. Any individual or firm that violated those laws would be prosecuted or be forced to leave. The successful strategy for disobedience in this case consisted in a large number of American firms agreeing that they would all publicly violate the apartheid laws by following the Sullivan Principles, which precluded discrimination. Together they were powerful enough that the South African government ignored their violations of its laws. Individual integrity was not enough, even though only individuals and firms with integrity would take the action that those individuals and firms took.

The moral to be drawn is that at the individual level or the level of the firm, unfair or corrupt competition can sometimes only be met by rising to a higher level, a level of cooperation among firms or countries that is adequate to deal with the injustice at the lower level. Integrity is required to muster the forces necessary to achieve the end at the higher level. But individual action is not enough.

In the case of Kuwait, its chief weapon was clearly ethical displacement. Unable to offset on its own the harm it suffered, integrity was not enough. Its recourse was to other nations, to the U.N., and through the U.N. ultimately to a coalition of forces to help it right a wrong that it was able to suffer but not combat.

When attacked by Iraq, Israel responded appropriately by exercising the technique of ethical displacement. It faced the dilemma of either continuing to suffer raids or of being provoked into doing what the enemy wanted to accomplish by the raids. The solution lay on a level higher than that at which the dilemma presented itself. Even had the Scud missiles been filled with poison gas, that response, rather than retaliation with a nuclear strike against Baghdad, would have been appropriate. Even had Israel faced the prospect of being overrun, the use of a nuclear bomb was morally precluded. Yet such an analysis will be acceptable to endangered countries only if other nations of the world, which are directly implicated in any such use of nuclear bombs, are willing to bear the burden of protecting and if necessary liberating nations that are so attacked. Ethical displacement in such instances depends on the rest of the world not allowing aggression against any nation to be such that the attacked nation feels it must use nuclear bombs against cities as its last resort. Eventually this requires that there be some global agreement against the use of nuclear bombs on cities and some enforcement mechanism whereby all such nuclear weapons are destroyed and effectively precluded from being built.

In situations of extreme danger, integrity on the part of those attacked is often not enough.

6. *In responding to an unethical adversary, use publicity to underscore the immoral actions.*

Publicity serves three functions. First, it opens up the unethical practice to public scrutiny and allows the public to judge it for what it is. Second, publicity makes it possible to mobilize public pressure against the practice and its perpetrators. What is tacitly accepted and quietly withstood becomes unbearable when brought to full light. Publicity demands a public reaction instead of a quiet individual one and often makes possible a joint reaction that individual persons may be too intimidated or frightened to make. Third, publicity forces a government at the least to be consistent in what it can demand of law-abiding citizens in conditions in which it is unable to protect them and unable to enforce its laws.

Since bribery always hurts someone, it cannot stand the light of publicity. No one openly admits engaging in it; much less does anyone engaged in it attempt to defend it in any particular instance. Where adequate background institutions do not yet exist, publicity helps generate support against bribery. When the Lockheed bribes to government officials were disclosed in Japan, where bribery was supposedly an acceptable norm, the government fell in disgrace, and one of the government ministers involved committed suicide. These are hardly the reactions to disclosure of practices that are morally permitted and acceptable. The technique can be generalized to other areas. In the Gulf War both sides used publicity to bring to public attention actions of the other side that they considered blatantly unethical.

7. *In responding to an immoral opponent, seek joint action with others and work for the creation of new social, legal, or popular institutions and structures.*

Individual or personal integrity is not enough when the structures within which one operates hinder rather than foster moral action and so lead to moral dilemmas.

Consider a situation in which a lower-level engineer in an airplane manufacturing firm detects a flaw in the design of the seat ejection mechanism. The flaw is such that it only occurs under certain conditions, and these conditions will not be detected in ordinary tests. The plane will be accepted, and the flaw will not become evident until after one or more fatalities that could have been prevented. The engineer reports this to his superior, who discounts its importance, argues that production has already begun and that it is too late to change the design, and orders the engineer to forget about it. The engineer, a person of integrity, goes above his superior's head and finds he is stonewalled all the way up the company. Finally, in desperation, he blows the whistle, leaking his concerns to an investigative reporter. Eventually, the truth comes out and the part is changed, but the engineer has been fired. Was integrity enough?

Society does not want planes with defective ejection mechanisms. A good society will not want its people of integrity to have to suffer the fate of our engineer. A wise society will not want the safety of its products dependent on the heroism of employees. Rather than only attempting to raise people with integrity who will be ready and perhaps even anxious to blow the whistle for the common good, we should see that integrity is not enough in this as well as in many other situations. Whistle-blowing is a symptom of inadequate corporate structures that prevent information about product defects from reaching the high levels of management in such a way and at such a time that they can be properly corrected. Asking people to act with integrity in blowing the whistle simply deals with the symptom rather than with the cause, and exacts too great a cost from individuals. Opening up lines of communication within a firm so that those with moral questions or qualms can make them known and have them fairly addressed requires a change in the structure of many firms. Only such changes, mandated if necessary by law, are the adequate response to the ills of which whistle-blowing is a symptom. A similar analysis applies in the military. Not only can existing structures be morally evaluated within the armed forces to see whether they foster or discourage unethical action, but nations should seek to develop new structures and reinforce existing ones that can help prevent war.

8. *In responding to unethical activity, be ready to act with moral courage.*

Moral courage requires not only that one determine what is consistent with one's values but also that one act in accordance with them. It may frequently be easier to ignore the unethical activities of others, even of one's opponents, than to take any action against them. And sometimes it is both proper and wise to do so. But in other cases and at some stage, it is necessary to face the perpetrator of injustice or terror. Knowing where to draw the line and when to respond rather than forebear requires prudence and judgment. But there are such lines to be drawn, and being willing to face that requires the courage of one's convictions and the willingness to stand up to immorality and to take the risk this involves. This is especially important when ignoring injustice will lead the perpetrator to continue similar actions or to escalate the degree of terror or injustice.

Responding with courage means being willing to stand up to immorality on one's own if necessary. But often more important is the realization that in unity there is strength, and that a collective response to injustice is usually stronger and more effective than an individual response. Moral courage thus also involves being willing to take the initiative in mobilizing others or to join the initiative of others who take a stand. The point of the claim that integrity is not enough is to emphasize that any individual is limited, and immoral forces generally can be overcome only by mobilizing forces at least equal to those on the other side.

The implication is that companies should be willing to join other companies to fight immorality and should join forces with legitimate governments and organizations as well. This general principle is one that is too often ignored by some American companies operating in Colombia, for instance, which prefer to negotiate with drug traffickers rather than join others in opposing them. The principle applies as well to countries when other countries are unjustly attacked or improperly treated. The United States might have responded to the call of Kuwait and Saudi Arabia on its own. Its response was enormously enhanced by joining forces with a coalition to enforce U.N. mandates.

9. In responding ethically to an unethical opponent, be prepared to pay a price, sometimes a high price.

Unethical activity may be initially cheap to the perpetrator. It is always costly to the victim. Ethical responses may be more costly still. Just as moral courage is required, so is willingness to bear the costs. The cost of an aggressive war on those attacked, as well as on those who attempt to fight against or defeat the aggressor, is obvious. We all hope that our ethically justified responses to immorality, despite the cost, will be cost-effective in the long run. In the short run, such responses may enhance the company's or nation's self-image and reputation and promote morale. Facing immorality or an immoral opponent early rather than late may cut one's eventual total cost. History teaches us that those who profit from immorality tend to continue more aggressively in their ways rather than resting content with ill-gotten gains. An aim of the rule of law is to make sure that immorality does not pay. But in the process we must pay the costs others impose on us by their actions.

10. In responding to unethical activity, apply the principle of accountability.

This principle demands that those who impose costs, do damage, and inflict harm on others be held accountable for their actions. This means that those who engage in immoral practices should know that they will be held accountable for what they do. The intent of accountability is to preclude anyone, to the extent possible, from benefiting from immoral activity, and thus to help remove any incentive for so acting. A rule of law imposes accountability and holds people responsible for their actions.

In a business situation accountability is often enforced through the courts and through civil suits in which those adversely affected seek to obtain redress from the guilty party. Criminal charges also come into play. In the insider trading scandals and the savings and loan debacle, we saw and will see both sorts of penalties imposed as those guilty are held accountable for their actions. In Colombia, the Colombian government is attempting to hold drug lords accountable for their actions, and the fear of the extraditables is that they will be held accountable in the American legal system, which they are less able to manipulate and coerce than the Colombian system.

Imposing accountability on multinational corporations is difficult, since they operate in more than one country and since there are still insufficient international rules and enforcement mechanisms in place. This both points up the need for such mechanisms and underlines the importance of accountability.

The situation is exacerbated when it comes to war. It is virtually impossible to hold any nation completely accountable for the damage it does during war. The lives lost are lost and cannot be replaced by any system of accountability. Those guilty of atrocities may in some instances be held individually accountable. Some reparations might be imposed on the country as a whole, depending on its ability to pay. The difficulties involved in assessing collective versus individual responsibility, and so accountability, are many. Accountability is imposed by the victor and may be one-sided. The Nuremberg trials and various U.N. declarations are attempts at holding the guilty accountable. The limitations of both demonstrate the need for more effective mechanisms for the international imposition of accountability.

Nonetheless, despite the difficulties of enforcing accountability, the principle is essential in dealing with unethical opponents. They must be held accountable by general public opinion—which shows again the importance of publicity; by legal bodies, where these have jurisdiction; and by the community of nations, where the offenses are between nations. Imposing them and enforcing them fairly set important precedents that can help preclude others from acting similarly in the future. The moral courage to impose them is as essential as developing adequate mechanisms to assess the proper reparations.

The ideal is to preclude the need for military responses to atrocities and actions such as the torching of Kuwaiti oil fields by making the price of terror, aggression, and wanton destruction too high for any nation or leader to bear. Holding nations and their leaders accountable for their actions and for the damage they do to others is part of what is necessary for a civilized world. The moral is that international mechanisms must be developed and supported that help preclude future destruction of the sort that Kuwait suffered.

Clearly, accountability in the senses I have described goes beyond the individual and hence beyond individual integrity. Those involved in the process of assessment must of course be people of integrity for the process to enjoy the moral support of others. But public accountability and the imposition of appropriate sanctions go beyond the scope of any individual. Otherwise we fall into the trap of vendettas, individual justice, and an eye-for-an-eye mentality, in which integrity quickly goes by the board.

These ten rules go together. They outline a pattern of response to unethical behavior on the part of one's opponents or enemies. Although I do not pretend the list is exhaustive, it is systematic in the sense that the rules are interrelated. They are rules of thumb in that they are not exact formulations of duties or obligations but rather describe and prescribe approaches to immoral opponents. They serve the purpose of organizing a number of disparate reactions and of precluding some that are inappropriate because immoral.

III

The ten rules of thumb apply to those on both sides of a competition or battle. In dealing with ethical responses to an unethical opponent we cannot assume, for instance, that one of the parties is engaged in a just war and the other not. Typically both sides will claim their war is just, although for different reasons. This does not mean that both sides—or that either side—is correct in its assertion.

The Gulf War has shown us that more is required of the side with technological superiority. Hence what is immoral for the technologically superior combatant may be morally permissible for the technologically inferior one. As a consequence what the winning side may consider immoral may on the part of the losing side be morally justifiable. The principles of proportionality and of restraint may apply differently in the two cases. Thus, for instance, those who cannot afford smart bombs cannot be held to the higher standard of those who can. The same moral minimum applies to both. But "ought" implies "can." The accuracy of the new weapons makes it easier to strike military targets without collateral damage to civilians. It thus makes that the norm and makes damage to civilians that much less tolerable. Yet only those with such weapons can be held to that new norm. Those with less sophisticated weapons cannot reach that norm and are thus allowed more leeway in collateral damage. Paradoxically, it seems to be to one's advantage not to have such bombs so one won't be held to a higher standard.

Moreover, those who can count on the enemy's observing the rules of war seem not completely unjustified in moving their military targets closer to civilian populations for protection. Why should one put one's military targets in the open when they are more vulnerable there? Why not protect them with civilians? The traditional answer is that concern for one's own population forbids this. But the paradox is that if one can count on the other side's being moral, the action does not actually put one's population at risk. The action rather forces the enemy to use smart, expensive bombs rather than the dumb, cheaper ones that might be used if civilians were not at risk.

A side effect of the Gulf War has been a great desire on the part of many nations to acquire smart weapons. The war showed that an army that relies on less is doomed to defeat if it engages in a war with a technologically superior opponent. This raises the stakes for everyone. Even *in extremis*, the moral minimum of respecting innocent life still applies. We may expect, however, that some of those in extremes will use whatever means they can to prevent their defeat, and if they have technologically advanced weapons, it may be more difficult to preclude disproportionate response, lack of restraint, and attacks on innocent people. The scenario of two technologically advanced nations opposing each other is still in the future. But we have already seen enough to know that the best alternative is to preclude the need for and possibility of war.

The moral we can draw is that it is not enough simply to teach people what is right and help form their characters. Integrity is central to morality. But individual integrity is not enough in many situations. We also need structures that help preclude immoral and destructive actions.

The principles that apply to nations apply in analogous ways to businesses, and vice versa. The new structures we need will vary, but they are necessary in all areas and on all levels. The need is pressing for global structures that preclude unfair competition and the need for war.

Perhaps we shall always have immoral opponents. The least we should do is put them on notice that they will be held accountable for the harm they do and for the costs they impose. In fighting them, we cannot let ourselves lose sight of and sacrifice the values and morals that we hold dear by responding in kind. More is demanded of those who can afford more. Restraint is demanded of the powerful. And accountability is rightly demanded of all.

In a complex world, where peoples and their interests are globally intertwined, moral structures are essential both in business and in international affairs. These can only be forged by people of integrity. Thus, although integrity is not all that is needed, and in many cases is not enough, it remains essential.

16

Conscience and Authority

Thomas E. Hill, Jr.

Introduction

My topic is conscience and its relation to authority. The problem is an old but persistent one. Some think it is a truism, boringly obvious: *One should always follow one's conscience*. But that is too quick. What if conscience conflicts with the direct commands of those who have authority over us? Such conflicts occur dramatically in war, but also in business affairs and in mundane, everyday life: one's superior officer, one's boss, or the law of the land insists, "Do it," but conscience objects, "Don't do it." Which should take precedence? Maybe the answer is "sometimes conscience, and at other times, authority." But then how can we reasonably decide *when* conscience should give way to authority, and when it should not?

In favor of conscience, some argue that we lack moral integrity if we violate our conscientious convictions just because someone told us to. But again, the issue is not that simple. Those who have legitimate authority over us are not simply "someone" who happened to tell us what to do. To acknowledge that they are authorities is to recognize that there are good reasons for them, rather than us, to have the right to make certain decisions. To ignore this crucial point can be disastrous, especially in times of crisis that call for immediate action. Even in the absence of crisis, when we have ample time to reflect, the need for authoritative decisions to coordinate group activities is a vitally important factor that our deliberations, and even our consciences, should take into account. If we were to ignore the moral reasons for having authorities, choosing instead to guide our conduct entirely by promptings of individual conscience formed in ignorance of these reasons, chaos would be the result in both civilian and military contexts.

So should we then adopt the extreme opposite policy: *Always obey the orders of our lawful superiors?* Unfortunately, from a moral point of view, this solution is also too simplistic. For practical purposes, it is, of course, necessary for legal and military codes to insist on unquestioning obedience to authorities in all but a few extraordinary situations—for example, where to obey would plainly be a crime against humanity. Virtually all moral traditions acknowledge that no secular authority is infallible or worthy of obedience in absolutely all possible circumstances. To be sure, even in the exceptional cases there are usually some good reasons to obey, but the reasons are not always decisive, not always sufficient grounds to override the moral repugnance of what has been ordered. My point here is not new or radical. It was affirmed in the Nuremberg trials, and it is presupposed by anyone who acknowledges that Germans in the early 1940s would have been justified in resisting Hitler's orders to exterminate European Jews.

In order to see the need to qualify a policy of always submitting to authority, we also should remember that such a policy would cover much more than the dramatic and dangerous cases that we typically see in films, where there is flagrant disobedience to direct orders (and even mutiny) in an emergency situation. (Think, for example, of *The Caine Mutiny*.) This unqualified policy would also dictate unquestioning conformity in less volatile situations, where there is ample time to reflect, minimum risk of harm, and a respectful alternative to outright defiance—for example, protest through recognized channels or resignation.

We face, then, a moral issue that is not amenable to simple solutions. We cannot hope to resolve it definitively here; but perhaps we can make some progress, at least in thinking more clearly about the problem. In philosophy the path to progress is typically to examine carefully the central ideas in a controversy. This is because ambiguities and misunderstandings often cloud the real issues. The key idea in our problem is *conscience*. Before we can say to what extent and why we should respect and follow our consciences, we need to examine the different sorts of things that conscience has been thought to be.

For this purpose, it is helpful to distinguish between various *particular* "conceptions" of conscience and a very *general* "concept" of conscience. The several conceptions of conscience are specific interpretations or more detailed under-standings of a general concept, or core idea, of conscience. This core idea that they have in common is, very roughly, the idea of a capacity, attributed to most human beings, that enables them to sense or immediately discern that their acts (or omissions) are morally wrong, bad, and worthy of disapproval.[1] The general concept also includes the idea that their consciences tend to influence their con-duct but rarely control it completely. Moreover, it is assumed that people tend to suffer mental discomfort and lower self-esteem when they act against their consciences. This general idea leaves open further questions about how con-science is acquired and developed, how it operates, what it purports to "say," how trustworthy it is as a moral guide, whether it is universal or found only in certain cultures, and what purposes it serves individuals and society. Particular concep-tions of conscience fill in these details in different ways.

My plan here is to describe briefly three particular conceptions of con-science, which I call the popular conception, the cultural relativist conception, and the Kantian conception.[2] More specifically, these conceptions are first, a popular idea that conscience is an instinct, designed by God or Nature to sig-nal us when our acts or intentions are wrong; second, a deflationary cultural relativism that regards conscience as nothing but our unreflective responses to whatever values we have picked up from our culture (or special subculture); and third, a familiar metaphor, described by Kant, that presents conscience as "an inner judge" that condemns (or acquits) us of the charge that we have not done our best, even to live up to our own judgments about what is right.

To preview my conclusions, I maintain that the last conception is the most plausible but that no matter which conception you choose, conscience is not a foolproof, completely reliable guide to what is morally right. Conscience, then, cannot always trump authoritative commands. But neither do authoritative commands always trump conscience. In fact, from a moral point of view, both should be seen as ultimately subject to review in a process of informed, reason-able moral deliberation and discussion. This process cannot *guarantee* that our conclusions are correct, but it would be an illusion to think that either con-science or authority provides a more basic or reliable guide. In fact, conscience presupposes willingness to engage in this process when time allows, for without this we can never be confident that we are even doing our best to do what is right. Moral integrity is not achieved by blind obedience to either conscience or authority. It is found only in resolute adherence to our best judgments after tak-ing into account, in the deliberative process, both the preliminary warnings of conscience and the grounds for respecting legitimate authorities.

The proper time for such moral deliberation is not in the heat of battle, of course, but in advance, when we can stop to think without causing anyone harm. This is one reason why military academies have courses in ethics and why it invites you to consider and challenge the opinions expressed in lectures such as this one.

I

Let us begin with a popular conception: *conscience as an instinctual access to moral truth, given to us by God or Nature.* There are many variations, but, for contrast, I describe an extreme version. Here are the main themes.

Each human being is born with a latent conscience, which normally emerges into its full working capacity in youth or young adulthood. It is a capacity to identify, among our own acts and intentions, those which are morally wrong and those which are morally permissible. Conscience, however, does not identify acts and motives as morally admirable or praiseworthy. At best, conscience is "clear" or "clean," not self-congratulating.

That certain acts, such as murder and adultery, are morally wrong is a matter of objective fact, independent of our consciences. That is, what makes such acts wrong is not just that conscience disapproves. Conscience merely alerts and warns us, like a gauge that indicates the presence of electrical problems but does not identify them specifically and is not itself the cause of trouble.

Conscience originates as a gift of God or Nature to human beings, a special access to moral truth that can work independently of church authority and rational reflection.[3] Appealing to conscience is not the same as using rational, reflective judgment to resolve moral questions. Conscience may be partly shaped and informed by such judgments, as well as by public debates, religious education, and so on; but it is not seen as an intellectual moral advisor, only as an instinctual inner "voice" or sign that indicates a moral problem, warns us when tempted, and prods us to reform when guilty.[4] If the signal is correctly identified and heard, conscience is thought to be a reliable source of moral knowledge. However, to explain the fact that outrageous acts are often committed in the name of conscience, the popular view admits that conscience is not always identified, heard, and interpreted correctly.

God or Nature is supposed to have designed conscience as a personal guide, not for judging or goading others. Judging that an act is wrong for oneself entails that it is wrong for anyone unless there is a relevant difference between the cases, but others' cases may differ in so many ways that one has no practical license to make extensive generalizations from what one "learns" from one's own conscience.

If we accept this popular conception of conscience, what should our attitude be toward what our consciences seem to tell us? Since the popular conception regards conscience (once properly identified) as a generally reliable access to moral truth, we would have good (moral) reason for not "dulling" our consciences, for "listening" carefully for the signals of conscience, and for being cautiously guided by what apparently it tells us to do. Several factors, however, combine to recommend caution, even to the firm believer in the popular conception. For example, though conscience is supposed to be a reliable signal of moral truth, it is not necessarily the only, or most direct, means of determining what we ought (and ought not) to do. When secular and religious authorities, together with the professed conscientious judgments of others, all stand opposed to what we initially took to be the voice of conscience, then these facts should raise doubts. Even assuming that "genuine" pronouncements of conscience are reliable, *we* may not be reliably distinguishing these from our wishes, fears, and the echoes in our heads from past lessons of parents and teachers. In effect, we need to check our supposed instinctual access to moral truth by reviewing evidence that is more directly relevant—for example, benefits and harms, promises fulfilled or broken, and the responsibilities of our social roles. To confirm that our instinctive response is a reflection of "true conscience" rather than some morally irrelevant feeling, we would need to consult other sources, such as seeing whether the response coincides with reflective moral judgment that is based on careful review of pertinent facts in consultation with others. Without such a check, there is no way to be confident that the instinct that we are about to rely on is really "conscience" rather than some baser instinct.

By analogy, suppose that we believe that we have an intuitive sense that somehow signals dishonesty in job applicants with considerable regularity when this "sense" is properly identified and used under ideal conditions. Although the suspicions we form by consulting this intuitive sense might provide useful warning signs, they would be no substitute for investigating candidates' records and seeking direct evidence of dishonest conduct. Only examination of the relevant facts could check whether what we take to be an accurate intuitive signal really is so.

Besides this practical problem, several considerations suggest that we would do well to look beyond the popular conception for a more adequate interpretation of conscience. For example, the popular conception draws major conclusions about ethics from assumptions about theology (or Nature) that are widely contested today. Many regard the alleged instinctual access to moral truth as unduly mysterious, scientifically unsupportable, and out of line with our best theories of moral development. Even among religious thinkers the popular view fails to muster strong support, for theologians are radically divided about how we come to know right and wrong and about the relative importance of conscience, reason, Scripture, and church authority.

A deeper problem is that the popular view of conscience as an instinctual indicator of morality neglects the prior and indispensable roles of reason and judgment in determining what is morally right and wrong. Basic morality, I believe, is ultimately a matter of what free and reasonable people, with mutual respect and proper understanding of their condition, would agree to accept as a constraint on the pursuit of self-interest and other goals. That is not the sort of thing that anyone could plausibly claim to know directly "by instinct." Once we have a basic grasp of the *reasons* for moral principles, our respect for these principles may be signaled by unbidden "pangs" and "proddings" that feel like instinctual responses. But these count as signs of conscience only because they reflect our prior *judgments* about what morality reasonably requires of us.

II

Some of those who cannot accept the just-described popular conception account of the origin and function of conscience adopt an extreme *cultural relativist conception.*[5] The term "relativism," of course, is used loosely to refer to many different ideas, but let us stipulate here that the cultural relativist conception is the view that the promptings of conscience are *nothing but* feelings that reflect the norms that one has internalized from one's culture. Such feelings are supposed to serve to promote social cohesion by disposing individuals toward conformity to group standards. This relativist conception replaces the theological story about the origin and function of conscience with a contemporary sociological hypothesis, but more radically, it goes beyond this empirical hypothesis by claiming that conscience reflects "nothing but" whatever cultural norms one has internalized. That is, the conception is actually a combination of two ideas: a common *sociological* explanation of the genesis and social function of the feelings we attribute to "conscience" and a controversial *philosophical* thesis that the cultural norms that express themselves in what we call "conscience" are inherently immune to objective moral assessment, that is, none are morally better or more justifiable than any others.

The cultural relativist conception, then, is not merely a view about the origin and function of conscience, but also a view about its reliability as a moral guide. Regarding origin, the cultural relativist explains the "conscientious" person's feelings of constraint as due to a learning process by which one inwardly accepts local cultural norms as one's standard of self-approval. Regarding function, the cultural relativist sees the development of conscience as a way by which social groups secure a measure of conformity to their local standards without relying entirely on external rewards and punishments. Regarding reliability, the cultural relativist holds that although conscience rather accurately reveals the local norms that we pick up from our environments, there is no objective standard by which we can ever determine that some cultural norms, but not others, are morally "true" or "justified."

What are the implications of cultural relativism for the attitude we should take toward our consciences? If cultural relativism is true, in every culture people will tend to feel "spontaneously" that certain acts are "bad" and "worthy of disapproval." But how *should* informed and reflective persons regard these feelings and respond to them if they think cultural relativism is true? Clearly, they should regard these feelings as just what they are (according to cultural relativism), namely, a fairly reliable sign that we are (or have been or soon will be) in violation of some cultural norm that we have internalized. Given this, we can expect that we are likely to experience further internal discomfort and to incur the disapproval of others if we continue to act as before (or as planned). These expectations give a prudent person *some* self-interested reason to "heed conscience"; and if the norms of a person's culture serve socially useful purposes, that person would have *some* altruistic reason to obey the promptings of "conscience."

But this is only one side of the picture. Those who accept cultural relativism also have reason to try to "see through" and get rid of their feeling that acts against conscience are "wrong," "immoral," or "unreasonable" by some objective, culturally independent standard. When the rewards of acting against conscience outweigh the unpleasantness of residual guilt feelings and predictable social disapproval, then the smart thing to do—assuming cultural relativism is true—would be to stifle conscience, or, if need be, simply tolerate the discomfort that conscience causes in order to gain the greater rewards to be had by violating it. In short, if we accept cultural relativism, we should not always follow conscience. Quite the contrary. Cultural relativists see the promptings of conscience as rather like beliefs that we can recognize as mere superstitions: we are tempted to accept them, but we really think they have no objective foundation. Given this attitude, relativists should often suppress or ignore their consciences, just as they would their superstitious beliefs.

Some may conclude that these implications, by themselves, are enough to show that cultural relativism is untenable; but quite aside from this, there are ample reasons to doubt the cultural relativist conception. It seems strikingly at odds with the ordinary understanding of conscience, and its radical denial that moral judgments can be objective is not supported by its observations of cultural diversity.

Consider first the cultural relativist's empirical hypothesis that people tend, unconsciously and passively, to internalize the values of their culture from an early age. No doubt this is partly true, but it ignores the role of active, mature deliberation and social debate in shaping the moral convictions that inform our consciences. No doubt conscience reflects moral standards that we have internalized, but these standards need not have been adopted uncritically, without reason.

Second, the cultural relativist's insistence that cultural standards are not subject to objective moral criticism is a methodological assumption, not a valid conclusion drawn from empirical studies. It is, in fact, a radical moral skepticism reached only by a giant step beyond science into an area of perennial philosophical controversy. The empirical observations that cultural standards differ and that people tend to internalize their local standards do not, by themselves, prove anything about objectivity in morals or any other field. What is objectively true or reasonable to believe, whether in normative or descriptive matters, is not constituted simply by the fact that people agree about it; by the same token, objectivity is not necessarily undermined by the fact that people disagree. The issues are more complicated than that.

Third, in its effort to avoid being unduly judgmental, cultural relativism interprets "conscience" as a morally neutral term, referring to internalized norms of any kind, no matter how cruel, oppressive, superstitious, or arbitrary these may be. Thus, for example, when Heinrich Himmler felt disapproval of himself for momentary feelings of pity for the Jews that he was gassing, the cultural relativist supposes this to be his "conscience speaking" just as much as when a reformed slave trader first felt a loathing for his dirty business.[6] Value neutrality may have its uses in empirical studies, but the most common and plausible understandings of "conscience" are not morally neutral. We presuppose that even though that person may be mistaken, anyone who has a

conscience and follows it must understand and endorse at least the basic elements of a moral point of view. When Himmler, governed entirely by self-
interest and Nazi ideology, felt bad about sympathizing with the innocent
people that he helped to slaughter in the Holocaust, those "bad feelings"
should not be confused with pangs of conscience.

III

Let us turn now to Kant's metaphor of *conscience as an inner judge.*[7] Kant's
idea is that we experience conscience *as if* we were brought to trial, accused,
scrutinized, and then either acquitted or found guilty. The pangs of conscience feel like a harsh but just sentence imposed by a judge who knows us all
too well. A crucial part of the metaphor is that in the inner court of conscience
we ourselves play all the roles: we are not only the accused, but also the prose-
cution, the defense, and the judge who reaches a verdict and imposes the sentence. A guilty verdict, in effect, is the painful realization that we have failed
to live up to our own moral standards. These standards are moral judgments
we have made previously—for example, in criticizing others. They become so
deeply embedded in our personalities that we experience an immediate disso-
nance, or involuntary discomfort, when our conduct violates them.

One standard that is particularly important for conscience, Kant reminds
us, is a "duty of due care": that is, at times we need to scrutinize carefully the
moral judgments that we normally take for granted in order to reassess whether
they are really as reasonable as we have supposed. Especially when simply sticking by our previous moral assumptions would inflict serious harm on others,
we need to rethink those assumptions carefully and honestly. Moral reason,
not conscience, imposes this duty, but it is a standard that every reasonable
person presumably has internalized. Conscience simply *alerts* us, painfully,
when we are neglecting this duty of due care. Conscience, then, not only
threatens to punish us for violating our previous standards of conduct; it also
warns us against moral complacency, that is, against always taking for granted,
despite evidence to the contrary, that our old standards are still reasonable
ones. Kant's example was the Spanish Inquisitioners, who burned at the stake
those they believed to be heretics. They may have acted according to their
moral beliefs, Kant concedes, but they failed in their *duty of due care*, a duty
to reexamine critically their moral assumption that burning heretics is right.

On the Kantian view, then, conscience has two important, but limited, tasks: the general task of judging whether our conduct lives up to the moral standards that we have accepted and the special task of prodding us to not neglect the duty to reexamine carefully our previous moral standards when there is some reason to question them. This idea has two striking advantages: first, it attributes to conscience a significant function that it can serve well; and, second, it does *not* assign to conscience a more ambitious function for which it is utterly unsuited. Let me explain.

The general function of conscience is to alert us when we are not doing our best to live up to our own moral standards. The pangs of conscience result from an implicit comparison of two things that each of us ordinarily knows well enough: the standards we accept for what we *should* be doing and our understanding of what we are *actually* doing. When there is a discrepancy between these things, it is usually obvious. You do not have to be a genius or a moral expert to see that what you are doing (or are about to do) is just what you have always believed to be wrong. This task of comparison, in fact, seems so easy and manageable that Kant remarked (with slight exaggeration) that there is no such thing as an erring conscience. His point was not that we always know what is *really* right, but merely that we can rather easily recognize when our acts violate what we *believe* is right.

The more ambitious task that Kant, quite rightly, does not ascribe to conscience is the difficult job of mustering all our best resources to find out what is really right—or, to put it more modestly, to make our most well-grounded, reasonable judgment about what is right. This is not the business of the "inner judge" of conscience, which only can apply our previous moral opinions. Trying to determine, as best we can, what is really right is the role of practical reason when it is actively employed in reviewing the facts, the alternatives, and the various complex considerations that favor one moral conclusion or another. Such reasoning requires consultation with others and confrontation with opinions that differ sharply from our own. It is not a purely intellectual process, for it must give due weight to human feelings. Nor is it reasoning in a vacuum, for it takes place within a framework of constraints that are widely accepted as fundamental for any moral thinking. Kantians have a view about how to describe this framework, but others do as well; and so, except for a brief postscript, this must remain a topic for another occasion.

Let us compare this Kantian conception of conscience with what I called the popular conception. Both acknowledge that the voice of conscience typically appears without an invitation: it warns, threatens, prods, and punishes us, even when the last thing we want is to engage in serious moral self-appraisal.

As Kant puts it, conscience is something we "hear" even when we try to run away, a voice that "speaks involuntarily and inevitably."[8] In this way, conscience is more like an instinct than a capacity for moral deliberation and reasoning. But unlike the popular conception, the Kantian view does not treat conscience as a mysterious "signal" inexplicably implanted in us as a guide to moral truth. Instead, the Kantian metaphor represents conscience as a familiar inner conflict experienced when we realize that what we are doing violates our own internalized moral judgments. This sort of inner conflict is not a mystery, but is in fact just what contemporary psychology would lead us to expect. Notice, too, that the Kantian conscience is not a nonverbal signal, like a flashing light. The metaphor represents it as *speaking* to us—accusing, examining, and passing sentence—in a familiar moral vocabulary. The point is that we are judging ourselves by standards that we understand and can articulate. The Kantian conscience, moreover, is not a private line to moral truth, something that might substitute for serious moral reasoning with others. What it reveals is not an objective truth about what we ought to do, but only that our conduct is out of line with what we have previously judged that we ought to do.

Now consider how the Kantian conception of conscience compares and contrasts with the cultural relativist conception. These are similar in one respect: both can explain the promptings of conscience naturally, as responses triggered by an awareness that we are deviating from internalized standards. Unlike the cultural relativist's conception, however, the Kantian conception of conscience is explicitly a *moral idea*—never meant to be neutral, for example, between Hitler's cohorts and those who conscientiously opposed them. And unlike relativism, the Kantian view does not hold that cultural norms are immune to objective moral evaluation. Like most of us, Kant would not hesitate to say that the Holocaust was really immoral, even if it was once the policy of a Nazi culture. That is a judgment that is no doubt deeply embedded in our consciences, but the task of showing why such judgments are justified is the business, not of conscience, but of public reasoning from the fundamentals of a moral point of view.

The implications of the Kantian conception regarding our attitude toward our own consciences should now be clear. Conscience is no substitute for moral reasoning and judgment, but it in fact presupposes them. A clear conscience is no guarantee that we acted in an objectively right way, and so it is no ground for self-righteous pride or the presumption that our moral judgment is superior to the judgment of those who conscientiously disagree. However, insofar as the warnings and pangs of conscience reflect our recognition that our conduct falls short of our moral standards, they are reliable at least as a sign that we are not doing our best. Conformity to conscience is necessary, and perhaps even sufficient, to avoid being worthy of moral blame (even though conscience cannot assure us that our conduct is morally correct).[9]

Of course, our impartial moral judgments (about what anyone in various situations should do), even when correct, will not have an effect on our conduct unless they are applied to our own case, which is a function of conscience. Thus, as Kant says, conscience ought to be "cultivated" and "sharpened" as well as heeded. Again, conscience makes one painfully aware of one's misdeeds, and so it also helps to motivate us to apologize, make restitution, and reform. In all these aspects conscience is to be respected, even though its functions are limited.

IV

Now let us return briefly to the initial problem of how conscience relates to authority. Admittedly, we have only examined three conceptions of conscience, and the moral grounds for respecting authorities have only been assumed, not discussed critically. Nonetheless, my reflections here point toward certain tentative practical conclusions. First, the most plausible conception of conscience, the Kantian one, gives us strong reasons to cultivate and respect our conscience but no reason to suppose that our consciences are infallible guides to morally justifiable conduct. It is a reliable guide as to whether we are living up to our own internalized moral standards, but it cannot *guarantee* that our standards are really justifiable as correct or reasonable.

But none of these conceptions of conscience guarantees that a conscientious decision is an objectively right one. The popular conception says that conscience, properly identified and used in ideal conditions, is a reliable sign of moral truth; but we have seen reasons to doubt this. Cultural relativism implies that we may be uncomfortable in acting against conscience; but it insists that this discomfort is purely subjective, having no firmer basis than the early, unconscious internalization of local norms. The Kantian conception gives reason to believe that conscience should be respected, but it insists that conscience is fallible and must be checked by public, reason-governed, critical discussion of the standards that our consciences habitually rely upon.

The upshot is that under any of our interpretations, conscience does not determine what it is objectively right to do. Under the best interpretation, it must be respected, for its judgments are reliable, within their limits. But given this view, conscience is never sufficient by itself: only explicit moral reasoning, together with others, enables us to live with a reasonable hope that our moral beliefs are justified. Ironically, assuming the "duty of due care," we cannot even have a clear conscience unless we are willing to check the opinions that our consciences rely upon by engaging in this process of moral reasoning. If this is right, there are good reasons for ethics courses in the military academies—and for continuing the moral dialogue long after the class is over.

Postscript

Regarding the conflict between conscience and authority, my theme has been a modest one: both should be respected, but neither is an infallible moral guide; and if we cannot satisfy both, there is a need, time permitting, to look for a resolution in a process of moral reasoning. In this process we survey the facts of the case, critically examine relevant arguments, and listen to diverse opinions, considering all this from a moral point of view.

This last qualification is important, but you would be right to wonder what features are inherent in a moral point of view. To ask this is to raise some of the deepest issues in moral theory, issues that have been debated for centuries. Obviously I cannot say much about them at this point, but I will conclude my remarks by sketching some basic points that I draw from Kant. There are four main points, corresponding roughly to Kant's different formulations of the basic principle of morality.[10]

First, in looking for *moral* policies we are not merely trying to find policies that serve our own interests or the interests of our favorite groups. Our policies must be such that we could reasonably choose them for anyone in comparable circumstances to act on. What is good for the goose must be good for the gander—at least when there are no morally relevant differences between geese and ganders.

Second, human beings are not mere expendable commodities, tools or toys that can be used and discarded. Enemies, then, are not *merely* enemies; we must grant to each person a basic respect as a human being. No one's interests, then, can be arbitrarily discounted, and when we think that the common good overrides an individual's interests, this must in principle be morally justifiable even to that individual.

Third, human beings are not mere animals or robots, to be manipulated or compelled to behave as we wish. They can be held responsible for their own conduct, responsible to control their passions and appetites by reason, and responsible to constrain themselves by moral principles, whether they feel inclined to or not. This is not simply a matter of the attitude we should take toward other people. First and foremost, morality requires each of us to hold ourselves responsible as moral persons, without pretending that we are merely the instruments or victims of others.

Fourth and finally, particular moral principles can be understood as just those principles that reasonable, responsible, mutually respecting persons can agree upon as a fair basis for reciprocal relations in a moral community. Even if universal agreement cannot be found, we do our best if we live by the principles that, in honest deliberation and dialogue, we would recommend for universal agreement.

These ideas are far from a complete framework for moral deliberation, and they do not always yield quick and easy answers. Nevertheless, I believe that they are a crucial part of a reasonable framework for further thinking about moral problems.

Notes

1. Roughly, to say that conscience is a capacity to "sense or immediately discern" is to say that it is a way of coming to the relevant moral beliefs about one's acts by means of feeling, instinct, or personal judgment. Becoming convinced *by conscience* that one's conduct is immoral is supposed to be distinct from reaching that conclusion by an explicit appeal to external authorities or by engaging in discussion with others, though perhaps most people would grant that public opinion and authoritative pronouncements tend to influence the development of consciences and so may indirectly affect what conscience "says" on particular occasions.

2. The three conceptions of conscience discussed here, along with another, are discussed more fully, with more extensive comparisons and citations, in my essay "Four Conceptions of Conscience," in *Integrity and Conscience*, edited by Ian Shapiro and Robert Merrihew Adams, Nomos, no. 40 (New York: New York University Press, 1998), 13–52.

3. It should be noted that the "natural law" tradition in Western religious ethics, unlike the "popular" religious conception, emphasizes individuals' *reason* as their mode of access to moral truth. This makes Aquinas's view more similar to Kant's, which is why, for starker contrast, I selected the "popular" view.

4. Typically one's conscience is pictured not as judging the moral quality of particular acts from first principles but rather as identifying a limited class of (one's own)

wrong acts by the means of characteristic painful feelings aroused in contemplating them. This is a feature of several conceptions of conscience that fits well the metaphor of conscience as a warning, nagging, and reprimanding Jiminy Cricket or a tiny angel that follows us through tempting times.

5. Types of relativism are usefully distinguished in Richard Brandt, *Ethical Theory* (Englewood Cliffs, N.J.: Prentice-Hall, 1959), ch. 11, 271–94; William Frankena, *Ethics* (Englewood Cliffs, N.J.: Prentice-Hall, 1973), ch. 6, esp. 109–10; and James Rachels, *The Elements of Moral Philosophy* (New York: Random House, 1986), 12–24. See also John Ladd, ed., *Relativism* (Belmont, Calif.: Wadsworth, 1973); and David Wong, *Moral Relativity* (Berkeley and Los Angeles: University of California Press, 1984).

6. Himmler's attitude is evident in the quotations cited in Jonathan Bennett, "The Conscience of Huckleberry Finn," *Philosophy* 49 (1974): 123–34, which is reprinted in Christina Sommers and Fred Sommers, *Vice and Virtue in Everyday Life*, 3rd ed. (New York: Harcourt Brace Jovanovich College Publishers, 1993), 25–39.

7. Kant's ideas about conscience are most fully expressed in two works: *The Metaphysics of Morals*, translated by Mary Gregor (Cambridge: Cambridge University Press, 1991), 59–60, 197, 233–35; and *Religion within the Limits of Reason Alone*, translated by T. M. Greene and H. H. Hudson (New York: Harper & Brothers, 1960), 173–74.

8. Immanuel Kant, *Lectures on Ethics*, trans. Louis Infield (New York: Harper & Row, 1963), 129.

9. "But when a man is aware of having acted according to his conscience, then as far as guilt or innocence is concerned, nothing more can be demanded." *The Metaphysics of Morals*, 59–60.

10. Kant's formulation of his basic principle of morality, which he called the "categorical imperative," is in Immanuel Kant, *Groundwork of the Metaphysic of Morals*, translated by H. J. Paton (New York: Harper and Row Publishers, 1964), 88–89, 96, 98–99, 104.

17

In the Line of Duty

The Complexity of Military Obligation

Nicholas Rescher

My theme will be the complexity of military obligation. But by way of an introduction, I want to insist straightaway that this is something that differs only in degree, and not in kind, from the complexity of human obligation in general. After all, any adult human being bears a substantial diversity of obligations—to one's employer, to one's client, to one's family, to one's friends, and so on. All of us owe various debts of duty to various individuals and groups—obligations that are rooted in the nature of the different relationships that exist among people. They result from the sort of role that each one of us plays in the lives and affairs of others—be it as their employee, their attorney, their brother, their friend, their neighbor, and so on.

These obligations will also be quite different in nature. Some are legal, some moral, some merely social and rooted in the custom of the country. But each sort of obligation has a certain force and legitimacy of its own, and all are important to maintaining a healthy and fully developed human existence. No one of them predominates to the exclusion of all the rest. For example, someone who says to all others, "I shall only give you what is legally your share, nothing else matters to me," and treats them on this basis—parent, child, friend, and colleague alike—is literally inhuman. In theory, this sort of thing is possible. One could write a story about such an individual. But the picture one would draw in the course of this story would be that of a monster, not of a person.

Some obligations are assumed voluntarily, others are involuntary, and still others are mixed. Your obligations to your parents are involuntary; those to your spouse or employer voluntary; those to your coworkers or your fellow citizens are mixed—because while you certainly do not choose them, you could, in principle, arrange to have others. Nevertheless, whether they are voluntary or not, all those various obligations are perfectly real and genuine. The obligations that one *finds* in place are just as authentic as those that one *puts* in place. One does not eliminate obligations by thinking them inconvenient and wishing they were not there.

Moreover, in taking on new roles and entering into new obligations you do not in general shed the old ones. When you change employers, you do, to be sure, exchange your erstwhile employment-related obligations for others, but you do not thereby cancel your obligations to a spouse or to your children. When you become a parent, you do not shed your obligations to your siblings or your fellow citizens. Our duties in life do not cancel one another out; they generally become combined and superimposed upon each other.

The coexistence of obligations means that they can compete and conflict. You cannot devote to your children the time you spend with a sick neighbor in the hospital. You cannot appropriately dedicate to your friends and relations the efforts and energies you owe to your employer. It is a fact of life that the obligations that we have will often compete and must, in such situations, be balanced off against each other.

In this life we are all servants of many masters. We have obligations to ourselves and to the other people who play a role in our lives. And it is not always easy to harmonize them—to figure out what is, in the circumstances, due to Caesar and what is due to God. The complexity of obligation is a phenomenon that pervades human life. It is something that every responsible adult has to learn to deal with.

But while this is a general phenomenon, it is one that is particularly acute for members of the military profession. And the reason for this is simple and straightforward. It lies in the fact that the obligation of the military person is—like that of a spouse or a parent—particularly large and pervasive in its scope. In the military, one's duty to one's country, to one's service, and one's unit looms very large indeed. It does not end with the time of day, the location of one's placement, or the extent of one's resources. When the going gets too tough, the discontented spouse can get a divorce, the dissatisfied employee can quit the job, but the reluctant soldier, sailor, or airman has no easy recourse.

All the same, the obligation of the military person, wide and deep though it is, does not become all-absorbing. It does not automatically overpower and abrogate all other obligations. Many of them remain in place—crowded into a narrower space, perhaps, but still very much present.

The member of the profession of arms accordingly has many foci of obligation. I shall limit myself here to considering just five of them: the chain of command, the service, the nation, civilization, and humanity at large. Each of these has its own characteristics and its own ramifications.

The Chain of Command

Let me begin with the chain of command. For the military person the first and most obvious source of obligation is clearly those duties that come into being through the injunction of those whom the military system has placed in positions of authority over oneself. The duty of obedience to legal command—personal preferences notwithstanding—is the most basic and most definitive commitment of those who belong to the profession of arms. Irrespective of whether one's affiliation is voluntarily self-generated (via enlistment) or generated through the action of one's fellow citizens (via the draft), one is by law, custom, and established practices bound to this chain of command and in consequence is subject to the separate and stringent code of justice to which the military stands bound.

However, if one's obligations to the chain of command were all—if they cancelled out all of one's other obligations—then the life of a member of the military profession would be much simpler than it is. It is precisely because this most characteristic and weighty of soldierly duties is not all that there is that the complexity of military obligation arises.

The Service

Beyond the chain of command lies first of all "the service"—the entire organization in its historical unity—to which the chain of command gives a concrete temporary embodiment. When it does its work well and serves its function appropriately, the chain of command generally implements the interests of the service. But every once in a while things go wrong. And then the conscientious professional has to ask him or herself the difficult question of whether the particular orders at hand or the larger interests of the service are to prevail. The legendary supply sergeant on Wake Island who, adhering to standing regulations, reportedly made his troops sign receipts for the live ammunition being issued them as the Japanese were storming ashore would be a clear example of someone who didn't get his competing duties properly prioritized.

The Nation, Civilization, and Humanity at Large

And beyond the service there loom the large issues of one's country, one's civilization, and also humanity at large. In being a member of the profession of arms one does not cease to be a citizen, a responsible person, or a human being. And at those levels of relationship, issues of potentially conflicting obligations also arise. Even in the heat of war there are some sorts of militarily useful things that are just not done. (One does not, for example, clear minefields by marching enemy civilians across them—or, for that matter, even prisoners of war.)

I would like to illustrate these complexities of military obligation with some concrete examples. Specifically, I propose to deal with four episodes that clearly bring to view the intricacies of obligation of the sort I have in mind. Quite deliberately, I have chosen these episodes from the pages of German rather than American military experiences. For when a situation comes too close to home, our personal loyalties and ideological leanings prevent our being able to view the matter with the objectivity and detachment that is needed in order to see clearly and objectively just what the issues are. Geographic and cultural distance improves the prospects of making a detached and dispassionate appraisal of the fundamental principles at stake.

The General and the Danish Jews

In the middle of World War II, the German occupation forces in Denmark were commanded by Infantry-General (General der Infanterie) Heinrich von Henneken, a professional soldier of proven ability. His was not, however, an autonomous command; his military jurisdiction was subordinate on all matters relating to specifically political affairs to the primacy of the ambassador. Since Denmark came under German control by political surrender rather than military conquest, the power of control was vested in the Foreign Office in Berlin, to which, in effect, Henneken was ultimately answerable.

In September 1943, orders went forth from Berlin decreeing that a state of emergency should be declared in Denmark and all Jews rounded up for deportation. On 23 September Henneken requested a postponement of this operation. Pleading a shortage of manpower support, he simply dug in his heels. When Berlin persisted, he strongly represented the impracticability and the undesirability of any army involvement in the operation, insisting that this would "injure the prestige of the Wehrmacht at home and in foreign countries." Instructions to the contrary notwithstanding, he refused the use of military personnel in the roundup and generally minimized cooperation. His intransigence created a delay during which most Danish Jews were successfully evacuated to Sweden.

The case of Henneken affords a clear and striking illustration of a soldier who put the best interests and good repute of his service ahead of the demands of the chain of command. As best as we can tell, Henneken's motivation was— as far as external appearance went, at any rate—not so much a humanitarian compassion for the fate of the victims as a sense of the inappropriateness of involving the military in their victimization. His concern was for the good name and repute of his service, taking the position that there are certain sorts of things that a self-respecting army just doesn't do. As far as Henneken was concerned, the best interests of the service took priority over any mere mechanical obedience to instructions. Fortunately for him, despite the irritation of Nazi authorities in Berlin, friends in high places were able to protect Henneken against unpleasant personal consequences—but this was something of which he had no real assurance at the time of action.[1]

The Army and the Country

Let me next turn to another, rather different sort of episode.

In September 1990, General Augusto Pinochet, Chile's former long-term head, still continuing as army commander, set off an international furor by his remarks in an address to the Rotary club in Santiago.[2] Using strong and biting terms, he characterized the postwar transformation of the German military as an unmitigated disaster, undermining the long-standing Prussian tradition of strict discipline, unquestioning obedience, and absence of discussion. According to Pinochet, the democratization of the German army and its acceptance of the individual rights of its members had brought a once proud military organization near to ruin. Pinochet viewed with alarm the prospect that there might be Chilean disciples of the generals who built the new German army and castigated the German commanders "who betrayed that institution by trying to

convert it into an army of inferior values." No doubt echoing a body of sentiment in the German military itself, Pinochet took the line that from a strictly
service point of view, the "democratization" of the military is a step toward its
emasculation. According to Pinochet, the general responsible for the changes
was "the biggest traitor Germany has had with respect to its army."

Pinochet's remarks understandably provoked an immediate reaction from
the German government—and from the German military as well. Their spokesmen responded by stressing the idea that "The soldier of today has to be a citizen." And they observed that the changes in the German military system since
the war were intended "to harmonize obedience and military discipline with the
principles and values of liberty and human dignity."

As the German military spokesmen emphasized, a duty to the service and
its strictly military values has to be balanced and coordinated—in Western democracies at least—with a duty to the nation and to the values that its military
is instituted to defend. Against Pinochet's narrow professional traditionalism,
the German military spokesmen gave voice to the widespread recognition that
the interests and values of the country and its citizenry have to play an important part in the management of military affairs. As they represented the matter, the modern soldier's duty to civic values is no less significant than his or
her duty to strictly military values.

The General and the City—Is Paris Burning?

Sometimes members of the profession of arms come up against obligations of
even a more far-reaching and—so to speak—ominous sort. This is exemplified
by my next illustrative episode.[3]

In 1944, the German commander of the Paris region was one General
Dietrich von Choltitz. He was a Prussian general of the old school. A third-
generation professional soldier, he had served in the airborne infantry with impressive success. He had led the unit that made the initial thrust into Holland
and devastated Rotterdam. Much further from home, he had commanded the
regiment that took the Russian stronghold of Sebastopol in the Crimea.

As the Allies were now converging on Paris, Hitler ordered an all-out,
house-to-house defense of the city. The high command, the OKW under
Rundstedt, put demolition teams at Choltitz's disposal and ordered him to
mount a Stalingrad-like defense of the city.

As the man on the spot, Choltitz saw the matter in a different light. He realized that a defense of Paris would lead to an immense loss of life, since there was no prospect of evacuating the civilian population. He also believed that an effective effort to hold the city was ultimately impracticable, that a house-to-house defense could achieve no goal beyond a modest delay of the Allies' overall advance, and that any serious steps in this direction would result in the physical destruction of Europe's most beautiful city. His considered professional judgment was that no valid military purpose could be served by an all-out effort to defend Paris. But orders are orders. Choltitz was in a deep and painful dilemma. And he resolved it in a bold and radical way.

Choltitz simply cut the chain of command. He ignored his orders, contacted the Allies, and arranged to surrender the city with minimal resistance.

There is little doubt that Choltitz's actions verged on the outright treasonable. And yet it could be argued that he was, in a way, justified—that his obligation to the chain of command was outweighed by obligations and interests of a higher order. Choltitz had made a very hard and very dangerous decision. As he was led away to internment, unknowing Frenchmen spat at him in the street. They would have done better to build him a statue.[4]

Choltitz realized that nations and peoples survive wars. Win or lose, Germans and French are destined to share the landmass of Europe as neighbors. And he recognized that an utterly pointless destruction of people and cultural treasures would provoke ill will and render peaceful coexistence difficult, if not impossible, for many years to come. From one point of view—that of the chain of command—we could say that Choltitz failed in his duty, perhaps even that he was a traitor. And yet it is difficult to deny that a responsible member of the profession of arms has obligations that extend beyond the chain of command, obligations to support the best interests of his country—and sometimes even the higher interests encompassed in the values that the traditions of the country profess.

The Anti-Hitler Conspiracy

This brings me to my fourth and last episode. It is undoubtedly the most drastic one—the 1944 attempt to assassinate Hitler.

I don't want to take time to describe the details; the story of Colonel Count Stauffenberg and his associates is too well known. The bomb that blew up on the wrong side of the conference table's supporting pedestal, the rallying of the shaken Führer's authority, the collapse of the conspiracy in the face of the opposition of military loyalists, the swift and cruel end of the conspirators and their sympathizers—all these are circumstances that do not need elaboration here. The point I want to make is that this was not a matter of the rising of an outraged populace or of a counterstroke launched by disaffected opposition politicians, but a conspiracy launched from deep within the traditional beliefs and values of the German military establishment.

The conspirators worked under difficult conditions. In some ways, they were less than highly competent; in others, they were just plain unlucky. But the important consideration for my present purposes is that these officers were actuated not by considerations of personal gain or political advantage, but by a genuine—and surely not really misguided—sense of duty to the German army, the German nation, and the German people. While these officers indeed violated their pledge of loyalty to Reich and Führer, they nevertheless acted out a deep sense of obligation to their country, their national traditions, and their higher duties.[5]

The episodes we have considered illustrate the complexity and potential conflicts of the obligations of those who exercise military authority. In Henneken's case, he had to choose between his good name as a soldier and the honor of his service on the one hand, and obedience to lawful orders on the other. Again, those German officers who responded to Pinochet placed the political values of their country ahead of the traditional values of its military establishment. Choltitz in Paris confronted the awesome choice between his straightforward duties as an officer on the one side, and a commitment to the long-range best interests of his country and his dedication to civilized values on the other. Finally, Stauffenberg and his co-conspirators put their lives on the line in placing their soldier's honor ahead of their soldier's oath and setting what they saw as the best interests of their service and of their country ahead of unquestioning obedience to constituted authority.

All of these cases exemplify in a particularly dramatic way the agonizing situations that arise when an officer faces a complex choice among conflicting obligations in situations fraught with difficulty and danger.

No doubt the episodes we considered involve rather extreme situations of conflicts of duty. But precisely because of the extremity of such cases, they serve to highlight sharply the complexity of obligation and the potential conflict of duty that—in some less dramatic way—faces virtually every responsible member of the profession of arms.

Most of you, perhaps all of you, will be lucky and will never have to face such conflict situations at a high level of visibility and historical significance, in circumstances where the duties to chain of command, to country, to civilization—and indeed even to yourself as an individual human being—come into conflict with one another. But each of you will certainly face less dramatic cases of this general sort of situation some of the time.

The fact is that at one point or another, every officer faces difficult choices among competing obligations. This is because the exercise of command responsibilities over the actions and situations of other people can all too easily create a condition of conflicting obligations—though (mercifully) usually of a minor and undramatic kind. But even in their milder forms, such experiences will bring home to you that the complexity of military obligation is not an abstract theoretical exercise, but something real that grabs you in the heart, the chest, and the stomach.

You may well wonder what advice I have to offer on this subject. And to my embarrassment, I must confess that I have no very satisfactory response. One reasonable tactic is to think of someone you admire very much as being placed in the same sort of situation, and then ask: "What would he or she do in my place?" Another tactic is to reverse the roles. Following the approach of the philosopher Immanuel Kant, one would ask, "If I myself were not personally involved but were charged with laying down a general rule that others would be called on to follow in such cases, what would I then stipulate?" In this sort of way one could, as it were, create one's own guidelines for choice in situations of conflicting obligations.

These different foci of obligation—one's lawful orders, one's service, one's country, one's values—represent valid and appropriate commitments upon every officer—commitments that make very real and pressing claims, be they legal or moral. When these claims clash with one another, there are no easy solutions and no mechanical formulas for working out the answer. Like any mature individual in a responsible position in life, an officer needs the ability to resolve conflicts thoughtfully—to examine an issue on every relevant side and to give each element of a difficult and controversial situation its due.

The conflicting claims that arise from complex obligations must be confronted and weighed and balanced and resolved. All one can do is work things out in one's heart and mind as thoughtfully and conscientiously as one can— and then do what one has to do. There are no simple, automatic rules, and to respond in a simple-minded and automatic way to problems of the sort at issue is to court disaster. One has no alternative but to worry and fret and sweat.

But there is one point I would like to emphasize particularly. It is this: When you exercise the responsibilities incumbent upon a military officer, you do not cease to be a citizen, and you do not cease to be a human being.

This may sound rather simple and naive, but it has substantial ramifications. For it means that the officer, though just another link in the chain of command, is nevertheless not a mere automaton responding to the will of others, but continues to bear responsibility for him- or herself as a person.

The officer cannot look simply to the wishes of a superior, to the practice of the group, or to what "the others" are doing, but continues as an individual, as a citizen, and as a human being—as someone who must to his or her own self be true, as someone who must act as a person in the light of his or her own values.

A fundamental recognition of right and wrong—a conscience, in short— is what makes one into a responsible person. It is a resource that every officer should and does have. It is what marks one as a responsible individual agent, capable of being answerable for his or her acts, even in the face of contrary custom and group disapproval. It is a manifestation of that most admirable and awesome human quality: the willingness to assume responsibility and stand by one's obligations as one sees them. And so in conclusion I would leave with you one important idea—the thought that in the larger scheme of things, the quality of moral courage is no less desirable and no less admirable in a military officer than the quality of physical courage.

Notes

1. For the episode at issue, see Raul Helberg, *The Destruction of the European Jews* (New York: Franklin Watts, 1985), 2:558–68.

2. For a detailed report on this episode, see the 8 September 1990 dispatch from Santiago filed by Shirley Christian of the *New York Times*, and published in that newspaper on 9 September 1990 under the title "Pinochet Irks the West Germans with a Potshot at Their Military."

3. The episode is described in detail in Larry Collins and Domonique Lapreire, *Is Paris Burning?* (New York: Simon & Schuster, 1965).

4. Choltitz survived to write his memoirs, *Soldat unter Soldaten*, published in 1951.

5. A useful source of information and appraisal is Hans-Adolf Jacobsen (ed.), *July 20, 1944: The German Opposition to Hitler as Viewed by Foreign Historians* (Bonn: Press and Information Office of the Federal Government, 1969).

TRADITIONS IN MORAL EDUCATION

18

The Education of Character

William J. Bennett

I 've had three jobs in government over the years: director of the Office of National Drug Control Policy, U.S. Secretary of Education, and chairman of the National Endowment for the Humanities. Since leaving those jobs, I've enjoyed just being a citizen of Washington, D.C. But over time, an old interest of mine as a former philosophy professor gradually began to reemerge: the whole question of the education of character. That is the subject of this essay.

A Character Deficit

Does character—do ideals—really matter? I'll state my conclusion first: I believe that few things matter more. In the long run of life it will be a person's character that allows him to sleep well at night and go into the next life with a clear conscience and a sense of satisfaction. And I view the education of character as one of the most important things we need to concern ourselves with today.

A big difficulty with the education of character in our time is that society at large seems confused by it. For one thing, broader society usually seems much more interested in celebrity than in character. The people that most Americans, according to opinion polls, want to meet more than any others are people from Hollywood, people from television, people from show business.

I understand that. I see what it is that people are excited by. But this is a substitution of image for substance. The hero is someone who's known for his good acts. The celebrity is someone who simply is known. The focus on celebrity, the focus on appearance, the focus on glitz and glamour, is part of the problem of our time. We're not getting to the heart of the matter; we're not treating and educating human beings as if they were moral and spiritual beings. As a result, we have a national character deficit. It is more important and of more consequence to this country than any budget deficit; in fact, it may very well be more important than any of the other problems we talk about in Washington.

This country has achieved a level of economic strength and self-sufficiency that is extraordinary. We are an economic miracle. The way people live in this society, in economic terms, is the fulfillment of a dream of two millennia. Yes, there's still poverty; we need to address it. But never have so many people lived so well. Militarily we are the only country that really makes a difference. We make the decisive difference. If there is a spot in the world that's having trouble, the U.N. might talk about it endlessly, other governments might send people in endlessly. But the only country that steps in that makes the decisive difference is the United States of America and its people. We are the military and economic power of the world.

In spite of all these great things, in the last thirty years we have suffered a degree of social and moral regression in this country that is extraordinary. We have seen a dramatic increase in crime. We have seen a dramatic increase in the disintegration of the family. We have seen a dramatic increase in the lack of commitment and the breaking of commitments.

In 1960, of all the children born in the United States, 6 percent were born out of wedlock. In 1991, 31 percent were born out of wedlock. From 1900 to 1960, the illegitimacy rate in this country ranged between 4.5 percent and 6 percent. That time span includes World War I, World War II, and the Great Depression: 4.5 to 6 percent. It then went from 6 percent in 1960 to 31 percent in 1991. Now, concern for this trend is not something that belongs to just one political party. Senator Daniel Patrick Moynihan has said if these rates keep going as they are, we will have 50 percent illegitimacy by the time we get to the early part of the twenty-first century.

This trend is particularly bad for poor people, for the lower class, mainly in black America. In fact, the trend in black America is *terrible*: the Moynihan Report cited in 1965 a 26 percent illegitimacy ratio in the black community. He said at the time that this was "a catastrophe." Today it's 68 percent. If 26 percent was a catastrophe, what is 68 percent? And in the white underclass, white illegitimacy is rising at an even faster rate. No society in the history of the world has ever had single parenthood as the norm for raising children. We have no precedent in history for this.

Can some single parents do it? You bet they can. There are plenty of success stories that start in single-parent homes, and those parents clearly did a great job. My mother raised my brother and me, and she did all right. (Some Democrats will disagree with that assessment about me; but my brother is President Clinton's lawyer, so some Republicans would disagree with that assessment about my brother.) She worked hard, she worked very hard, she worked extraordinarily hard. But she did it.

But she is the exception. This does not happen most of the time. My hat is off to the single parents who do their best, but there's no longer any serious debate about whether children do better in two-parent families. Of course they don't do well in two-parent families where people fight all the time, where there's violence, where there's abuse. But statistically, according to almost all available evidence, there's no serious question about this anymore. Single parenthood is not a good social norm to generate examples.

In spite of this, I read a newspaper account recently that reported most people think it's all right to be a single parent. Nearly 70 percent of Americans between the ages of 18 and 35 do not think it is wrong to have a child out of wedlock. They do not think any moral reproach at all is appropriate for someone having a child out of wedlock. But consider the research about children out of wedlock and their chances in life. We're not talking about the miracle story, this wonderful thing, the minority of people who have made it. Look at the general outcome. You can also grow up in Beirut and live to a ripe old age; but statistically the chances aren't great. Given the information I cited, why don't we think having children out of wedlock is wrong?

I've been asked if I think information-age technology might make single parenthood more manageable for some people, because they will be able to work at home. I don't think that will make any difference at all. We have put our hopes in technology too many times before. Think back to what was said about television in the thirties and forties. You know what almost everybody said about television? "One thing will happen for sure; our kids will be a lot smarter because of television."

The returns are now in. It wasn't true. I think television—despite some great stuff—has basically rotted people's minds. Do you want to know an interesting fact about American life? American people complain that they do not have enough time to spend with their children; they do not have enough

258 ◆ William J. Bennett

time to teach them. But the average American adult also spends four hours a day watching television. What about that? They say, "Well, I mean, I can't give up television." Why not? A recent article in the *New York Times* reported on a poll in which parents were asked: "Do you deprive your children of television as a form of punishment?" Astonishingly, 40 percent of parents said no, because they thought taking away television was too harsh.

You can work at home in front of that information-age computer, or you can sit there in front of the TV, or you can be away at work. The important thing is the *lessons* you're teaching while you're away at work, or when you're sitting there at home. If the reasoning is, "I'm sitting here at home because I want to be here and be close to you," that's an important message. If the reasoning about being at work is, "I'm at work because it's for you that I'm at work," that message comes across too. But I don't think that technology is the answer to the lessons we teach or the time we have to teach them. I don't think that technology and the computer is the answer any more than television was. The problem is, generally, a problem of character.

We must also face another problem: the problem with men. Mostly it is the women who are making the effort to raise children, not the men. For some reason yet to be adequately explained, the sexual revolution succeeded in liberating men from their sense of responsibility, and unless we can get men back, reattached to a sense of responsibility, we will continue to see this decline. I said this the other day and someone asked, "Well, are you in favor of the 'shotgun' marriage?" Compared to no marriage, yes, absolutely. Maybe we need to insist on saying, "You're marrying that girl, or at least you're proposing to her." Now, she may not want to marry the jerk. That's all right. But there is a sense among a lot of young men in this society that marriage and childrearing simply aren't their responsibility anymore. And unless we can reattach young men to that notion, we're not going to improve this situation. This is a problem of character.

Divorce also brings many people into single parenthood. If people are not committed when they get married, I don't think they should get married. A friend of mine got married ten years ago and sent out cards that made it clear they weren't making any of the traditional vows. They promised to stay together only as long as it felt good, as long as it was exciting, as long as they turned each other on. As a gift I sent him paper plates. Kidding aside, you can't sustain a society without that basic commitment to the family unit. That's the fundamental one. Regardless of the heroics of many women in this society, the alienation of many men from this sense of responsibility is a big problem.

Why has this happened? Well, I think a lot of things may have contributed to it. I think it's modernism and I think it's affluence. But importantly, I also think it's the erosion of the notion of commitment; I think it's the erosion of the notion of honor. Instead of notions of honor and commitment and character, we have an entirely different set of messages coming across at our young people. "Just do it; if it feels good, do it; peel off the road and find your own way." If you get those things drummed into your head for a very long time, they don't mesh well with commitment. And commitment is what we need to keep a country going, to keep a marriage going, to keep a family going, to keep an educational system going. Unless we restore character—the education of virtue, as I call it in another context—back to an important place in our educational system, we will continue this ruinous slide.

The rules people are now willing to live by are extraordinary. I am not a prude. I am not a bluenose. I grew up in Brooklyn, New York, in a tough neighborhood. I played a lot of football. I played semipro football in Mississippi. I've been in a lot of locker rooms and a lot of bars. I know about the real world. I've been in it, lived in it, made a lot of mistakes in it, and am still making mistakes in it. But the depths to which this culture has gone today are such that if we don't lift it up, it will take us down.

Let me give you an example. There is an entry in Bob Packwood's diary that is a document for our times. Good Republicans stood up and wept that he left. I say they should have thrown him out the door. First of all there is the behavior; and second, there is the narcissism of entering these things in his diary. I thought our legislators were so busy they couldn't even turn around. He's sitting there writing, "Really good-looking girl with her blouse unbuttoned." What the heck is going on here, Senator? Anyway, he writes in his diary, "I told my wife I just didn't want any part of her, I didn't want any part of the children. All I wanted to be was a US. Senator; that's the only thing I wanted to be." Well, look how that one came out. Do you think he's leaving self-satisfied? I don't think so. I was sorry for Packwood, but once I saw what was in those diaries, I didn't shed any tears for him. This was rampant self-indulgence. And the fact that more people don't recognize it is a big problem.

I'll cite another example. The Calvin Klein ads we are seeing are child pornography. Pictures of young girls with a voice-over of a man in his fifties, my age, deep-voiced, sounds like he's been smoking two packs a day and drinking a bottle of Wild Turkey every day, saying to the little girl, "Do you like to take orders?" This is simply pornography. This is the bottom of the human order. This is the bottom of the human psyche. If you don't know that's bad, you don't know anything is bad.

This kind of thing probably is going to be good for my cause. It probably is going to be good for my political party. It's going to be good for conservatism because people are going to react with such revulsion to this. A friend of mine who is a former liberal said the new definition of conservative in the last five years is anybody with a teenage daughter, because you look out at the world and you say, "I'm for protection; I'm for protecting from the onslaught." We all know there is now a serious deficit of character.

The Causes

There is, however, some good news. At least some people in this country realize what we have done wrong on these issues. They know we have abandoned the education of character. They know that in the sixties and seventies, instead of the education of character, we substituted things like values clarification, which did no good and did a great deal of harm. They know, as well, that the kinds of behavioral patterns we see being played out in the streets of this country are a product of a deficit in family structures, educational structures, moral structures, and community structures.

One of the tragedies that's occurred here is that we have reduced the notion of character and the education of character to a mere academic exercise. When I was a philosophy professor, teaching freshman philosophy, the answers I started to get from students in the sixties were, "I think each person should do his own thing. I mean if they want to do something, who am I to say something's right, who am I to say something's wrong?" But the idea that each person should do his own thing and that there are no common responsibilities or common values is a *real* notion which, if taken seriously, will lead to the end of society and the end of all these institutions.

The good news is that not one of my students *really* believed it. You know how I know? Because I cut through the rhetoric and got to the point. In Philosophy 101, a student would say that there are no values, no right and wrong. "Who are you to impose your values on me?" Whenever I heard this, I always did the same thing. I'd say, "You don't think there are values, you don't think there's a right and wrong? You don't think there's a difference?" "No." I said, "Well, you are wrong." And they said, "Well, who are you to say?" I said, "I'm the professor in this class, and if you don't agree with me, you're flunked and I will have you removed from this institution because you're too stupid to be here." You know what the students invariably did? They stood up and said, "You can't do that!" And I said, "Why not?" And they said, "It's not fair." "It's not what?" "It's not fair." My reply: "Don't impose your values on me, son." Next time you run into a moral relativist, steal his wallet!

We can't live the doctrine of moral relativism consistently. But what many in this country are trying to figure out, amidst our affluence, amidst our entertainment media, amidst a host of other things, is whether you *can* just go for it, whether you *can* just have a good time, and whether you really *need* to pay any attention to responsibilities and to the notions of right and wrong. Many of us are trying to make a way to do the impossible.

Well, what has happened was bound to happen. The first place it was going to come out was in the streets, in crime, and we're seeing that. The second place it would come out is in family settings, in bad family situations, and we're seeing that too. And of course the family setting predicts and generates more of the crime, because if you don't raise children to notions of right and wrong early and emphatically, the odds that they're going to make it and grow into responsible and decent human beings are very small. Human beings are very fragile things, and the hold of civilization on human beings, people of culture, people of virtue, people of decency, is fragile.

I used to coach soccer. Why did I coach soccer? Because my wife signed me up to coach soccer. That's how a lot of guys get into it. Anyway, I was the coach of these little boys, fifteen little boys. They come from the suburbs of Washington, D.C., my neighborhood. They have lots of parents. Each of those kids has at least two parents; some of them have three, four, or five. They go to good schools. They've got everything money can buy. They go to church, they have good health care. Little boys at six years old out on the soccer field, running around before the game starts, and you turn and look, and there's trouble. Somebody's got somebody in a headlock. Somebody's kicking somebody. And these are the best children we have in terms of what we are able to offer them, and there's trouble.

Not all of them are going to make it. You can give them every advantage, and still some of them aren't going to make it. Now take away the fathers, take away the good schools, take away the neighborhoods, take away all those advantages. Are you surprised that we have the kind of social dislocation we're seeing, that we have the kind of people running around doing the things to other people that we're seeing?

It is hard to raise children. It is hard to keep a family together. A cultural anthropologist told me that in our cities we now have what is tantamount to a state of nature. And men in a state of nature are interested in violence, in immediate gratification, and in being sexual predators. He also said, "Men are interested in that in a civilized state too . . . but their wives won't let them do it." Seriously, that may be too dark a view of human nature. But I was brought up as a Catholic, and I believe in original sin. I believe there is a tendency and a partiality of human beings to go in the wrong direction. And that's not just a matter of faith for me. I think that is proved every day, and that original sin is one of the clearly empirically verifiable doctrines of Christianity. All you need to know is some history and you'll know the capacity of human beings to get themselves into trouble.

So we have to work on this issue of character. The results of our failures in this area are obvious and predictable. Thomas Jefferson said of education that we should aim at the development of the intellectual *and* moral faculties. When the American public school system was established in the nineteenth century, it was established primarily so that the American people could have a common moral code, a common moral code so that we could talk with each other and work with each other and live with each other. But now we too often say, "Well, I don't know; maybe it isn't right, maybe it is right." All these moral doubts are at the root of a lot of what is going wrong with American society.

When I was secretary of education I read a story in the *New York Times* that I cut out and sent to Ronald Reagan. He used to put it in his speeches all the time. It was a very typical story from the early eighties. It's the story of a young woman, a junior high-school student who found a purse in the street. It had a lot of money in it. She brought it to school, she asked to use the office telephone, she called the woman who owned the purse, and gave it back to her. The woman gave her a ten-dollar reward, as there were several hundred dollars in the purse. She told her counselor about it.

Her counselor said, "We'll make a counseling session out of this." He told the story to the class—this was in suburban New York—and asked the class under the guise of democracy, "Do you think she did the right thing or the wrong thing?" Half the class said she did the right thing, half the class said she did the wrong thing. He said, "We'll vote on it." Feeling besieged by the critics who said she was a fool, she said she should never have done it. When asked what she owed this woman, she looked beseechingly at her teacher, the counselor. And he said, "I don't have an opinion; I'm just a facilitator."

Now that story certainly seems more banal, more harmless, than a story of people going down a wrong alley and getting shot, but that story portends the end of a civilization every bit as much as a shooting in an alley does. Because if you can't tell the difference between right and wrong, if you can't tell that young lady, "Good for you, you did the right thing," you're going to fall apart; you're going to disintegrate. Because this society is not held together by a tyrant. It's not held together by a totalitarian government, it's not held together, indeed, by the Supreme Court, by the legislature, by the Congress, or by the president of the United States. This country is held together by the people, their institutions, their beliefs, their principles, and their practices.

James Madison said it in the Federalist Papers. We depend critically on what he called "virtue in the people." All the other things—the rule of law, the balance of powers, elections, all of that—are auxiliary to the main thing: virtue and a sense of justice in the people. And if that goes, we all go.

Of course, it's not just in the education of character that we're failing in public education. I visited Chicago. While there I said, "These are the worst public schools in the United States of America." A spokesman from the mayor's office stood up and said indignantly, "What do you mean?" I said, "That is a perfectly clear sentence. These are the worst schools in the United States of America." In 1986 they spent $4,000 per child per year, but still had a 50 percent dropout rate. Of the kids who stayed in school, 50 percent of them scored in the bottom 1 percent of the country. There was even a high school in the city with a 100 percent dropout rate. No customers. Now, for those of you in business, if you don't have customers, you don't have a business, right? I don't know if they were doing announcements over the loudspeaker, but there weren't any students there. The staff was getting its salary with a 100% dropout rate—no accountability. You've got to have accountability in the system.

That is meltdown. That is disaster. We know where those kids are going. They're not going to Harvard or Princeton or the United States Air Force Academy. But there are some kids there who *could* go to those sorts of places. And we all know Chicago isn't the only place where this kind of meltdown is taking place.

Fixes

Where are we then? We've been conducting a social experiment for thirty years in this country, and it's gone like this: let's have babies; let's not raise them in families; let's not pay much attention to their education; let's give them a lot of garbage over TV and in the movies and on the radio; let's not have them brought up to understand the concepts of right and wrong; and let's see how they turn out. Had enough?

I think we've had enough. I know a lot of people in neighborhoods in Washington and New York who are trying to raise children, and they are living in a free-fire zone. People say, "Well, it's modernization; it's not enough government programs." No, it isn't. It's that we've forgotten the things that are most important.

We either get back to some sense of commitment and taking commitment seriously, or I think we see a very different country. I'm not sure how we do this in the larger society. School programs could give us a start. Service programs could work too. I don't know about military service for all. But maybe we ought to have young men and women in a national-service program. Have them walking the streets and neighborhoods with orange slickers, walkie-talkies, and flashlights so we can get some massive presence out there in the streets. Get them to take on the bad guys, the drug pushers and the others. This might help to teach young people that the common interest is part of their interest.

I talk to a lot of people after they've gone through military training. I ask them what they think after two or three years when they go back to their neighborhoods and hang out with their old friends. They have told me, "It just doesn't look very good." You get to a place where there is honor, where there is self-discipline, where there's hard work, where there's a sense of community, where there is aspiration. Sure there are problems, sure there is rigidity, sure there are things that could be better, but you're in a serious place with a serious enterprise. And then you go back into the rest of American life, and the reaction of a lot of the young people I know is "This is a joke." People want to horse around, they want to smoke dope, they don't care about anything, they don't work.

I'm tempted by the idea of national standards in the secondary schools. When I was secretary of education I used to travel around the world and meet with my counterparts. I met with the minister of education of France, and we had a nice chat. And at one point I said, "How are the schools?" He said, "Let's see; it's 2:15, they are all reading Racine." The minister could look at his watch and tell me what French schoolchildren were doing all over the country. Ask the secretary of education of the United States the same question. It's 2:15 . . . I'd have said, "God knows, I hope they're there. I hope somebody's doing some math, English, history, and science."

In the last fifteen years, every time we've done an assessment of our students against kids from other countries, we come in last or next to last among industrialized countries. We entered our thirteen-year-olds in an international competition about two years ago. We came in last in math. South Koreans came in first. But there was a question on the test which asked: "What do you think about your abilities in math?" On that question we came in first. "How do you feel about your knowledge in math?" "Great." "What do you know?" "I don't know anything." We think it's important in America in a classroom to say how you feel about it. It doesn't matter what you know about quadratic equations.

I think a lot more assessments would have a very positive effect on performance. That doesn't mean everybody should take a test a week. Just do samples, and advertise the results, put it out there. The commissioner of the State of Pennsylvania lost his job because he posted the results of his schools' test scores in the newspaper. But we *should* post the test scores and see how much we're learning. Justice Louis Brandeis said, "Sunlight is the best disinfectant," and we should have these international assessments published. Couple that with school choice, so there can be competition, so some can be better than others, and standards would go up on their own.

So I would assess, evaluate, and publish. I would have a choice. And the third thing I would put into the system—which would come automatically if you had competition—is accountability. If you serve up a rotten hamburger in this country, you get closed down by state, local, or federal authorities faster than you can flip another one. You serve up a rotten education in this country year after year after year in schools, and you get more money because the argument is made that lack of money is the problem. We now have a few schools with some sense of competition. And these are the schools that can make a difference. That's what we need for real standards.

But as for the character deficit in particular, I think there's some good news. First piece of good news: What do you suppose was behind the appeal of Colin Powell's possible run for the presidency? Now, I may have supported him, I may not have. There are some things I disagree with him on. But his appeal is undeniable. What is behind that appeal? I think what a lot of the American people see when they see Colin Powell is character. They see a man who seems to have his life and his act together. They also see a patriot, a good father, and a good husband. They see a man who seems to walk it like he talks it, and they are interested in him.

Quite apart from any level of political agreement or disagreement you may have about Colin Powell, I submit to you that you should step back and think about his appeal. Before we knew any of his views, why did he finish, in almost every opinion poll, ahead of the other major candidates? Because the American people see in him, perhaps, an embodiment of what they think we need. He may have it, he may not; he may have disappointed, he may not have. But what his supporters were looking for is what we're talking about: character. The fact that it counts for so much is, I think, good news.

Imagine this possible scenario, just to further illustrate my point. Colin Powell goes to the Republican convention, stands up, and says: "I'm running for president for one simple reason. I want to do what I can to help save this country and help save my people. Not black Americans, not military Americans, but the American people." I bet there would be a fourteen-minute standing ovation, maybe even longer than for Cal Ripken. (But it would be about the same thing, wouldn't it? What was Ripken's record all about? It was about showing up, it was about consistency, it was about character.) Suppose Powell is elected and then says, "For four years, we're not going to talk about legislative issues so much. We're going to talk about what we need to do as individuals." Suppose he makes the following claim, which I believe to be true: "We're looking too much to Washington for solutions. The answer lies in our character-forming institutions: churches, families, neighborhoods, schools, communities. Those are the things we have to work on." And suppose he says it every day on TV and on the radio. Every day he says it in a different way, and he keeps saying it.

And for four years the American people would turn on the TV and say, "There's the president; I agree with him, I don't agree with him," whatever. But every one of them would be able to say, "See that? That is a real man. He honors his wife, he's raised his children, he's served his country. He tells us what he thinks. He speaks the truth. Be like that man, or find someone like that man, and things will be better for this country and in your life." The country could do worse for four years.

Of course, a critical question for those of us faced with political choices is the actual plan of action, the platform. But the turnaround plan, who the cabinet members will be, how you are going to execute the plan, what you are going to do about welfare, what you are going to do about budget, what you are going to do about taxes, what you are going to do about deficit—these are, in a sense, of secondary importance. The reason for the Powell appeal and the reason that the American people are restive on this issue, I think, is that they're looking for what is the first priority, which is a moral lift.

Sure, I think this country needs tough fixing. The government needs to scale down, not up. It needs to do what a lot of businesses have done. But what this country needs more than those remedies, more than anything else, is a lift. People need to start raising their sights. There is a great old hymn that says

"We Shall Raise Them Up." We've got to raise it up, because when you watch television or you talk to young people, they're talking down, they're talking too low. We're not raising it up. Sample the afternoon talk shows. That is some of the worst stuff. People don't like it, but people watch it. But what people *want* is a certain degree of lift.

What is on people's minds, what is becoming a part of our society's ethos, is character and leadership. These things are crucial to a democracy. There's a reason we still revere George Washington. There's a reason we still revere Abraham Lincoln. What's central in the stories about Washington and Lincoln? They are stories that reveal virtues. They are stories that reveal certain deep core beliefs and convictions.

There's a great old country and western song called "Looking for Love in All the Wrong Places." It's a great song with a great lesson. For thirty years, we have been looking to Washington to solve our problems. Problems can't all be solved in Washington. First of all, a lot of the people there don't have the foggiest idea. Shakespeare said, "Don't trouble the poor with begging." And second, the problems are in River City, not Washington. There is trouble in River City, and that's where we need to address it. And last, if you could get a sensible plan for revitalizing this government, for scaling it down, for the devolution of power to the states, that would be great. All of these things are important. But more important is what happens in those classrooms and in those family circles and in those churches and communities. We shouldn't look to a government plan, much less a government plan from Washington, to solve problems that have a *moral* root. Only *moral* lift will begin to address these kinds of problems.

I'm a religious man, so I'm sure that God has to play a role in all this, and I'm sure He can and will play a role. But it's not His part that's bothering me. It's what people are doing that's all wrong. Cultural anthropologists tell me that the only precedent for turning around this sort of thing, providing this kind of moral lift, has got to be some kind of twentieth-century equivalent to the Great Awakening, some equivalent of a spiritual awakening. (That would make a very interesting research project. What have been the things that have turned societies around?) I'm not sure—the situation in this country is extremely unusual. Our society is already one of the most church-going, but at the same time, is extremely secular in its outlook in many ways. Great Awakening or no, I think that at the end of the day, the final argument for character is an argument that you are, indeed, a moral and spiritual being. You either you pay attention to that or you miss the point.

In any case, this public concern for moral lift in public and private life is the first piece of good news. The second piece is more personal, but it tells an interesting story of our time. I visited schools when I was the secretary of education. My wife said, "Instead of just standing there in Washington and making speeches, why don't you go out and visit schools, teach class? I've heard you teach. You're a good teacher. Teach class; teach third grade, seventh grade, eleventh grade and find out what's going on, and then make your pronouncements." I stood up, kind of huffy, and I said, "Elayne, I'm the secretary of education of the United States. I don't do retail. I do wholesale." She said, "Do good retail, and you'll do better wholesale." Of course she was right.

So I visited schools, and I taught classes back and forth across this country. During my visits, I'd ask people what they were doing about the education of character. And people would say, in America's public schools, "Well, we can't do that." And I asked, "Why?" And they said, "Because it violates church and state." I said, "And how does it violate church and state?" "Well, it gets into sort of moral/spiritual things." I'd show them the passages from Jefferson, show them the passages from Lincoln, show them other things they could rely on without violating the separation of church and state. But people were still afraid of it because we have so mangled our historical understanding of what's involved here. They finally would say, "We don't even know what kind of materials we could use."

So I promised myself that when I left office I was going to do a book that parents could use, or that teachers could use in a private school or public school, that would help in the education of character. So I put together this book, a collection of a lot of old stories. Is there a market for it? Well, I will now boast, I have sold 2.2 million copies of *The Book of Virtues*.

I fought recently with the people at Time-Warner about gangster rap lyrics. They said to me, sitting in the board room, "People buy it." I said, "You can sell anything and American people will buy it. It's a great big country with a lot of variety. People have too much money. They're spending it on stuff they don't need and they don't want and they're just trying it. Some people are doing it to be outrageous. But you guys could make a living without selling this garbage. You could make a living by selling good stuff." By then we had passed out the lyrics to some of these songs, and I said, "Will any of you read the lyrics to the songs that you're selling to kids?" Not one of the people at Time-Warner—not the board members, not the Time-Warner executives—would read their own lyrics out loud.

And one of them said to me, "You know, you come from government, and you don't understand the private sector." And I said, "No, no, no. I'm in the private sector. I *used* to be in government. I'm in the same business you're in. I do books, I do entertainment, I'm doing a cartoon series of *The Book of Virtues.*" I said, "You know something? It sells. You can aim low and make a sale. You can also aim high and make a sale." As Aristotle said, there is an interest in men—even though there may be this downward pull that Christianity calls original sin—there is this interest in men in reaching out and aspiring to be something better. The commercial success of this kind of material is encouraging. It is my second piece of good news.

The question I have is this: With something like *The Book of Virtues* making its way, with something like the appeal of Colin Powell, with some other things stirring in this land, can we get it together, and can we get it together in time? Aristotle said that we form character and virtue through habit, through precept, and through example. We need to work on the habits, we need to work on the precepts, and Lord knows we need to work on the examples. Every little boy wants to be a man; every little girl wants to be a woman. But they don't know what it means exactly. What we tell them it means—through television, through the movies, through teaching, through talking, and through our behavior—is what they take it to mean. That's where the education of character comes home. It is the most real thing in the world.

Martin Buber, the great Jewish theologian, said, "All education that is worth it is the education of character." It's not the lectures about character; it's not the lectures about ethics. It matters more to the long run of a student's life how an ethics professor treats his students than how well he lectures on the subject. If you have a bunch of people teaching ethics who don't treat students with regard and respect, the lessons don't matter.

I'll give you an example of the difference between talking a good game and living a good game. I remember this from when I was teaching philosophy, that freshman ethics course I always volunteered for. During one semester, there was a seminar, a graduate seminar in ethics taught by another professor, that met at night. I was in my office one of those nights and heard the seminar going on. Then I heard them all leaving, going down the hall to what we called the Robot Room, where we could get soft drinks and snacks. All of a sudden I heard a crash, and I went in to see what had happened. Apparently, they had put their coins in, and it broke the coin box, and coins were scattered all over the place. The machine was broken, cans were coming out, money was coming out, and everybody was grabbing some of it.

The next day I saw this professor, and I said, "What went on last night?" And he said, "Well, the machine broke, so we had a party. You know, we took the money and took the cans." I said, "Who did?" He said, "The advanced seminar on ethics. Any problem with that?" I said, "Do you know that the guy who comes and empties that is probably going to get hit for the bill, and if he complains, the company will just take it out of his hide?"

He started giving me a lecture about corrupt corporate systems and so on, but it didn't really matter. This was a man who was published in prestigious philosophy journals, but he didn't know the difference between right and wrong. He didn't know the basic difference between right and wrong, talking the game and walking the game. Be careful of philosophy. It's a wonderful discipline, but pay as much attention to example, to precept, and to habit as you do to anything else. Precept is important, habit is important, and example is important.

I think I learned that most profoundly not through my study, not through my jobs, but through being a father. Before I was a father, a friend of mine said to me, "God's love is so great He loves the sinner no matter what he does." And I said, "I don't understand why. Some people are so awful you just wouldn't love them. I don't know why He loves me, I've done so many horrible things." He said, "When you have a child, you will understand."

Now I'm the father of two sons, and I understand. I get mad, I get impatient, I feel all sorts of things. But the love never goes away. Now when I look at those boys, what I want them to be more than anything else—more than I want them to be happy, more than I want them to be smart, more than I want them to be successful—is to be good boys. And I want to be a better example to them as a father because I now know that what I do has an awful lot to do with what they do. I can say something or preach something. They hear that, but above all they're looking at my actions.

For most of us, the most important parts of our characters are already formed. They were formed early on. And for most of us, there will be situations in which those things we've learned are going to be tested, and then we'll see. Over the course of a life, as I said earlier, a number of our decisions are going to tell us the kind of persons we are. A friend of mine, a philosopher, said, "Who are you? You are in the end, morally, what you are in other people's lives. Don't ask yourself; ask them, and they'll tell you."

But a lot of this is already formed. It was formed because somebody, maybe a lot of people, took the trouble to teach us, to take time with us, to bring us along. The great sociologist Robert Nisbet said that the struggle to make civilized human beings is a struggle between the forces of composition and the forces of decomposition. Now, if he'd said that in religious terms, he might have called it a struggle between good and evil. But the point is the same. You know what brings the person together and what doesn't, and a lot of that has to do with examples that are set early on.

I think in the end every human being in a free society has to make one fundamental kind of judgment. They must come to grips with the judgment about who they are and what their life is about. It doesn't matter whether it's the seventies, the eighties, the nineties, the fifties, or the forties. In the conversations I have with young people, the big question is still what it's always been, as old as the questions the young people have in Plato's dialogues: What's it all about? What does it come to in the end? What's the meaning of it all?

We decide the kind of people we are through some series of decisions, through some series of actions over the course of a life. I have come to believe fervently as an adult what I was taught as a child—that in the end we are, indeed, moral and spiritual beings. It is the example we set which in the end, I think, tells the tale. There is behavior talked about, and there is behavior exemplified. The education of character is finally a matter of human being to human being. The existential decision, the decision about who you are and what matters in your life, no one can take from you. That's the decision that you, and you alone, make.

In the end, that decision about who you think you are and where you think you're going will be the most important decision you will make in the education of your own character. And those decisions made by millions of American citizens this year, next year, and the year after will determine whether we keep this republic. I no longer believe it is a certainty that we will keep this republic. I believe it is now an open question, and I think it will be decided by the decisions made by the millions of American citizens, particularly the young ones, about who they think they are, what they think their aspirations should be, and what they think is worthy of their character.

19

Liberal Education and Its Enemies

ALLAN BLOOM

The year 1991 was quite a year for the US. military. The Gulf War demonstrated many things, but perhaps the most important among them is that force is still an essential component of political life and that the United States is capable of exercising force. At that moment it became clear that the United States is the greatest, most unchallenged power since the Roman Empire.

The end of the Cold War was for certain groups the proof that military power is no longer needed in the world. Most of these people have tended to go so far as to say that the dangers of the Cold War were exaggerated or even nonexistent. This is all part of an attempt to delegitimize the use of national force and especially American force, which is held to be at least as selfish and pernicious as other nations' force. The Cold War is treated as a kind of sham to justify America's national interest, and the end of the Cold War is treated as a kind of proof that we should never use force again. The exploitation of the Vietnam War by the legions of the Left has been and continues to be used in this intention, trying to destroy the will to fight in the defense of justice.

The Gulf War and the great outpouring of public support for it proved once again that the American people trust our military and believe in the decency of our political goals. And the actual performance of the military dispelled so many illusions about the competence of our generals; the courage, dedication, and intelligence of our fighting men; and the value of the weapons, so complex, expensive, and controversial. It was in every way a splendid and inspiring performance.

But why is the country now in such a grouchy mood, and why have the media so quickly learned to denigrate this magnificent achievement? Behind this lies a story that helps us to understand the intellectual crisis of our times and the character of our intellectual elites, which are so eager to educate the great unwashed public. These are the same people who said we should not enter the war because of the terrible casualties that would result, and now tell us that the war had no significance because it was so easily won.

The issue is directly linked to the collapse of communism and the problem created for the Left by that collapse. The Left is motivated much more by hatred of modern democracy, or what they call capitalism, than by any idealism about the perfect socialist society. For a set of various interesting reasons, the most intolerable thing for them is the bourgeoisie and the bourgeois individual. What has happened is that the absolutely definitive end of any movements or regimes that are antidemocratic has left radicals without a rudder and a polestar. Marxist socialism promised a rational, universal society with plenty for all. What has happened is that hated capitalism has turned out to be the truly universal rational principle of order. The Left has nowhere to go but is not willing to reconcile itself with reality. Therefore, they have turned in large measure toward an attempt to delegitimize the West and its democratic philosophy, which is linked with the idea of rational rights belonging to all people. And by successful manipulation of tensions within American society, they are having a spectacular success in making the United States look like a failure, not a promoter of freedom and equality, but a hegemonic oppressor whose reason is only a tool of its oppression. The Gulf War is in their view to be understood as an effort only at preserving American control of Middle Eastern oil and preventing the autonomy of alien cultures. Very early on in this new kind of assault on the West, the French writer Michel Foucault condemned the Soviet Union while breaking with the fellow-traveling French intellectuals; and then he turned to praising Khomeini. The attraction now is the quasi-fascistic and reactionary attack on democratic values and technology in the name of Iran and Islam. Such sympathies are wholly new on the Left.

Let us look at this in another way. From the perspective of the Americans and their European allies, we have engaged throughout this century in a heroic struggle in defense of the rights of man against two colossal threats aimed directly at our destruction, fascism and communism. This was no battle for national aggrandizement, like the traditional wars between the English and the French or the Russians and the Austro-Hungarians. This was like a cosmic morality play, where each of the characters represented a great idea. Against all odds, we won and affirmed our principles of individual rights and freedoms. We fought great battles, and we spilled much blood. But even more impressive was our resolve and our political responsibility. Think only about the last forty-five years: the maintenance of a policy with a clear goal—containment and the ultimate destruction of the Soviet empire—by democratic nations with changing, popularly elected leaders, and in an alliance of very diverse nations, is an unexampled achievement. What Harry Truman outlined in the forties remained unwaveringly our policy and the policy of Western Europe and Japan until the goal was achieved. We have every right to be proud of ourselves and triumphant because in great majority we believe that our cause was just and the cause of our opponents was demonstrably unjust. This was enough in itself to make us gloriously remembered throughout all future history, and perhaps more gloriously than any other nations that were simply splendid in their empires. I am simply astounded by the fact that we have not rejoiced in the triumph of those democratic principles enunciated in the Declaration of Independence for a tiny and obscure people, principles that have grown great and have become the only serious alternative for all peoples on earth. Ours was the just cause; we made many and continuing sacrifices for a long time, and yet we hate ourselves.

This nation has been made to seem a system of unjust hegemonies, and a whole series of extreme complaints have captured our way of looking at things. Corporate greed, assaults on the environment, unremitting tyranny over women, blacks, and other minorities, and indifference to the homeless are only a small part of the list of intolerable evils that must be cured by some kind of new revolution. Something like this is what is meant when President George Bush, Sr., was criticized for not having a domestic agenda and spending all his time in that world outside, where we encourage all the worst forms of oppression. The expression that has caught on and is used all over the place is "white Western male." The term implies that whites must incurably want to enslave nonwhites, that Westerners, who are connected with the use of modern natural science and its technology, are exploiters of nature and destroyers of other cultures, and that men dominate women in patriarchal structures and can never understand them. These are taken to be incurable vices of the white Western male, so no rational self-consciousness could correct the distortions in their *perspective*: their minds are fixed by their cultural and gender origins, and only by replacing them with other *powers*—that is the important word—is there hope of justice on earth. These are really radical assertions, because the issue is no longer one of reform of mistaken or inadequate policies but the need to change the human mind utterly.

Let me recount to you a bit of essential autobiography in order to make my point clear. A few years ago I wrote a book that was a reflection on liberal education in our times in America. I can tell you very simply what I meant by "liberal education." The theme of liberal education is the good and just life, a theme treated in no other discipline, but on the face of it, the most important of all studies. I argued in my book that the primary way of approaching this subject matter is by reading the writers who thought best about these questions, but that such education was being squeezed out of the curricula of universities.

Of course, much of any course of study will contain technical education. But as citizens in our kind of open democratic society, we have a responsibility to have thought, and to continue to think, about the nature of this political regime and its claims to justice, particularly in relation to the claims of other kinds of regimes. We also have to think about a choice of career and what it means for the polity and ourselves. Otherwise we would be simply thoughtless, and other people would be making the most fundamental decisions for us.

For the United States it is pretty obvious that one would have to begin with study of the Declaration of Independence, the Constitution, and the Federalist Papers. The Federalist Papers explicitly leads back to even profounder and more comprehensive writers, like Montesquieu and Locke, on whom the American founders relied in their founding. This is but one example among many of how a liberal education must proceed if we wish to understand ourselves at all. We all talk about rights, but hardly anyone can say what they are, let alone defend them against those who say, for example, that duties are much more important than rights. My simple proposal was that a considerable part of the education of serious persons should consist in reading some of the good books that address our most urgent questions. For example, it was characteristic in the past that a great general, like George Marshall, kept Thucydides' *History of the Peloponnesian War* on his desk for real guidance about the nature of war and peace. Such people have become rarer and rarer, and the fact that so many Pentagon generals have Ph.D.s only obscures the fact that they are narrow technicians and never reflect on these absolutely central questions.

I expected that my book would get almost no attention, just another professor's complaints. But it got enormous, unprecedented attention, obviously appealing to something the American people admire, if they do not actually possess it. However, the academic and public intellectual establishment reacted with an absolutely ferocious hostility and anger, and I was characterized, and continue to be characterized, as, at the very least, sexist, racist, homophobic, and elitist. It was then that I became fully aware that the establishment in the humanities, which usually cares for the kinds of books I championed, had gone through a radical transformation and now regarded these books as the source of all the worst prejudices and dominations that characterize the West. What they call "the canon" is the real source of our problem, for the ideas that feed our prejudices come from it. The heart of that part of the American community which was given the task of civilizing us has turned know-nothing and hostile to civilization. Now one of its greatest efforts is to prove that the lowest-level, gutter expressions of culture are equal to the most noble production of philosophy, poetry, art, and music. The barbarians are not at the gate; they, without our knowing it, have taken over the citadel. It is almost impossible to make sensible people outside the universities believe how extreme this all is, although the flap about political correctness has helped alert the public.

Illustrative of what is going on are events of the last days. Some time ago I gave a talk to a group of congressmen in Washington. I showed them the scarlet letters—R and G—that I am forced to wear and described the university horrors about race and gender. They all laughed and said that none of this nonsense ever touched Washington.

Two weeks later came the Clarence Thomas–Anita Hill affair. And you must remember that the issue had very little to do with whether Justice Thomas sexually harassed Anita Hill but concerned consciousness-raising. It was designed to show, as a *New York Times* op-ed piece said, that all men are pigs, that women are systematically abused by male domination, that men cannot understand women or justly judge them. It is *prima facie* unjust that there are ninety-eight male senators and only two women. Senator Bill Bradley, formerly a sensible fellow, who has been radicalized, perhaps by his literary critic wife, spoke about "structures of power," perhaps unawares parroting Michel Foucault, who is the great hero in the universities. What was being asked for was a soul transformation, and the senators in general accepted the principle, if they did not all agree about its relevance to this case. A new ideology was promoted by this story: Western males and their institutions are corrupt. Relations between men and women were said to be primarily power relations, and almost everybody swallowed this way of speaking.

But this is nonsense. Men and women are in the first place naturally attracted to each other in the gentlest and most mutually respectful way, and their relations can have, in addition, a sweet and noble goal in the production of children, who belong to men and women equally. Obviously, these naturally good motives can be corrupted or abused, but it is a terrible thing to persuade people that such abuses are their essence. This is part of a new philosophy that tells us that the will to power is the central human motive. If it were true, all relations between human beings would be like those between warring nations. That this point of view should be routinely accepted is a sign of the political forces that are being unleashed. It is possible to begin to look at all human relationships in power terms, just as it is possible to look at them in economic terms, but such ways of looking at them destroy their reality. It is perfectly possible to discuss things like sexual harassment or political representation in commonsense terms, but this was not done, and it was not done because the goal was, to repeat, to delegitimize our institutions, which claim to be able to bring justice on the grounds of principles that all human beings, including women and blacks, not to mention white Western males, can affirm.

Another aspect of the Clarence Thomas hearings is also indicative of the way academic views have come to be part of the political mainstream. It was perfectly scandalous, from my point of view, that it was constantly asserted that unless there was a black justice on the Supreme Court, there could be no justice for blacks. Whatever happened to the common good and the view that decent people, no matter what their color, their sex, or where they originally came from, can act rationally for the sake of the common good? Thomas was asked over and over again whether he actually represented the black community as it wished to be represented. What a transformation in the understanding of what the Supreme Court is, or of what our political institutions in general are! They all become a messy aggregation of competing interests fighting for dominance without any true common ground. When John Kennedy ran for president, it was asked whether he could forget or overcome his Catholic attachments in order to think about the national good, as opposed to the interests of the Catholic Church. In the case of Kennedy the questions may have been irrelevant, but they reflected a natural, healthy view about what a president or a judge should be. This is all part of the attempt to say that the U.S. Constitution, for example, is not a thing to be taken seriously other than as a reflection of the class consciousness of slaveholders. What could one be committed to or fight for if this is the meaning of our political life? We are asked to believe that the situation of blacks and women in this society is as grave as that of the persons incarcerated in the Nazi death camps or the Communist Gulag archipelago. Triumph? We should be racked with guilt, they claim, for doing exactly the same things our enemies did. If such a point of view succeeds—and it is well on the way to doing so—you can understand why the country is down in the mouth.

A further note about the Gulf War that is relevant to the foregoing considerations is the magnificent behavior of the black men and women in the armed services. A great effort had been made to make us believe that the blacks were there as cannon fodder, exploited by the whites to do their dying for them and, some went so far as to say, put there in order to be killed. Also, the air was filled with rumors about their ignorance, demoralization, and use of drugs. All of this turned out to be lies. The blacks were uniformly the most moving aspect of the war. Clever reporters tried to get these youngsters to speak of their suffering and the injustice done to them. Without exception, they expressed satisfaction and pride in their roles. They did not feel they lived in a world utterly separated from the whites and expressed group solidarity that went beyond the corrosive of race. They denied that they could not get promotion on merit and pointed to their black officers and commanders, not only to the chairman of the Joint Chiefs of Staff. In addition to their decency, they all seemed highly competent, explaining to the reporters their complicated weapons systems with clarity and authority. This was a perfect achievement of American ideals, and of course none of the American intellectual elites wanted to notice it. This is almost criminal, because it deprived these excellent young men and women of their right to say, "We have contributed notably to one of the most important aspects of political life, and we deserve respect for it." The same thing was done in Vietnam, where blacks fought so notably and so well. What is the cause of the military's success in the relation between the races? Perfect concentration on merit and no affirmative action. When a black holds a position of command, no one can say that he does not deserve it.

But the universities are going in the absolutely contrary direction. The chairman of the University of Chicago's English department and the editor of *Critical Inquiry*, the sacred text of deconstructionism or postmodernism, wrote a letter to the *Chicago Tribune* in response to a lighthearted article that ridiculed some of the titles of papers at the Modern Language Association meetings, such as "Jane Austen and the Masturbating Girl" and "The Female Penis." He asked rhetorically, "What are we supposed to do when racism, sexism, and homophobia are rampant?" This is quite an interesting statement of the vocation of humanities professors. Formerly, while most humanities professors deplored those vices, they thought their function was to study books and transmit the taste for reading them. This modest function has come to be seen as demeaning to them. Now they think that they can play the decisive role in transforming the minds of American men and women so that they will no longer contain these ugly dispositions. This is really an astonishing change if you think about it for a moment.

How do professors of literature liberate us from racism, sexism, and homophobia? By teaching that the books they teach, which they once taught so respectfully, are the sources of these terrible prejudices. They are all written by "dead, white Western males." They make up the "canon" that imprisons us.

The canon is treated as though it were the city council of a corrupt and segregated city in which there are no black, Asiatic, or female faces to be seen. If you look at the curriculum that way, of course it is a matter of simple justice to fight to get such faces in the city council. The composition of the city council is a sure indication of where the power lies in that city.

But what a nutty way to look at books. Always, men and women pick up books to find out, for example, what love is, what democracy is. If you find a better account of courage than the one in Aristotle's *Ethics*, then you must turn to it. But you will find it hard to do so. This is why Aristotle has been read for so long. What these critics tell us is, "Don't trust Aristotle. He is lying, he is deceiving you. You can't trust your judgment. Trust us." This Eurocentric or phallocentric stuff is intended to validate such claims.

They do not openly say, although they want to, that the natural sciences themselves are susceptible to the same critique, and you can understand better what they mean if you look at it in this way. We need, they believe, to have 50 percent of our physics curriculum non-Western. Moreover, our physics of force is a male or phallocentric physics, which would change to a nurturing physics if women were *empowered*. Aerodynamics is a mere tool of Western imperialism, which has no serious scientific basis. So many people I meet say, "All the books you propose are written by dead, white Western males," believing that by making that remark they are saying something significant. But apply that same remark to mathematics, physics, and biology, and you see how ridiculous this all is.

Now I want to discuss one of the buzzwords of our Newspeak, "diversity." Diversity is taken to be something sacred, not something one can think about, but a kind of trump card. The accusation that someone is not favoring diversity is enough to send him scampering with his tail between his legs. The good thing about America, if there is any good thing about it, is, they say, its wonderful diversity of cultures rather than, as an older way of looking at it would say, its miraculous forming of a unity out of great diversity. It is alleged that we are now much more diverse than we ever were and therefore must transform our education so as to encourage and fertilize our present diversity. How you get unity out of heterogeneity of human types and principles has disappeared as a theme. Personally, I am very doubtful whether America today is any more diverse than it was in 1900, when it was teeming with immigrant Irish, Italians, and Poles, as well as the despised WASPS and the blacks. And there were even, so far as I can determine, women here. One might argue that the Asians today do indeed represent something different, unlike the others, who were all raised, one way or the other, in the Judeo-Christian tradition. But in general, the proposition about our new diversity requires examination, and in this, as in so many other things, one should not roll over and let such claims go unexamined when so much depends upon it.

I would suggest that the change is much more in the status of diversity and in the stridency of the voices that promote it. In the past, right up through the civil rights movement, prior to the emergence of the Black *power* movement in the late sixties, the various groups strove to become Americans. Now they are told by intellectuals and the leaders of these groups that they should be inspired by what they once were and what separates them from the American public as a whole. Nothing could be further from Martin Luther King's insistence that blacks are the true Americans than the assertion that blacks are distinguished by forming a separate culture, one that is irreducibly opposed to Eurocentrism. It is argued that no education can be a good one without the presence of diversity in the student population. The conclusion of this line of reasoning is that Athens, Rome, Britain, France, and Germany did not have a serious system of education or a high intellectual life. The political success of Rome and England was clearly founded on the homogeneity of their ruling classes. The "decline and fall" of Rome has usually been attributed to the bewildering diversity of nations and religions incorporated into it by the empire. There was no common ground left for political action. The American founders wanted—and this is what is new in their understanding—to form a true nation or people in spite of the diversity of the elements that were to compose it. They concentrated on what men simply are, as in "all men are created equal." They planned a nation capable of common purpose and political determination without the harshness of the ancient legislators, who imposed a unity of belief and action on their citizens. It was not known whether this would be possible. They took it to be a great gamble, combining nation-building with gentle tolerance. They would not interfere with diverse ways of life or religion, except within the very narrow limits imposed by absolute political necessity. But they would never encourage the extremes of diversity or regard them, as such, as a good thing. They would have expected that the differences brought here from elsewhere or fostered by the terrible fact of slavery would gradually be attenuated by the common experience of the nation's life. This democracy was understood to be future-oriented rather than past-oriented. Its inhabitants—again with the notable exception of the blacks—immigrated here because they wanted to get away from the horrors of the lands from which they came. The nostalgia for the "culture" of their distant fatherlands is an indulgence of the third and fourth generations in this country, and the intellectuals want to impose this diversity on populations that frequently have little taste for it.

The changed status of diversity is a fascinating phenomenon, and we could set up a number of interesting courses to understand how it came to pass. But the current insistence in America today on diversity, or the latching on to the idea of diversity celebrated by certain European thinkers, is fairly easily explicable. It is founded on the conviction that liberal democracy has failed in its project of treating individuals as individuals and offering them equal opportunity along with a relatively high degree of tolerance for the diversity of the groups that persist within it. The new project attempts to replace the old one with a scheme for treating this land as a mosaic of groups and forcing what are alleged to be the previously dominant groups to abandon their spurious sense of superiority. For whatever it is worth, this is the idea.

A serious intellectual life requires a diversity of well thought-out opinions about the fundamental questions if there is to be any hope of the diversity of opinions being replaced by the unity of the truth. The truth is our goal, no matter how much the demagogues try to suppress our love of the truth in the name of sensitivity; but since we do not have full access to the truth, this high-level diversity in thought is very desirable for us. Political correctness undertakes to stifle the profound diversity that existed in the past, the dangerous and attractive diversity that opposed believers to nonbelievers, materialists to idealists, democrats to aristocrats. I believe that we are, to our great loss, much less diverse than men and women of the past were in this decisive respect, and that the range of respectable alternatives has been narrowed. Milton Friedman may be opposed to the socialism of John Kenneth Galbraith, but only on the basis of a profound agreement that the purpose of society is to provide material well-being to the population at large. The difference consists in a disagreement about the means to the actualization of their shared good. No one in this country is conservative in the sense of being able to believe or to speak publicly, as conservatives did in the past, about limiting the franchise to a small aristocracy or, as theologians once did, about dedicating society to the renunciation of worldly goods for the sake of salvation. Our diversity of groups is more like the Coca-Cola ad, where persons of different races, nations, and genders sing the same thing "in perfect harmony." Such harmony is achieved by a reasoning akin to this: "If the beautiful think they are beautiful, they will try to dominate the not-beautiful and make them have low self-esteem. Therefore, we must abandon the idea of the beautiful and suppress our longing for it for the sake of tolerance and everyone's feeling good about themselves." Aristophanes wrote a comedy about this named the *Assembly of Women*, and I recommend it to all of you. The question is whether this maiming of our best instincts is really required for a reasonably tolerant society and whether this fragmentation is actually the royal road to our all getting along together.

It is one thing to argue that there are not enough black professors in universities because they have been discriminated against due to their skin color. It is an entirely different thing to insist that there be an African-American perspective in the universities represented by African-Americans, who alone have the qualities of soul to promote it. It is not so much the pernicious political consequences of this move that alarm me but the intellectual confusion, thinness, and deceptions that are its necessary accompaniments. It stands in the way of each person's thinking seriously about his individual situation with the help of those great thinkers who have stated the alternatives. Students are made to believe, before examining them, that such thinkers are the exclusive oppressors.

We survey a bleak and dangerous intellectual scene. What I have described here is just the tip of the iceberg. Very extreme theory has plugged into political practice, and it would require a series of essays to cover the scene. But the bottom line is that with class, race, and gender dominating the humanities, alleged to be the only serious issues, and demanding revolution as the solution, the classical problems of philosophy and literature are systematically being suppressed.

The result is that young persons who are going to be citizens, statesmen, or soldiers can no longer learn from Thucydides, Plato, Machiavelli, and Hegel how to address the great issues of the relation between power and justice. This is a very influential movement, and I really do not know what can be done about it, as its adherents gradually take control of all tenured posts in the university humanities departments, with the enthusiastic support of TV anchormen and the trendier parts of the press. I hope we can manage to not be too intimidated by all the propaganda that is being generated by those disciplines. Maybe we can be heartened to try a new start for ourselves. Most of all, we must not be intimidated by words like "Eurocentric," "empowerment," and "diversity." Our sense of national purpose depends on it.

20

The Hazards of Repudiating Tradition

CHRISTINA HOFF SOMMERS

In the late sixties a group of hippies living in the Haight-Ashbury District of San Francisco decided that hygiene was a middle class hang-up that they could best do without. So they lived without it. For example, baths and showers, though not actually banned, were frowned upon as retrograde practices. The essayist and novelist Tom Wolfe was intrigued by these hippies who, he said, "sought nothing less than to sweep aside all codes and restraints of the past and start out from zero."[1]

After a while the hippies' principled aversion to modern hygiene had consequences as unpleasant as they were unforeseen. Wolfe describes them thus:

At the Haight-Ashbury Free Clinic there were doctors who were treating diseases no living doctor had ever encountered before, diseases that had disappeared so long ago they had never even picked up Latin names, diseases such as the mange, the grunge, the itch, the twitch, the thrush, the scroff, the rot.[2]

The itching and the manginess eventually began to vex the hippies, leading them individually to seek help from the local free clinics. Step by step, they had to rediscover for themselves the rudiments of modern hygiene. Wolfe refers to it as the "Great Relearning." The Great Relearning is what has to happen whenever earnest reformers extirpate too much, whenever, "starting from zero," they jettison basic social practices and institutions, abandoning common routines, defying common sense, reason, conventional wisdom—and sometimes sanity itself.

Wolfe draws attention to other, more consequential experiments of our century: Marxist-Leninism, Maoism, fascism. Each movement had its share of zealots and social engineers who believed in "starting from zero." They had faith in a new order and ruthlessly cast aside the traditional arrangements. Among the unforeseen consequences of these experiments were mass suffering and genocide on an unprecedented scale. Eastern Europeans are just beginning their own "Great Relearning," reviving religious institutions and the teachings of the older ethic that many thought had been lost forever. They now realize, to their dismay, that starting from zero had been a calamity, that the structural damage wrought by the political zealots has handicapped their societies for decades to come. They are learning that it is far easier to tear apart a social fabric than it is to piece it together again.

America too has had its share of revolutionary developments—not so much political as moral. We have been living though a great experiment of "moral deregulation" whose first principle seems to be that there is no right or wrong, it's just what works for you. Not everyone has joined in this experiment, but even those who have are becoming increasingly alarmed at the outcome.

Concerned observers point to some of the ways the social fabric has been unraveling in recent decades—with signs of greater entropy to come. Most worrying of all are facts about teenagers. We are daily numbed by stories of sociopathic violence. Sexually transmitted disease is a rampant problem. Teenage suicide has tripled since the sixties. Teenage pregnancy has doubled and now nearly one in every three babies is born to an unwed mother.

How are educators, government officials, and social critics responding? One word I would use to describe the reaction is "denial." The strategy seems to be to put a nice label on it and then maybe it will go away.

Consider how we deny the social crises called "the breakdown of the traditional family." Sixteen-year-old unwed mothers on drugs are "nontraditional parenting teens." A mother with two children she cannot take care of and with a third on the way and no husband anywhere in sight is an "alternative family." There are no more "broken homes" anymore. We speak blandly and sometimes even glowingly of "single parenting."

Many of the problems we now have are the unintended and unforeseen consequences of revolutionary social policies that seemed right and good to perhaps the majority of young Americans. Consider the divorce revolution.

There is a lot to be said for it, not least because making divorce easy meant that many were freed from loveless marriages. It was part of the sexual revolution, and there is a lot to be said for that too. But these things happened so fast that no one had time to do an "environmental impact study." Well, now enough time has elapsed and sociologists are stunned by what they are seeing. Easy divorce has affected children far more seriously and adversely than anyone had predicted.

Of course, there are many cases where the children make admirable adjustments. But statistically, the children of divorced parents are at a distinct disadvantage. This has come as a rude surprise to many contemporary observers. Each year there are another 1.25 million divorces in the United States, involving over one million children. Studies by Lenore Weitzman and others show a correlation between coming from a broken home and a variety of ills ranging from depression to poor scholastic performance and social violence.[3]

Most often the child from a broken home loses the father. As if to make light of this loss, we have begun to speak neutrally of "parenting," thereby avoiding reference to the distinct roles that the mother and the father play in the rearing of a child. Twenty-five years ago you could not find the androgynous verb "parenting" in any dictionary. But in the euphemistic lexicon of today, parenting has become the favored way of referring to child rearing. It is as if nothing mothers and fathers do is distinct to their genders: it's all just parenting. Yet even when they passively watch their children play, mothers and fathers engage in quite different ways with their children. Here is how the essayist William Raspberry contrasts them:

> It is not a question of right or wrong, but of **difference** that a mother seeing her small child on a jungle gym is more likely to say, "Be careful!" while the father may say, "Can you climb to the top?" The mother who asks, "Where does it hurt?" is not wrong, but neither is the father who says, "You're okay, shake it off."[4]

Recent studies show clearly that the absence of a father from the home is linked to a high incidence of violence in male children. Seventy percent of juveniles in long-term correctional custody grew up in homes that had no fathers. In her book *Boys Will Be Boys*, Myriam Miedzian shows cross-culturally that the link between inadequate fathering and male violence is *universal*.[5] In other words, the amount of social violence is inversely proportional to the amount of fathering: less fathering, much more social violence. Fathers appear to be central in helping sons develop a conscience and a sense of responsible manhood. Fathers teach boys that being manly need not mean being aggressive. By contrast, when the father is absent, male children tend to get their ideas of what it means to be a man from violent peers—often in gangs. Or they imitate the ways of violent pop heroes. In short, fathers play an indispensable civilizing role in the social ecosystem.

Instead of facing this stark truth and instituting social policies to recover some of the stability we have lost, many social thinkers engage in sophisticated denial that the problem of the missing fathers is serious. One Wellesley College sociologist argues that the absence of a father would not matter so much if men were brought up to be more caring and less aggressive. But that puts the cart in front of the horse, for it is precisely when the father is absent and boys are forced to form their conception of masculinity from figures outside the home that they are at greater risk of growing up to become violent and uncaring. It would be unfair to say that the Wellesley sociologist and others like him are not distressed by the findings that children and society at large suffer from the absence of the fathers. But such findings conflict with the new dogma that parental roles are interchangeable, so there is the temptation to deny that the problem is serious and to explain it away. Among intellectuals the Great Relearning is often preceded by the Great Explaining Away.

We now jokingly call looters "nontraditional shoppers." Serial killers like Jeffrey Dahmer are described as "morally challenged"—again jokingly, but the truth behind the jokes is that moral deregulation is the order of the day. We are poking fun at our own society for its lack of moral clarity. People today seem to be unable to reach clear moral decisions in condemning evil, the kind of decisions that used to be automatic. We have been denigrating our moral and social traditions for so long that the fabric of norms that have held our society together is worn out and discredited. So now we are reduced to hoping that something or someone—perhaps the social workers, or the police, or three strikes and you're out—can hold the center together.

We have to go back—but not to a new drawing board, for that again would mean just another start from zero. Instead we must concentrate on strengthening, reviving, revitalizing, and repairing the normative foundations of our society. But here we run into a second problem. Many of us are aware that the center is not holding—but we have *unlearned* the truths that our forebears knew: that the center was the country, the military, the church and temple, the school, and marriage and the family.

Plato versus Aristotle

Ever since its very beginnings in ancient Greece, social philosophy has moved between the two poles of Plato's *Republic* and Aristotle's *Politics*. Plato was in many ways a conservative, but the Plato of the *Republic* has been very influential, and that Plato was a radical utopian who was quite ready to scrap customs and traditions and start again from zero. Aristotle, on the other hand, respected the traditional arrangements and sought always to reform them from within.

I should like to elaborate a bit on this historic contrast between the Platonist and Aristotelian temper, since, in my opinion, we are now philosophically, socially, and intellectually in a Platonist period, while the real problems we face call for an Aristotelian temper and approach.

Social criticism is an engaging pastime to which philosophers are professionally addicted. One approach, Aristotelian in method and character, is antiradical. It is conservationist and cautious in its recommendations for change. It is not given to such proposals as radically altering the family or abolishing private property, and indeed, does not look kindly on such proposals from other philosophers. Aristotle believed in giving great moral weight to traditional arrangements, and he saw common opinion as a primary source of moral truth. Many of our greatest social and moral philosophers have adopted an Aristotelian model of social criticism: philosophers as diverse as John Locke, David Hume, Henry Sidgwick, William James, and Bertrand Russell share with Aristotle the conservative conviction that traditional arrangements have great moral weight and that common opinion is a primary source of moral truth.

The more exciting genre of social criticism is not Aristotelian but Platonist in spirit. Plato's *Republic* is a radical treatise. In the *Republic*, Plato stood above all social institutions and placed them under "supernal" scrutiny. Looking down on society as a cave that distorted real values, Plato showed a great readiness to discount all traditional arrangements. He was the first philosopher to inspire generations of utopian social philosophers by constructing an ideal of a society that reflected principles of justice. For Plato, reform of the existing arrangements would not suffice: instead, massive efforts at consciousness-raising and a complete refashioning of the system, including the family and the schools, were deemed necessary. Thus Plato was the original radical utopian social engineer. Plato is the philosopher behind the idea of "starting out from zero."

In my opinion, Aristotle instinctively understood something that Plato's admirers overlook and that Plato himself failed to appreciate: traditional societies are in their own way natural, and there are important similarities between natural systems and moral systems.

We today have become aware that large-scale human intervention into natural systems can be disastrous. We know that natural history has its reasons and its wisdom, and we have learned that we are largely ignorant of that wisdom. For the present, at any rate, ecology is a modest science whose practical advice seems to be confined to telling us to *desist* from any large-scale interventions because of our appalling ignorance. Acting in ignorance can have, and has had, many fateful consequences. I believe that much of this same cautionary moral applies to the proponents of radical social reform.

But here we come up against a deplorable paradox. For it is ironically true that many of the people who are so prominent in urging caution and sensitivity in ecological matters—the very people who counsel us wisely to be careful and conservative and to avoid making serious changes in nature's traditions—are irresponsibly different when it comes to embracing an activist social philosophy whose radical goals may include such measures as eliminating the traditional family and other traditional institutional arrangements.

Change is fine. Change is inevitable. But looking at what the rapid revolutionary changes have effected in our stressed society, it would seem that we need a group of moral ecologists who would be concerned to protect our fragile but vital social institutions (some of which have taken millennia to evolve) in just the way ecologists are counseling us to protect systems in nature.

To be sure, this comparison between moral and natural systems must be made carefully. After all, could it not be used to justify unjust traditions or cruel customs? Institutions such as slavery and practices like human sacrifice or suttee (burning the widow along with the dead husband on the funeral pyre) have long histories, and many have argued that they too have some inherent logic of their own. Such "established customs" seem to constitute serious contradictions to the proposition that tradition has moral authority. To this objection, the brief but somewhat oversimplified rejoinder begins by admitting that institutions are generally imperfect and almost always in need of reform. However, some institutions and practices are *essentially* unjust and must be eliminated. The practices of slavery and suttee are essentially unjust and not subject to reform. (What would it mean to introduce "reforms" into the practice of human sacrifice?) By contrast, an institution like marriage, the family, or an imperfect democracy—such as the one we live in—will have many unjust features, but these basic social arrangements do not need to be abolished but rather repaired and made better.

So it is possible to practice moral ecology without being a hidebound conservative. It is possible to be an Aristotelian, rejecting utopian approaches and solutions, while being sympathetic to and active in bringing about social changes that amend our institutions without repudiating them and "starting from zero." I think of Aristotle as an advocate of moral ecology, not so much a conservative as a conservationist. Just as the conservationist often opposes radical interventions into a sensitive ecology, so the moral conservationist opposes what Sir Karl Popper calls utopian social engineering, favoring instead reforms that remedy injustice without starting from zero, reforms that do not destroy imperfect but necessary institutions. For the conservationist, morality is just as much a matter of mores as it is of abstract moral principles, and the actual norms of any tradition—with the exception of those that are essentially unjust—have a *prima facie* moral force.

Nothing I have said should be taken to mean that I believe there is no place for the Platonist temper in social criticism. Sometimes the traditional social arrangements are intolerable and unjust; in such cases revolutionary measures may be called for. But today, in our contemporary democratic Western culture, it is Aristotle that we need. Our culture is under radical stress. And we need badly to be reminded that the more radical the solution, the more it is subject to the law of unintended consequences.

Deconstructing American Institutions

It is a matter of serious concern that in the modern university environment there are far too many Platos and too few Aristotles. Our schools have their full quota of would-be social engineers, consciousness-raisers, utopians, philosopher kings and queens who, like Plato, are eager to describe for us the evils of the cave we live in and even more eager to take the lead in showing us the way out into their own brave new, just social order. On campuses throughout the United States, the new historians, poststructuralists, Marxists, radical feminists, deconstructionists, and other debunkers are busy "critiquing," denouncing, excoriating the cave culture and advocating its replacement, mostly without attending to *any* of the unintended consequences of the alternatives they are promoting.

As a lecturer around the country I meet more and more students who have little or no respect for the United States. I don't mean merely that they find fault with certain aspects of our society—that is healthy, good, and to be encouraged; I mean they seem to view it as an evil empire—a military industrial complex or a fascist patriarchy—unworthy of respect. Many condemn the established culture by deriding our philosophical, artistic, and literary greats as a bunch of "DWEMS"—dead white European males. They see Christopher Columbus as a genocidal villain; the founding fathers are "patriarchal oppressors," as are the military commanders who led American armed forces to victory in the global conflicts of this century.

Being a feminist myself, I am disturbed that many of my academic feminist colleagues are playing so central a role in denigrating our culture. The passion for attacking our established customs and traditions is running so high that we all now seem willing to believe even the most outrageous statistics—especially those that "prove" what a morally suspect creature the American male really is. There are quite a few feminists who are anxious to educate us about this and to recruit us in a socially divisive gender war. I shall give you some examples of how this works and how it affects our attitudes to the family.

In her book *Revolution from Within*, Gloria Steinem informs her readers that "in this country alone . . . about 150,000 females die of anorexia each year."[6] That is more than three times the annual number of fatalities from car accidents for the total population. Steinem cites another feminist best-seller, Naomi Wolf's *The Beauty Myth*, as her source. And in Ms. Wolf's book one does indeed find the statistic, along with the author's outrage. "How," she asks, "would America react to the mass self-immolation by hunger of its favorite sons?"[7] Although "nothing justifies comparison with the Holocaust," she cannot refrain from making it anyway. "When confronted with a vast number of emaciated bodies starved not by nature *but by men*, one must notice a certain resemblance" (my emphasis).[8]

Where did Ms. Wolf get her figures? Her source is *Fasting Girls* by Joan Brumberg,[9] a historian and former director of women's studies at Cornell University. Brumberg gives the American Anorexia Association as her source. I called that association and spoke to Dr. Diane Mickley, its president. "We were misquoted," she said. In a 1985 newsletter the association had referred to 150,000–200,000 *sufferers* of eating disorders. Apparently, someone misread this as 150,000 anorectic *fatalities* per year.

What is the correct morbidity rate? According to the Division of Vital Statistics at the National Center for Health Statistics, there are fewer than 100 deaths from anorexia per year. In 1991, for example, there were 54 deaths.

But now the false figure of 150,000 fatalities—such dramatic evidence for the view that our "sexist society" demeans women by objectifying their bodies—is widely accepted as true. Ann Landers repeated it in her syndicated column in

April 1992. "Every year, 150,000 American women die from complications associated with anorexia and bulimia."[10]

The anorexia "crisis" is only one example of the kind of provocative misinformation being purveyed. It has the effect of portraying us as a society divided against itself along the lines of gender: misogynist males "objectify" women. Women, seeking desperately to please men, sacrifice their very lives.

The message of a divided society is being sent in many different ways. In January 1993 newspapers and television networks reported an alarming finding: incidence of domestic battery tended to rise by 40 percent on Super Bowl Sunday. NBC, which was broadcasting the game that year, made special pleas to men to stay calm. The feminists called for emergency preparations in anticipation of the expected increase in violence. They also used the occasion to drive home the message that maleness and violence against women are synonymous. Nancy Isaac, a research associate who specializes in domestic violence at the Harvard School of Public Health, told the *Boston Globe:* "It's a day for men to revel in their maleness and unfortunately, for a lot of men that includes being violent toward women if they want to be."[11]

Almost all journalists accepted the 40 percent figure at face value and duly reported the bleak tidings. The sole blessed exception was Ken Ringle, a reporter at the *Washington Post*, who decided to check on the sources. He quickly found that the story had no basis in fact.[12] It turns out that Super Bowl Sunday is in no way different from other days in the amount of domestic violence. Though Ringle exposed the falsity of the rumor, it had done its work: millions of American women who heard about it are not aware that it is not true.

To the question: "Why is everyone so credulous?" we must add another: "Why is there so much enthusiasm for putting husbands and fathers in a sinister light?" I have written a book to answer these questions. Suffice it to say that the campaign to denigrate men is widespread and unrelenting. Gloria Steinem's portrait of male-female intimacy under "patriarchy" is typical:

> Patriarchy *requires* violence or the subliminal threat of violence in order to maintain itself. . . . The most dangerous situation for a woman is not an unknown man in the street, or even the enemy in wartime, but a husband or lover in the isolation of their own home.[13]

But the more careful studies on domestic violence simply do not bear out the implied claim that the average American man—the husband, the sports fan, the boyfriend—is a violent bully. Richard J. Gelles and Murray A. Straus are academic social scientists (from the University of Rhode Island and the University of New Hampshire, respectively) who have been studying domestic violence for more than twenty-five years. Their research is among the most respected and frequently cited by other social scientists, by police, by the FBI, and by the personnel in domestic violence agencies. They have found that violence occurs in approximately 12 percent of American families, but that most of the violence consists of occasionally "shoving, pushing, grabbing and slapping," with no intimidation and no physical harm. And women do it to men just as often as men do it to women. The truly brutal violence (hitting, punching, beating up) is found in approximately 3–4 percent of homes.[14] Here too the women do it as well, but the injuries are mainly caused by men. In a country as large as ours, that translates into a tragically large number of violent homes. Clearly we need sound social policy and effective law enforcement to help deal with this problem. But if 88 percent of families have no violence at all, and only about 3–4 percent have serious violence, why is the *average* family being impugned? Some men are indeed violent bullies, and any humane and moral person should want to see them brought down. But why impugn all men? Why portray all families as unsafe, unjust, and abusive?

The American family is under severe stress; it badly needs to be fortified and renewed. Yet at the very moment the growing disintegration of the family is posing serious threats to the future of our social order, we find a host of articulate and angry social critics attacking the family. These Platonist critics regard the family as an unjust institution, a "bulwark of patriarchy" that reinforces the subjugation of women in distinct gender roles. They look forward to the day when the traditional family will be replaced by "more just" institutions, a day when women will no longer have the main responsibility for the rearing of children. It is unfortunate and sad that at a time of social entropy in which families are endangered and weak and millions of our children are at risk, these clever feminist critics are on the side of the forces that seek to destroy the family as we have known it.

The feminist radicals portray us as a misogynist "rape culture." Other radicals portray us as an imperialist culture that leads the advantaged nations in exploiting a hapless third world. Neither type of radical has affection for us as we are, and both want radical change. I have my special bones to pick with the feminist utopians, who speak glibly of "dismantling the patriarchy." But we should be looking with alarm as well as skepticism upon the preachments of *all* utopians. My advice to students who find themselves mesmerized by their radical teachers, who are "critiquing" everything in sight and promoting their utopian solutions, is to ask: "Where are the Aristotelians? Who is making the case for tradition, for common sense, for conservationism? The social consequences of the revolutionary contempt for tradition are becoming increasingly evident. Who, among those urging the radical solutions, knows anything about how to reduce the level of violence in our society today?"

I do not say we should summarily dismiss the modern-day utopians. They are the contemporary heirs of a social critique that does not hesitate to start from zero. This kind of social critique is always exciting and provocative. But we should be demanding the Aristotelian counterpoise, we should be examining the unintended consequences of a rampant radical distrust for tradition and the traditional institutions. We badly need a perspective that abjures the Platonist impulse to totalizing solutions that start from zero.

People's Soup

I was a kind of radical in the sixties. Without knowing what it meant, I called myself a Marxist in my freshman year of college. I was on the periphery of a group of students who occupied a building at New York University and held a computer hostage for a few days. My mother recalls a poster of Che Guevara on my wall. "When did you stop being a radical?" people sometimes ask me. It did not happen all at once. It was a gradual process of disillusionment. But I have a clear and distinct memory of my first moment of disenchantment.

It happened in 1968 at a peace march I was attending in Washington, D.C. Thousands of protesters had turned out, so the demonstration organizers set up makeshift food and drink stations. It was cold and rainy, and I waited in a long line for a cup of hot soup. When I finally reached the front of the line and saw a steaming vat of liquid, I politely and diffidently asked, "What kind of soup is it?" An angry young revolutionary woman in charge of the soup looked up at me in disgust for having asked such a bourgeois question. "It's people's soup," she snarled. (It made me think of little people swimming around in broth.) I withdrew, sans soup, as the kitchen commissar, her comrades, and some of the people in line snickered and sneered at me. The entire event lasted no more than twenty seconds. But I would never forget it. I saw in that young woman and her cohorts an authoritarianism, an intolerance, and a self-righteousness that I had thought existed only on the right.

At the time it was fashionable to speak of overthrowing the U.S. government. "Power to the People," we chanted. Until that moment, I never really thought about what it would really mean if The People took over. I was only seventeen and it would be a few years before I read Plato or Aristotle, or George Orwell or Tom Wolfe, but I sensed even then that a radical uprising could mean the seizure of power by a frightening horde, forcing People's Soup on everyone. You might say it was the beginning of my disenchantment with the idea of starting from zero.

Later I was to learn who my philosophical mentors were. I learned that I preferred Aristotle to Plato, John Locke to Karl Marx, John Stuart Mill to Simone de Beauvoir. I learned how much easier it was to "critique" and to jeer at our institutions and culture than to understand and appreciate them. I was to learn—and it shocked me to learn it—that those who would transform our society along some party line blueprint almost *always* do far more harm than good. That was dismaying; I would much rather have believed that a utopia was realizable—that society could be radically transformed for the better. Milan Kundera writes about the *temptation to believe* even in the face of disillusionment:

> People like to say: Revolution is beautiful, it is only the terror arising from it which is evil. But that is not true. The evil is already present in the beautiful. Hell is already contained in the dream of paradise.[15]

I am now convinced that the hell contained in the dream is manifest in the *contempt* that revolutionaries have for the reality they wish to destroy. Karl Marx once suggested that those who seek to understand the world are missing the point. The point, he said, is not to understand the world, but to change it. Many a utopian is attracted to this counsel. They neither understand nor sympathize with the world they are assaulting; in fact, they learn to hate it. And when they succeed in destroying their society, the ensuing misery is mainly borne by the children who live in the new order.

In my opinion, we today are not unlike those confused hippies in the late 1960s who showed up at the doors of the free clinics in Haight-Ashbury to get their dose of traditional medicine. I pray we have the good sense to do that too. The cures for what ails us are known and they are available. We need to take an active stand against the divisive unlearning that is corrupting the integrity of our society and political culture. The poet William Butler Yeats talked of the center and warned us that it was not holding. Others talk of the social fabric and of tradition. We need to reinforce the center. We need to repair the social fabric. We need to teach and to pass on the traditions that bind us.

The past few decades have seen an assault on the sustaining institutions of our society, and these now need our *conscious* protection and care if they are to be preserved. Our American society is in many ways admirable and enviable; in any case, it is *our* society, and in preserving it we preserve ourselves. We need to devote ourselves to strengthening the institutions and social arrangements that nurture us. If we again become alive to the value of our traditions and our institutions, if we become determined to preserve and protect them, we will be doing what needs to be done to redeem and to safeguard our future: our own lives and those of our children will be more secure, more dignified, more humane.

Notes

1. Tom Wolfe, "The Great Relearning," *The American Spectator*, December 1987, vol. 20; reprinted as "A Eulogy for the Twentieth Century," *The Utne Reader*, March/April 1988.

2. Ibid.

3. See, for example, Lenore Weitzman, *The Divorce Revolution: The Unexpected Social and Economic Consequences for Women and Children in America* (New York: The Free Press, 1985), or Barbara Dafoe Whitehead, "Dan Quayle Was Right," *The Atlantic Monthly*, April 1993. The Institute of American Values, a research center in New York City, has done a large number of studies showing a strong connection between social ills and the absence of fathers.

4. William Raspberry, "Phasing Out Father," *Washington Post*, January 22, 1992.

5. Myriam Miedzian, *Boys Will Be Boys* (New York: Doubleday, 1991).

6. Gloria Steinem, *Revolution from Within: A Book of Self-Esteem* (Boston: Little Brown and Company, 1992), 222.

7. Naomi Wolf, *The Beauty Myth* (New York: Doubleday, 1992), 180–82.

8. Wolf, 207.

9. Joan Jacobs Brumberg, *Fasting Girls: The Emergence of Anorexia Nervosa as a Modern Disease* (Cambridge, Mass.: Harvard University Press, 1988), 19–20.

10. Ann Landers, "Women and Distorted Body Images," *The Boston Globe*, April 29, 1992.

11. *The Boston Globe*, January 29, 1993.

12. Ken Ringle, *Washington Post*, January 31, 1993.

13. Steinem, *Revolution from Within*, 259–61.

14. See Murray Straus, Richard Gelles, and Suzanne Steinmetz, *Behind Closed Doors: Violence in the American Family* (New York: Anchor Books, 1980). See also Murray Straus and Richard Gelles, *Intimate Violence* (New York: Simon and Schuster, 1988), 324–25. According to Straus and Gelles, in 3 to 4 percent of couples there was

at least one incident of severe violence. But in their surveys they also found that "women assault their partners at about the same rate as men assault their partners. This applies to both minor and severe assaults." Gelles and Straus are careful to say that women are *far more likely* to be injured and to need medical care. But overall, the percentage of women who are injured seriously enough to need medical care is still relatively small compared to the inflated claims of the activists and journalists—fewer than 1 percent. Murray Straus estimates that approximately 100,000 women per year are victims of the severe kinds of violence shown in the film *The Burning Bed*. That is a shockingly high number of victims, but it is far short of claims we now routinely see cited in the media.

15. Milan Kundera, *The Book of Laughter and Forgetting*, Afterword: "A Talk with the Author" (New York: Penguin Books, 1981), 234.

Contributors

PROFESSOR HADLEY ARKES is the Edward Ney Professor of Jurisprudence and American Institutions at Amherst College. He serves on the editorial advisory boards of *First Things: A Monthly Journal of Religion and Public Life* and the *American Journal of Jurisprudence*. He has been a fellow for the National Endowment for the Humanities and a visiting Leavey Professor on the Foundations of American Freedom at Georgetown University. He has written many articles for scholarly as well as popular publications, such as *National Review,* the *Wall Street Journal*, and the *Washington Post*. He has written four books, including *First Things: An Inquiry into the First Principles of Morals and Justice* and *The Return of George Sutherland.*

DR. WILLIAM J. BENNETT is presently the co-director of the Empower America Organization. He has served the United States as chairman of the National Endowment for the Humanities, Director of National Drug Policy, and US. Secretary of Education. He has authored a number of scholarly articles and books, including the best-seller *The Book of Virtues.*

PROFESSOR ALLAN BLOOM was, before his death, a professor at the University of Chicago and codirector of the John M. Olin Center for Inquiry into the Theory and Practice of Democracy. He had also taught at Yale University, Cornell University, the University of Tel Aviv, the University of Paris, and the University of Toronto. Professor Bloom authored a very large number of scholarly articles and eight books, including the best-seller *The Closing of the American Mind.*

GENERAL GEORGE LEE BUTLER retired from the US. Air Force in 1994 after thirty-three years of military service. General Butler currently serves as a member of the Council on Foreign Relations as well as the Committee on International Security and Arms Control for the National Academy of Sciences and the Canberra Commission. While on active duty he was the Commander-in-

Chief of the Strategic Air Command and subsequently Commander-in-Chief of the United States Strategic Command, Offutt Air Force Base, Nebraska. In this capacity, he had responsibility for all U.S. strategic nuclear forces. He is a command pilot with over 3,000 flying hours. General Butler is a 1961 graduate of the U.S. Air Force Academy and later attended the University of Paris, France, as an Olmsted scholar, where he earned a master's degree in international affairs.

PROFESSOR JAMES F. CHILDRESS is the Edwin B. Kyle Professor of Religious Studies and professor of medical education at the University of Virginia. A leading thinker on problems in medical ethics, he has served as vice chairman of the Task Force on Organ Transplantation and on the board of directors of the United Network for Organ Sharing (UNOS), the Recombinant DNA Advisory Committee, the Human Gene Therapy Subcommittee, and the Biomedical Ethics Advisory Committee. He has received more than fourteen major fellowships, published over one hundred scholarly articles, and authored or co-authored seven books, including *Principles of Biomedical Ethics*.

PROFESSOR MARTIN L. COOK teaches at the Army War College. He has also held academic posts at Santa Clara University, the U.S. Air Force Academy, the Pritzker School of Medicine at the University of Chicago, Gustavus Adolphus College, St. Xavier College, and the College of William and Mary. Professor Cook has lectured on ethics to many organizations and served as an ethics consultant to many hospitals, public service groups, and acquisition agencies for the Department of Defense. He has authored a significant number of scholarly papers and journal articles and the highly praised book *The Open Circle: Confessional Method in Theology*.

PROFESSOR MANUEL DAVENPORT was, before his death, a professor in the Department of Philosophy at Texas A&M University, a department he founded in 1967. He also held faculty posts at Colorado College, the University of Colorado, Colorado State University, and the U.S. Air Force Academy. Professor Davenport published over sixty articles and essays, made more than forty distinguished presentations at scholarly gatherings, and was awarded twenty-eight research and travel grants. The range of his work was impressive and included military ethics, the life and work of Albert Schweitzer, existentialism and phenomenology, and the teaching of philosophy.

PROFESSOR RICHARD DE GEORGE is University Distinguished Professor of Philosophy and Courtesy Professor of Business Administration at the University of Kansas. He has been a research fellow at Yale University, Columbia University, Stanford University, and the Hoover Institute. Has was the Charles J. Dirksen Professor of Business Ethics at Santa Clara University in 1986 and a visiting professor at the Graduate School of Business at the University of St. Gallen, Switzerland in 1985. Professor De George has served as the president of the American Philosophical Association and the Society for Business Ethics. He has written prolifically in applied ethics, publishing over one hundred articles and sixteen books, including *Ethics, Free Enterprise, and Public Policy* and *Business Ethics*.

GENERAL RONALD FOGLEMAN retired from the US. Air Force in 1997 after an exceptional career that culminated in his appointment as the Chief of Staff of the Air Force. A trained historian who taught history at the Air Force Academy, he was also a command pilot with over 6,800 flying hours. He flew 315 combat missions and logged 806 hours of combat flying in fighter aircraft. Prior to assuming the Air Force's top uniformed position, during the course of his career he also commanded a wing, a numbered air force, and major command, and a unified command.

PROFESSOR PETER A. FRENCH holds the Lincoln Chair in Ethics and is director of the Lincoln Center for Applied Ethics at Arizona State University. Previously, he was director of the Ethics Center and chair of the Department of Philosophy at the University of South Florida. He has also taught at Trinity University, the University of Northern Arizona, the University of Minnesota, and Dalhousie University in Nova Scotia. He is senior editor for *Midwest Studies in Philosophy*, editor of the *Journal of Social Philosophy*, and the general editor of the *Issues in Contemporary Ethics* series. He has written many scholarly articles and produced sixteen books, including *Corporate Ethics*, *Ethics and Government*, and *Cowboy Metaphysics: Ethics and Philosophy*.

PROFESSOR THOMAS HILL, JR., is Kenan Professor of Philosophy at the University of North Carolina, Chapel Hill. He has also taught at Pomona College, Johns Hopkins University, and Stanford University. Professor Hill has written extensively in ethics, the history of ethics, and political philosophy, and he is one of the leading Kant scholars of his generation. He has authored three books: *Autonomy and Self-Respect*, *Dignity and Practical Reason*, and *Respect, Pluralism, and Justice*. He has also authored over forty articles.

LIEUTENANT GENERAL BRADLEY HOSMER retired from the US. Air Force in 1994. In his last assignment he served as the superintendent of the US. Air Force Academy. Prior to that time, he commanded a number of Air Force organizations and served in several high-level staff positions. He is a command pilot with over 4,000 flying hours. He was the number-one graduate of the Air Force Academy's first graduating class, and was later a Rhodes Scholar at Oxford, England, where he earned an MA degree in international relations.

PROFESSOR JAMES TURNER JOHNSON is University Director of International Programs, a professor in the Department of Religion, and an associate in the Graduate Department of Political Science at Rutgers University. He has also taught at Newberry College, Vassar College, Douglass College, and New Brunswick College. The recipient of over fifteen fellowships and grants, he has also published more than fifty articles and ten books, including the influential text *Can Modern War Be Just?*

FATHER EDWARD A. MALLOY is president of Notre Dame University. He has taught theology at Notre Dame since 1974. He has a long record of public service in a number of different capacities. Moreover, he is a scholar of distinction, having published many articles and reviews and two books.

PROFESSOR JOHN J. MCDERMOTT is Distinguished Professor of Philosophy and Humanities at Texas A&M University. There he has served in many capacities, including professor and head of the Department of Philosophy and Humanities and professor and head of the Department of Humanities and Medicine, College of Medicine. In 1986 he was named an Abell Endowed Professor in Liberal Arts. Professor McDermott has also served on the National Board of Officers of the American Philosophical Association. He has written numerous articles for professional and scholarly journals and authored or edited many books, including *A Cultural Introduction to Philosophy: From Antiquity to Descartes* and *Streams of Experience: Reflections on the History and Philosophy of American Culture.*

THE HONORABLE JOHN T. NOONAN, JR., is an extremely influential jurist and is presently a judge for the United States Court of Appeals, Ninth Circuit. He was a professor of law at the University of Notre Dame Law School and is professor emeritus at the School of Law, University of California, Berkley. He holds honorary degrees from many prominent universities, including Notre Dame, Loyola Catholic University, Seton Hall, Holy Cross, and the University of San Francisco. Judge Noonan has authored over 140 articles and over a dozen books, including *The Lustre of Our Country: The American Experience of Religious Liberty.*

PROFESSOR NICHOLAS RESCHER is professor emeritus in philosophy at the University of Pittsburgh. One of the leading philosophers of the twentieth century, he is a past president of the American Philosophical Association, the C. S. Pierce Society, and the G. W. Leibniz Society of America. Professor Rescher has edited the *American Philosophical Quarterly* and the *History of Philosophy Quarterly.* He has received a very large number of fellowships, grants, and awards, and has authored more than a hundred articles and over fifty books.

PROFESSOR CHRISTINA HOFF SOMMERS is a resident scholar at the American Enterprise Institute in Washington, D.C. She has taught philosophy at Clark University, Brandeis, the University of Massachusetts, and the University of Pittsburgh's Semester at Sea program. She has edited and co-edited two basic ethics texts and over twenty-five scholarly articles, which have appeared in journals and as chapters in several books. Professor Sommers has read a large number of papers to scholarly conferences and campus gatherings and has won seven major grants and fellowships. She has been cited in many discussions of "political correctness" on campus by *Time, New York Magazine,* the *Wall Street Journal,* the *Boston Herald,* and on CNBC. She has been interviewed by NBC, the Phil Donahue Show, the *Christian Science Monitor,* and *US News & World Report.* She is also well known for her book *Who Stole Feminism?—How Women Have Betrayed Women.*

BRIGADIER GENERAL MALHAM WAKIN is retired from the U.S. Air Force and is a professor emeritus in the Department of Philosophy at the U.S. Air Force Academy. He taught at the Academy from 1959 until his retirement in 1995, where he served as head of the department, chair of the Humanities Division, and assistant dean of the institution. He also occupied the William Lyon Chair in Professional Ethics. For thirteen years he served as the national chairman of the Joint Services Conference on Professional Ethics and is currently a member of the Ethics Oversight Committee of the U.S. Olympic Committee. In 1975 he was featured in *People Magazine* as one of twelve "great professors" and in 1984 was the subject of a feature article in *Newsweek.* He speaks to dozens of audiences each year, has participated in nationally televised video courses with The Learning Channel, written many scholarly articles, and authored or edited four books, including the very widely used anthology *War, Morality and the Military Profession.*

PROFESSOR MICHAEL WALZER has been a member of the permanent faculty at the Institute for Advanced Study at Princeton University since 1980. Prior to that he taught at Harvard and Princeton. He has had editorial responsibilities at *Dissent*, *The New Republic*, and *Philosophy and Public Affairs*. Professor Walzer has also authored a large number of articles and over ten very highly regarded books, including *Spheres of Justice* and *Just and Unjust Wars*.

Index